The World Book of House Plants

The World Book of House Plants

Revised Edition

ELVIN McDONALD

*Line drawings by Kathleen Bourke
and Peter Kalberkamp*

*Photographs by Larry B. Nicholson, Jr.,
and Others*

Funk & Wagnalls   *New York*

Manufactured in the United States of America

ISBN 0-308-10087-5

Library of Congress Cataloging in Publication Data

McDonald, Elvin.
   The world book of house plants.

   Bibliography: p.
   Includes index.
   1. House plants. I. Title.
SB419.M25   1975   635.9′65   74-23165
ISBN 0-308-10087-5

2   3   4   5   6   7   8   9   10

In Memory of

BERNICE GAINES BRILMAYER

*for the many happy hours
we shared as editor and writer*

CONTENTS

PART II: AN ILLUSTRATED ENCYCLOPEDIA OF INDOOR PLANTS

PART III: A USEFUL MISCELLANY

CHARTS AND TABLES

PHOTOGRAPHS

INTRODUCTION

Gardening indoors can be a fascinating hobby or avocation for persons of all ages. I know, because my interest began when I was a child on a small ranch in western Oklahoma. It has grown through all my adult years. Looking back, I am somewhat surprised that as a suburbanite on Long Island and in Kansas City, indoor plants were just as vital to me as they are now in Manhattan. In writing *The World Book of House Plants,* my aim has been that it would serve as a complete guide to indoor plants, one or many. Part I deals with all the ways and means of growing plants in containers, usually indoors. Part II describes several hundred plants, and outlines the cultural requirements of each. Part III includes a glossary of terms, the titles of books and periodicals of interest to indoor gardeners, and a listing of mail-order sources for indoor plants and supplies for growing them.

Officially, I wrote this book in 1962, but its beginning goes back many years—all the way to the winter of 1940, when at the age of three I grew a bean plant in our family living room.

Even now, one of my favorite childhood memories is the Christmas my grandmother gave me a poinsettia. My fondness for plants and gardens grew along with me, and at twelve I had a 6 x 9 lean-to greenhouse. By 1951, my admiration for gloxinias had led me to found the American Gloxinia Society (now called the American Gloxinia and Gesneriad Society), and for some ten years I served as editor of its publication, *The Gloxinian*.

In 1956, one year out of high school, I became Indoor Gardening Editor of a new magazine, *Flower and Garden*, based in Kansas City. Fresh from the country and naive about everything and everybody, I took a dark, basement apartment which had nothing going for it except a grand piano, and on second thought, it was I who put the piano there. One thing for sure, no plant in the world could live in that place. I didn't last there for long, but I learned a good lesson. I really have to have living plants in my environment. To survive constant travel, some people carry their own pillow, or take pills. Me, I check in at the hotel and rush out to the nearest florist for a bouquet of fresh flowers or a plant. Then I can honestly say I feel at home anywhere.

The more books I write (originally this was my fourth, the second published; now it is around number thirty), the more I realize how many persons help me. In my 1963 Introduction the standouts were Kathleen Bourke, Vera Dillard, Larry B. Nicholson, Jr., Peggie Schulz, Katherine B. Walker and Carol H. Woodward. Today, for reasons each of them will know, I add to the list Sarah T. Lee and Wallace Guenther, my former and present Editors-in-Chief of *House Beautiful*.

ELVIN McDONALD

New York City
April 1974

part 1

GARDENING
INDOORS

1. The pleasures of house plants

THERE is something elusive and wonderful about growing a plant in a pot. It is the joy of seeing a flowering Christmas cactus or begonia on the window sill with snowflakes falling on the other side of the glass. It's the fragrance of good moist earth, the perfume of a gardenia, the spiciness of a scented geranium leaf. For you it may be the magic of waiting for a night-blooming cereus to burst into pristine loveliness on a summer evening, the challenge of training an ivy to frame a window, or the delight of propagating your favorite pot plant to share with a friend.

Many growers like the feel of house plant leaves—to touch a velvety gloxinia, a pebbly pilea, or a waxy hoya. Others enjoy strange and picturesque cacti, bizarre bromeliads, or gnarled dwarf trees. The person with a passion for neatness will find special pleasure in symmetrically grown African violets. For some people, indoor gardening has no meaning unless the plants produce bumper floral crops. Others find the gem-toned foliage of rex begonias and episcias even more appealing than flowers.

23

A HOBBY FOR PEOPLE OF ALL AGES

It is a matter of family record that I began a window-sill garden at the age of three and a half years. It consisted of young beans transplanted from outdoors before frost in autumn, a pot of pink oxalis from a great aunt, and wax begonias from a neighbor. Today, preschool children stare in wide-eyed wonder at my potted holly and Norfolk Island pine, which they call "Christmas trees." To the kindergarten set, sharing a potted plant with classmates is a real adventure. I know elderly people whose lives are made far less lonely by house plants. And, conversely, some of the busiest people I know find peace in caring for a collection of indoor plants.

Since that winter years ago when I carefully tended three house plants, I have found every phase of indoor gardening full of its own special delights. There is the thrill of having an orchid produce its yearly crop of long-lasting flowers. There is pleasure in hearing guests exclaim over the huge fruit on a small potted Ponderosa lemon tree. And, every autumn I find buds pushing upward from amaryllis bulbs, promising pure white, pink, and velvety crimson flowers for the holidays. There is great satisfaction, too, in reflowering a poinsettia or an azalea the year after its purchase from the florist. Eagerly I anticipate the blooming of all seedling house plants, for there is always a chance that one of them will be better than were its parents. Finally, there is the daily pleasure my family and I derive from seeing house plants express a measure of warmth, individuality, and charm in each room of our home.

RIGHT: *Collection of plants for a bedroom occasional table. They grow in standard clay and plastic pots slipped inside elegant white porcelain containers. Left to right, the plants include angel-wing begonia, coleus, and 'Fluffy Ruffles' fern. They are situated near an east-facing window which receives full sun in winter.* Interior by Sermon-Anderson. (Photograph by Nicholson)

A PLACE FOR PLANTS IN EVERY HOUSE

Praise is due the designers of many of the houses and apartments being built today, because their great expanses of glass admit life-giving sunlight to indoor plants. While window sills are becoming narrower and narrower and are excluded from some houses, rooms are getting brighter and sunnier; architects are designing more and larger built-in planters; and, central heating, cooling, and humidifying combine to make a year-round climate that provides a congenial atmosphere for hundreds of different plants.

The multitude of indoor gardeners who live in older houses will find that their wider window sills can accommodate an array of plants without the addition of extra planters. Lack of light need not be a problem. Install fluorescent fixtures above an indoor garden and the plants will receive all the illumination they need.

Lack of central heating can give dividends such as more space for growing plants that require coolness in winter (see page 35).

DECORATING WITH HOUSE PLANTS

Highlight a coffee table, a fireplace mantel, or a piano with a single pot plant, or bedeck a bay window with a collection of them. Bring early spring to the indoor garden with the freshness and fragrance of spring-flowering bulbs. Add sparkle to your kitchen with a few geraniums, miniature roses, or herbs. Dramatize an entrance with a splash of green foliage plants.

Use house plants as room dividers and screens. In rooms where the dining area is a part of the living room, let a planter screen one section from the other, affording a measure of privacy.

If your home has a picture window, one that people look into as well as out of, this would be a perfect place for a collection of pot plants. They will give you pleasure as you come and go, and neighbors will appreciate the view from outdoors. Arrange plants on saucers atop a low wooden bench, or set them in a metal-lined planter box. Group potted plants on a plastic-covered window seat, display them on tiered tables, or use Lazy Susan plant stands. Any of these will provide a delightful staging for a collection of potted plants.

Portable planters equipped with rollers are convenient and practical. Redwood boxes and large pottery pieces are frequently set on dollies (wheeled platforms) which allow them to be moved around wherever a plant decoration is indicated.

A variation of this idea is a teacart for plants. It might be an old one you find at a secondhand store, or a bright new one. Either could become the center of attraction in an entire room

Large, shallow containers carpeted with pebbles kept moist make an ideal place for grouping a collection of potted plants. Here an antique pewter tray has white stones which contrast beautifully with the natural clay pots, and variegated sansevieria, chlorophytum (spider or airplane plant), English ivy, and euonymus. The plain green leaves of Chamaedorea elegans *(miniature palm) add a pleasant background.* Interior by Sermon-Anderson. (Photograph by Nicholson)

"A teacart for plants . . . the center of attraction in an entire room." The one shown includes, left to right, a small bottle garden, polyscias (tall, ferny plant), Norfolk Island pine, sunset ivy-leaf geranium, aglaonema (Chinese evergreen), aralia, peperomia, and episcia. Interior by Sermon-Anderson. (Photograph by Nicholson)

when converted to a plant stand. Group plants in colored plastic pots to complement the color scheme of the room. Make a conversation piece by setting a tall plant in a large pot by a miniature in a two-inch container. Set porous clay pots inside glazed jardinieres, or make a terrarium landscape. However you use it, a teacart of house plants will be a delight. And think of the convenience at watering time! Move cart and plants to the kitchen; feed and water, wash foliage, spray if you detect signs of insect infestation, prune branches, and pick off withered flowers and leaves. Then wheel the plants, refreshed, back to the living quarters.

PLANTS FOR THE OFFICE

Lavish displays of thriving foliage plants have changed thousands of offices into more pleasant places to work. Properly air-conditioned buildings no longer chill plants in summer, or dry them to a crisp in winter. Usually this year-round temperature comfort is maintained even on weekends.

Plant enthusiasts bud in every office; in fact, plants are more likely to be overpampered than neglected. It's a good idea in such a situation to leave the care of the plants to one person at a time; otherwise overfeeding and overwatering may result. Where masses of plants cover a major area of an office, a professional gardener can be hired to take regular care of the planting.

Many offices have no windows, and living plant material is out of the question unless artificial lights can be recessed into a ceiling or wall to keep plants in good growth. For more information about gardening indoors under lights, see Chapter 11.

2. Setting the scene for gardening indoors

ULTIMATELY, the pleasure of having potted plants comes from displaying them at home. They bring freshness and individuality to any room. Through the four seasons, a collection of house plants has many faces. The idea is to put the best of these forward in an always changing array of plant decorations.

ALL PLANTS NEED LIGHT

In any given situation, the amount of light available is the first consideration in growing healthy plants. Even the few kinds which are seemingly indifferent to the intensity of light respond to ideal lighting. For example, the Chinese evergreen (*Aglaonema modestum*) will exist on pebbles and water in a dark corner, or in front of a sunny window. However, when it is grown in humusy, moist soil and filtered light, the result is a longer lived, more handsome plant.

Flowering house plants need more light than those grown exclusively for foliage. Indoor gardens of flowering plants should be situated where they will receive direct sunlight part of each day in the winter. Except in the South, windows facing east, southeast, and south are preferred locations. Growers in the southern parts of Florida, Texas, Arizona, and other sunshiny states may find southern and eastern exposures too bright for flowering plants, except cacti and most other succulents. For these fortunate people, day-long light from northern windows or partially shaded south-facing locations give satisfactory results with many flowering house plants.

During the darkest days of winter, there is little chance of having indoor plants harmed by too much sun. A possible exception to this occurs where winter snow comes early and stays late. One friend, a most successful window gardener in Minneapolis, Minnesota, says that rays of the sun on snow bounce back through her house windows, admitting up to 30 percent additional light. When snow cover is constant, this grower finds it possible to flower wax begonias and African violets in a picture window on the northern side of her home. By this same token, gardeners whose north windows face white-painted buildings or an expanse of unshaded land find they can grow African violets, begonias, and some other flowering tropicals in this exposure.

HOUSE PLANTS THAT PREFER A SEMI-SUNNY LOCATION

Semi-sunny indicates a situation that receives two to five hours of direct sunlight in the winter. Most windows, except those facing directly south or north, fit into this classification. In the spring and summer these plants do well in bright light with little or no direct sun. They can be grown in a sunny location if protected by a curtain, or a screen of sun-loving plants.

ACAMPE	AERIDES	ALPINIA	ASARINA
ACANTHUS	AESCHYNANTHUS	ANGRAECUM	ASCOCENTRUM
ACHIMENES	ALLOPHYTON	APHELANDRA	ASPARAGUS
AECHMEA	ALLOPLECTUS	ARAUCARIA	BEGONIA
AEONIUM	ALOCASIA	ARDISIA	BELOPERONE

House Plants That Prefer a Semi-Sunny Location (cont.)

BLETIA	DIEFFENBACHIA	IPOMOEA	PLATYCERIUM
BORONIA	DION	JACOBINIA	PLECTRANTHUS
BOWIEA	DIPLADENIA	KAEMPFERIA	PLEOMELE
BRASSAVOLA	DIZYGOTHECA	KOELLIKERIA	PODOCARPUS
BROWALLIA	DRACAENA	KOHLERIA	POLYPODIUM
BRUNFELSIA	DUDLEYA	LAPAGERIA	PRIMULA
CALADIUM	DYCKIA	LEEA	PSEUDERANTHEMUM
CALATHEA	ELAEAGNUS	LICUALA	PSEUDOPANAX
CALCEOLARIA	ENSETE	LYCASTE	RECHSTEINERIA
CALLISIA	EPIDENDRUM	LYGODIUM	REINHARDTIA
CAMELLIA	EPIPHYLLUM	NEOMARICA	RHAPIS
CAREX	EPISCIA	NEOREGELIA	RHIPSALIS
CARYOTA	ERANTHEMUM	NEPETA	RHOEO
CATTLEYA	EUCHARIS	NEPHROLEPIS	RHOICISSUS
CEROPEGIA	EUONYMUS	NERTERA	RIVINA
CHAMAEDOREA	EUPHORBIA	NIDULARIUM	RUELLIA
CHIRITA	EURYA	ONCIDIUM	SAINTPAULIA
CHLOROPHYTUM	EXACUM	OPHIOPOGON	SANSEVIERIA
CHRYSALIDOCARPUS	FATSHEDERA	OPLISMENUS	SARCOCOCCA
CIBOTIUM	FATSIA	MALPIGHIA	SASA
CISSUS	FICUS	MANETTIA	SAXIFRAGA
CLERODENDRUM	FITTONIA	MANIHOT	SCHEFFLERA
CLIVIA	FRAGARIA	MARANTA	SCHISMATOGLOTTIS
CLUSIA	FUCHSIA	MIKANIA	SCHIZOCENTRON
COCCOLOBA	GARDENIA	MIMOSA	SCHLUMBERGERA
CODONANTHE	GASTERIA	MONSTERA	SCILLA
COFFEA	GEOGENANTHUS	MUEHLENBECKIA	SCINDAPSUS
COLEUS	GESNERIA	MUSA	SCIRPUS
COLOCASIA	GLOXINERA	NAUTILOCALYX	SELENICEREUS
COLUMNEA	GLOXINIA	NEOFINETIA	SENECIO
COMMELINA	GUZMANIA	PANDANUS	SERISSA
CONVALLARIA	GYNURA	PAPHIOPEDILUM	SERJANIA
CORDYLINE	HABENARIA	PARTHENOCISSUS	SIDERASIS
COSTUS	HATIORA	PEDILANTHUS	SINNINGIA
CRASSULA	HAWORTHIA	PELLIONIA	SMILAX
CROSSANDRA	HEDERA	PEPEROMIA	SMITHIANTHA
CRYPTANTHUS	HEDYCHIUM	PERESKIA	SONERILA
CTENANTHE	HELICONIA	PETREA	SOPHRONITIS
CURCUMA	HIPPEASTRUM	PETROCOSMEA	SPARMANNIA
CYCAS	HOFFMANNIA	PHAIUS	SPATHICARPA
CYCLAMEN	HOMALOMENA	PHILODENDRON	SPATHIPHYLLUM
CYCNOCHES	HOWEA	PHOENIX	STENANDRIUM
CYMBALARIA	HOYA	PILEA	STREPTOCARPUS
CYMBIDIUM	HUERNIA	PIPER	STROBILANTHES
CYPERUS	HYPOCYRTA	PISTIA	SYNGONIUM
DENDROBIUM	HYPOESTES	PITCAIRNIA	TIBOUCHINA
DICHORISANDRA	IMPATIENS	PITTOSPORUM	TILLANDSIA

House Plants That Prefer a Semi-Sunny Location (cont.)

TOLMIEA	VANILLA	WITTROCKIA	ZANTEDESCHIA
TRADESCANTIA	VELTHEIMIA	WOODWARDIA	ZEBRINA
VANDA	VRIESIA	ZAMIA	ZYGOCACTUS

HOUSE PLANTS THAT PREFER A SUNNY LOCATION

Sunny *indicates a situation which receives at least five hours of direct sunlight in the winter. Most windows that face east, southeast, or south fit into this classification.*

ABUTILON	CARISSA	EUCALYPTUS	IMPATIENS
ACACIA	CENTAUREA	EUCOMIS	IPOMOEA
ACALYPHA	CEPHALOCEREUS	EUGENIA	IRESINE
ACAMPE	CEREUS	EUPHORBIA	IXORA
ADROMISCHUS	CESTRUM	FATSHEDERA	JASMINUM
AGAPANTHUS	CHAENOSTOMA	FAUCARIA	JATROPHA
AGAVE	CHAMAECEREUS	FEIJOA	KALANCHOE
ALLAMANDA	CHAMAEROPS	FELICIA	KLEINIA
ALOE	CHORIZEMA	FENESTRARIA	LACHENALIA
ALTERNANTHERA	CHRYSANTHEMUM	FORTUNELLA	LAMPRANTHUS
AMARCRINUM	CITRUS	FRAGARIA	LANTANA
AMARYLLIS	COBAEA	FREESIA	LAPEIROUSIA
ANACAMPSEROS	COCCOLOBA	GARDENIA	LEPTOSPERMUM
ANANAS	CODIAEUM	GAZANIA	LIGUSTRUM
APOROCACTUS	COLEUS	GERBERA	LILIUM
APTENIA	CONOPHYTUM	GLORIOSA	LITHOPS
ASTROPHYTUM	COTYLEDON	GLOTTIPHYLLUM	LOBIVIA
AZALEA	CRASSULA	GRAPTOPETALUM	LOTUS
BAMBUSA	CRINUM	GREVILLEA	LYCORIS
BAUHINIA	CUPHEA	GYMNOCALYCIUM	MAHERNIA
BEAUCARNEA	CYANOTIS	GYNURA	MALPIGHIA
BEGONIA	CYPELLA	HABRANTHUS	MAMMILLARIA
BELOPERONE	CYRTANTHUS	HAEMANTHUS	MESEMBRYANTHEMUM
BILLBERGIA	CYTISUS	HEBE	MIMULUS
BOUGAINVILLEA	DINTERANTHUS	HEDERA	MORAEA
BOUVARDIA	DIONAEA	HELICONIA	MUSA
BRUNSVIGIA	ECHEVERIA	HIBISCUS	MYRSINE
CALADIUM	ECHINOCACTUS	HIPPEASTRUM	MYRTUS
CALLIANDRA	ECHINOCEREUS	HOODIA	NERINE
CALLISTEMON	ECHINOPSIS	HOYA	NERIUM
CALLUNA	ENSETE	HYDRANGEA	NICODEMIA
CAMPANULA	ERICA	HYDROSME	NICOTIANA
CAPSICUM	ERVATAMIA	HYLOCEREUS	NOTOCACTUS

House Plants That Prefer a Sunny Location (cont.)

OLIVERANTHUS	PITTOSPORUM	SANTOLINA	STRELITZIA
OPLISMENUS	PLEISPILOS	SASA	STREPTOSOLEN
OPUNTIA	PLUMBAGO	SAXIFRAGA	SYNADENIUM
OREOPANAX	POINCIANA	SCHEFFLERA	TAVARESIA
ORNITHOGALUM	POLYSCIAS	SCILLA	TETRAPANAX
OSMANTHUS	PORTULACARIA	SCUTELLARIA	THEVETIA
OXALIS	PSEUDOSASA	SEDUM	THUNBERGIA
PACHYPHYTUM	PUNICA	SEMPERVIVUM	TITANOPSIS
PACHYVERIA	PYRACANTHA	SENECIO	TRIFOLIUM
PARTHENOCISSUS	REBUTIA	SETCREASEA	TULBAGHIA
PASSIFLORA	RIVINA	SOLANUM	VALLOTA
PELARGONIUM	ROCHEA	SPREKELIA	VELTHEIMIA
PENTAS	ROSA	STAPELIA	VITIS
PETUNIA	RUTA	STENOTAPHRUM	ZANTEDESCHIA
PHORMIUM	SANSEVIERIA	STEPHANOTIS	ZEPHYRANTHES

HOUSE PLANTS FOR A
SEMI-SHADY LOCATION

Semi-shady *indicates an area that receives bright light most of the day in winter, but little or no direct sun. In this situation, very few plants cultivated for flowers grow well, but those which do are followed by the abbreviation* fl.

ACHIMENES *fl.*	CHLOROPHYTUM	MILTONIA *fl.*
ACORUS	CISSUS	MONSTERA
ADIANTUM	CORDYLINE	NEPHROLEPIS
AECHMEA *fl.*	CYPERUS	NEPHTHYTIS
AGLAONEMA	CYRTOMIUM	ODONTOGLOSSUM *fl.*
AMOMUM	DARLINGTONIA *fl.*	ORNITHOCEPHALUS *fl.*
ANTHURIUM *fl.*	DAVALLIA	PANDANUS
ASPIDISTRA	DIEFFENBACHIA	PAPHIOPEDILUM *fl.*
ASPLENIUM	DRACAENA	PELLAEA
ATHYRIUM	EPISCIA *fl.*	PELLIONIA
AUCUBA	FICUS	PEPEROMIA
BEGONIA *fl.*	FUCHSIA *fl.*	PHALAENOPSIS *fl.*
BERTOLONIA	HAEMARIA *fl.*	PHILODENDRON
BLECHNUM	HEDERA	PHOENIX
BRASSAVOLA *fl.*	HELXINE	PHYLLITIS
CALADIUM	HEMIGRAPHIS *fl.*	PHYSOSIPHON *fl.*
CALATHEA	HOWEA	PILEA
CEROPEGIA *fl.*	LAPAGERIA *fl.*	PITTOSPORUM
CHAMAEDOREA	LYGODIUM	PODOCARPUS
CHAMAERANTHEMUM *fl.*	MARANTA	POLYPODIUM

House Plants for a Semi-Shady Location (cont.)

POLYSTICHUM
PTERIS
SAINTPAULIA *fl.*
SANSEVIERIA

SCHEFFLERA
SCINDAPSUS
SELAGINELLA
SPATHIPHYLLUM *fl.*

SYNGONIUM
WOODWARDIA
ZAMIA

HOUSE PLANTS FOR A
SHADY LOCATION

Shady *indicates an area that may be dimly lighted even in the middle of a sunny day. The plants in this category tolerate low-light intensity but seldom thrive in it. To decorate with potted plants in such a situation, a rotation plan like this can be used: While one group of plants occupies the shady area, rejuvenate another in a semi-sunny place. Or, use fluorescent light (Chapter 11).*

AGLAONEMA
AMOMUM
ASPARAGUS
ASPIDISTRA
CHAMAEDOREA
CHLOROPHYTUM

CYPERUS
DIEFFENBACHIA
FICUS
HEDERA
MONSTERA
NEPHROLEPIS

NEPHTHYTIS
OPHIOPOGON
PHILODENDRON
PITTOSPORUM
PODOCARPUS
POLYPODIUM

POLYSTICHUM
PTERIS
SANSEVIERIA
SCHEFFLERA
SCINDAPSUS
SPATHIPHYLLUM

HOUSE PLANTS THAT NEED COOLNESS

60-65° F. in the daytime, with a drop into the 50's at night.

ACACIA
ACORUS
ATHYRIUM
AUCUBA
AZALEA
BORONIA
CALCEOLARIA
CALLUNA
CAMELLIA
CAMPANULA
CHRYSANTHEMUM
CONVALLARIA
CYCLAMEN
CYMBALARIA
CYMBIDIUM

CYPELLA
CYTISUS
DAPHNE
DARLINGTONIA
DIONAEA
ERICA
EUONYMUS
FATSHEDERA
FATSIA
FRAGARIA
FREESIA
FUCHSIA
GERBERA
GYMNOCALYCIUM
HABENARIA

HEBE
HEDERA
LACHENALIA
LANTANA
LAPAGERIA
LIGULARIA
LIGUSTRUM
LILIUM
LIRIOPE
LYCASTE
MILTONIA
MORAEA
NERINE
NERTERA
NOTOCACTUS

ODONTOGLOSSUM
ORNITHOGALUM
OSMANTHUS
PHYLLITIS
PHYSOSIPHON
PRIMULA •
REBUTIA
SENECIO
SOPHRONITIS
STREPTOCARPUS
TRIFOLIUM
TULBAGHIA
VELTHEIMIA
VIBURNUM
ZEPHYRANTHES

The Daily Quarter Turn. There is an ageless rule that says potted plants in a window need to be rotated a quarter turn each day. If you have time to do this, fine, but unless plants are being groomed for exhibition, it isn't really necessary. The idea is that plants turned like this develop symmetrically because each side receives its share of light.

If having perfectly symmetrical plants appeals, and you haven't time to give each its daily quarter turn, try rotating the pots whenever you water them. I confess that in my collection the pots are turned infrequently if at all. I don't object to plants that face one direction. In fact, when I want to display several of them for a special occasion, plants with one exceptionally good side are better than those which face all directions and have no obvious front.

MOST HOUSE PLANTS NEED WARMTH

A temperature range of 65-75°F. satisfies the majority of house plants. The few kinds that need coolness, especially during fall, winter, and spring, are listed in the accompanying table. They can be grown on a frost-free sun porch, or in a seldom used sunny bedroom. For special occasions, enjoy them anywhere in the house, but spare them the torture of long sessions in hot, dry air.

In severe winter climates where cold weather keeps frost on the windows at night, slip a newspaper or cardboard between plants and the window pane to keep them from freezing. Often the space on a window sill in this kind of climate is so chilly in the winter that cool-loving plants can be grown there, even though the interior of the room is warm.

AMPLE HUMIDITY SPELLS SUCCESS WITH HOUSE PLANTS

Pleasantly moist air is a boon to healthy house plants. Specifically, a range of 30 to 60 per cent relative humidity satisfies the majority. The most nearly perfect combination for plants and people is a temperature near 72°F. with about 50 per cent humidity.

Even if your plants are doing well, you will find it convenient to own a hygrometer (about $10 at local hardware stores, or by mail from house plant specialists). This instrument measures the quantity of moisture in the air. One of my friends did everything to make a new collection of African violets thrive. Within a few days all flower buds dried up, and the leaves were beginning to wither. A hygrometer placed nearby registered only 5 per cent relative humidity! This knowledge made it possible for him to correct the problem before valuable plants were permanently harmed.

How To Provide More Humidity. If you desire lush green foliage and quantities of bloom on house plants, use every possible device to heighten humidity around them. The old rule of safety in numbers applies. Group pot plants in a deep brass or wooden planter and place moist sphagnum or peat moss around them. Another way to increase humidity and display plants at the same time is to set pots on the surface of pebbles kept moist inside a plastic or metal tray. One of my friends who grows luxuriant house plants keeps water in deep galvanized trays. She sets bricks or pieces of redwood into the water and places the plants atop these. The bases of the pots never touch the water, but evaporation from beneath them benefits the plants.

A slip cover of transparent polyethylene plastic can be made and placed over non-display gardens (plants on a porch, or those growing under lights in a basement or attic). This will hold enough moisture to provide an atmosphere conducive to good plant growth. Some growers report success when they place drinking glasses filled with water among their plants. This practice can enhance the beauty of a window garden if the containers are of colored glass. Some of them could include cuttings of English ivy, wax plant, Chinese evergreen, or philodendron.

The kitchen of an active homemaker yields considerable

humidity. For example, a boiling teakettle, the steam escaping from a dishwasher, or a simmering pot—all do their part in humidifying the house. Terrarium gardens in glass containers are assured an atmosphere that is always moist (Chapter 7).

Another way to increase relative humidity is to spray leaves often with water that is at room temperature. The sprayer can be anything from a plastic tube and nozzle, such as one uses for cleaning windows, to a fogger designed specifically for house plants. Inexpensive metal ones tend to rust after a few months, but those of plastic last indefinitely.

An almost automatic way to mist your plants is to invest in a cool-vapor humidifier. Room-size units are sold by every neighborhood pharmacy, usually priced at around $20. One of these will hold one or two gallons of water and when operated constantly will need refilling once or twice every 24 hours. The next step up from one of these is an apartment- or small house-size portable humidifier. The one I use holds six gallons of water and when set on "high" in the middle of winter when the heat is on full blast, it needs refilling every other day. This unit, with one supplementary room-size humidifier, maintains a range of 50 to 60 percent relative humidity during the winter in my two-bedroom apartment. In combination with temperatures around 68 to 72 degrees, this amount of humidity produces healthy plant growth and is also desirable for people, furniture and the piano. If you live in a house, consider installing a humidifier in your heating system. Do not run a humidifier while an air conditioner is operating; cooling unit removes moisture from the air.

SOIL: THE FOUNDATION FOR HEALTHY HOUSE PLANTS

The texture of potting soil is more important than its richness. Porous soil having enough leaf mold or peat moss in it can be supplied with necessary nutrients in the form of fertilizers. Indeed, with added care in their fertilizing, plants can be grown in sterile mediums such as vermiculite, sphagnum moss, sand, or Perlite.

It is possible to purchase prepared potting soils at plant counters, greenhouses, florists, seed stores, and from mail-order specialists. Most of these mixtures are well balanced and, for a small plant collection, they save the bother of soil preparation. The newest prepared growing mediums on the market are called "soilless." These are based on formulas perfected at Cornell University and the University of California. You can buy them under such trade names as Jiffy Mix, Super Soil and Redi-Earth. To mix your own, I recommend this recipe from grower Michael Kartuz: 2 quarts sphagnum peat moss, screened; 1 quart Terralite vermiculite; 1 quart coarse Perlite; 1 tablespoon ground limestone. Moisten mix prior to use. Feed a little each time you water when growing in this mix; use one-fourth to one-fifth the usual amount recommended on the container of fertilizer.

There are hundreds of soil formulas, many of them originated by hobbyists to fill the special requirements of such plants as African violets, amaryllis, begonias, cacti, gloxinias, and fuchsias. If you have a mixture that grows one of these plants to perfection, by all means keep on using it. The basic soil recipe given below will provide a good medium for all plants except some cacti, orchids, bromeliads, and possibly geraniums.

The Basic Potting Soil Mixture:
>   1 part garden loam
>   1 part sand
>   1 part peat moss or leaf mold

When growing instructions call for charcoal or Perlite in the soil, add to 2 quarts of the dry basic mixture 1 cup Perlite or ½ cup charcoal chips.

For cacti (except Christmas cactus which needs regular potting soil) instead of the basic mixture, use:
>   ½ part garden loam
>   2 parts sand
>   ½ part peat moss or leaf mold

Most orchids and some bromeliads require an entirely different potting mixture, such as osmunda fiber, redwood chips, or shredded fir bark. Bromeliads and terrestrial orchids, such as paphiopedilums, can be grown in a mixture of 3 parts shredded bark (½-in. size) and 1 part dried crushed oak leaves. The epidendrum orchids grow easily in unmilled sphagnum moss kept moist and fertilized regularly.

For geraniums (pelargoniums), instead of the basic potting soil mixture, use this recipe:

> 2 parts garden loam
> ½ part sand
> ½ part peat moss or leaf mold

Plants like citrus fruits and azaleas, which require an acid soil, can be grown in the basic mixture given above, and fed an iron chelate (Sequestrene, for example), according to package directions.

Pasteurizing Potting Soil. It is wise to pasteurize, or sterilize, all home-mixed house plant soil. Most commercial mixtures have been steamed before you buy them, and will be labeled "sterilized." Sterilizing done through heat, or by chemical fumigation, kills harmful germs and insect larvae or eggs which might be lodged in the soil. The simplest way to sterilize a potting medium is to put it in a roaster pan, add a cup of water to each gallon of the mixture, and bake forty-five minutes at 180°F. Turn out on a clean newspaper and allow to cool for twenty-four hours before using.

To sterilize a bushel of soil chemically, mix 2½ tablespoons of formaldehyde in a cup of water and pour this solution over the top of the soil. Cover it for twenty-four hours with a large sheet of polyethylene plastic, and then air the soil. Other commercial soil sterilants may be used according to package directions.

CONTAINERS FOR HOUSE PLANTS

Selecting pots, tubs, and other planters is part of the pleasure derived from cultivating house plants. Containers can be complementary accessories, even objects of art, at the same time that they provide a place for roots and soil.

The Unglazed Clay Pot. This container is inexpensive and makes a good starting place for young plants. New clay pots have an orange-red color that may clash with some flowers and surroundings, but this weathers to a certain neutrality that goes well with almost anything. The top of a standard clay pot is as wide as it is high. For example, the smallest size commonly used is two inches tall and two inches wide across the top. The complete size range starts with a 1¼-inch thumb pot, and extends to an 18-inch tub. A three-quarter or azalea pot is three fourths as tall as it is wide. Bulb pans are half as tall as they are wide.

Italian clay pots are enjoying increasing availability in this country. Some of them have smooth walls extending to the rounded edge at the top. These do not have the "lip" along the top edge that characterizes our standard clay pot. The more ornate Italian pots are decorated on the outside with floral garlands.

The important thing to remember about unglazed clay pots is that they evaporate moisture through the sides as well as at the soil surface. This action keeps roots cooler in hot, dry weather but, at the same time, it may be impossible to keep the soil and plant roots sufficiently moist without constant watering. To prevent rapid evaporation, place the clay pot inside a glazed jardiniere, or mulch the soil surface with pebbles. All kinds of clay containers are now in short supply, especially the matching saucers. Take good care of, indeed cherish, those you have.

Because unglazed clay pots do not hold moisture, they are recommended for cacti and other succulents. Orchids, bromeliads, and other epiphytes do well in clay pots made with special drainage holes which extend up the sides.

Plastic Pots. These lightweight plant containers come in the same sizes and shapes as clay pots. In addition, they are sometimes square. Although plastic pots are made in many colors, the creamy white kinds look best with plants, especially those grown for flowers. Sometimes, however, colored plastic pots may be used effectively in a decorating scheme. For example, red pots complement wax begonias and most geraniums. Or, foliage plants in pale-blue pots add visual coolness to a summer display.

Moisture does not evaporate through the sides of plastic pots, and plants growing in them require less frequent watering. It is interesting to note that while roots of plants in clay pots tend to stay near the pot walls, in plastic they penetrate the entire body of soil.

Glazed Ceramic Pots. This kind of container is available in many sizes and shapes. Sometimes the colors are too vibrant, and distract from the plants, but, when chosen carefully, they make attractive furnishings. If a drainage hole is provided, glazed ceramic pots can be used in the same way as those made of plastic. Evaporation of moisture occurs only through the soil surface and the plant itself. Glazed as well as unglazed ceramic containers which do not have drainage holes can be used as slip covers for slightly smaller clay or plastic pots. To make ready, put in an inch of pebbles, then place the plant pot on these. If you plant directly in a drainless pot, water very carefully.

Saucers for Pots. Except when pots are grouped together in a waterproof tray or planter, a saucer is needed for each to protect the window sill, floor, or other surface. Plastic pot saucers are available in all sizes and colors, and most glazed ceramic pots come with a saucer attached. Unglazed clay saucers complement matching pots, but they are not completely moisture-proof. Where a little dampness over a long period of time might harm a wooden surface or a rug, cut pieces of cork to fit under unglazed clay saucers. Moisture will then evaporate through the cork. The inside surface of a saucer can also be sealed with shellac or paint and a circle of felt added on the bottom as a final protective measure for a fine wood surface.

Cleaning Pots. Plastic and glazed ceramic flowerpots can be cleaned in detergent and warm water just as if they were dishes; unglazed clay requires more strenuous activity. When subjected to constant moisture, the sides of clay pots become mossy, and often they display a white crusting from fertilizer salts. Use a stiff brush and hot, sudsy water to clean them. To clean empty clay pots, place them in a pail of hot water to which a half cup of household bleach has been added. Let stand a few hours, then scrub and rinse clean.

Trays for Pot Plant Collections. The grouping of potted plants in a shallow tray filled with moist gravel dates from the time when steam radiators first became a part of dwellings, and indoor gardeners found this a means of growing house plants. Today this practice retains its utilitarian value, but at the same time it gives the imaginative person an opportunity to create pleasing arrangements of plants in all kinds of trays filled with interesting pebbles or stones. The oriental influence now apparent in American gardens has much to do with our present awareness of simple plant displays and natural surfaces.

Ready-made trays vary in size from about twelve inches to several feet in diameter. For pure utility, a shallow Pyrex baking dish from the kitchen can be used for one or two large plants or several small ones. One West Coast orchid grower manufactures round trays of brass or black plastic up to 18 inches in diameter. In Cleveland, Ohio, Tube Craft, Inc., makes a Fiberglas tray 1½ inches deep, 19 inches wide, and 49 inches long. This is especially useful in front of double, or picture windows. Antique shops and country auctions often yield trays suitable for house plants.

Any sheet metal shop can make a galvanized tray to fit individual needs. A depth of two inches is usually ample. Any exposed surface of the tray can be covered with waterproof paint to harmonize with the setting.

While small pebbles or uniform, water-polished stones may be more attractive in a tray, there are other moisture-holding materials which can be used. These include coarse vermiculite, Perlite, dolomite gravel, peat moss, and sand. It is important that the pots themselves not touch the water contained by the tray.

"Many windows do not have sills wide enough to accommodate flowerpots. If this is your problem, try a self-attaching plant shelf." This one, of Swedish design, includes, *left to right, scirpus (miniature bulrush), caladium 'Red Flash,' crassula hybrid, tangerine, ornamental pepper,* Anigozanthus flavidus, *and pelargonium 'Inferno.'* (Photograph by Nicholson)

Stands and Shelves for Pot Plant Display. Metal plant stands with rings, or Lazy Susan circular trays for holding pots are useful for exhibiting flowering plants. For example, use a white-painted wrought-iron stand to hold a dozen flower-laden wax begonias or African violets, each growing in a spotless white plastic pot.

Many windows do not have sills wide enough to accommodate flowerpots. If this is your problem, try a self-attaching plant shelf. There are several of these on the market. They are inexpensive yet practical and attractive.

Hanging window shelves offer a place for plants in the absence of a wide sill. These can be of simple designs utilizing glass shelves and wrought-iron hangers. They can be attached to wooden window frames in such a way as to do no permanent damage.

Tubs for Large Plants. The first plant tubs were probably wooden kegs, barrels, or kits. These are still useful where a round, rustic container fits the setting. Other wooden tubs made of moisture-resistant cedar, cypress, or redwood may be round, square, rectangular, triangular, hexagonal, or octagonal. Whether made commercially or at home, they may be stained, painted, or left natural. Many handsome plastic planters have been designed to go with contemporary furnishings.

Soy tubs made of wood and bamboo can be used with any decorating scheme, but they are especially useful with an oriental décor. Large porcelain urns from Japan are also appropriate to this kind of interior. If the container includes elaborate floral decoration, it is better used for a foliage plant such as asparagus-fern than for something that bears flowers.

Decorators often place urns of cast iron, clay, or concrete in a formal entranceway. Foliage plants, when added, give the urns a final touch of elegance.

Any large jardiniere, kettle, or decorative bucket may be used as a plant tub. A copper cooking kettle or coal bucket is often used as a planter with early American interiors. The basic requirement for such a container is that it be moisture-resistant. If the one you select is not, grow the plants in regular pots and wrap the base of each in aluminum foil or set it in a saucer inside your decorative container. Water carefully so that soil remains moist, but never saturated. The edges of the pots can be concealed by filling the space between them and the container, and carpeting the surface with pebbles or florists' sheet moss.

Built-in Planters. One of the most enjoyable ways to garden indoors is in a built-in planter. This can be of any size, shape, or height to fit the location. Sometimes a planter is recessed into the floor in front of a large window. The most vital consideration is availability of light. When built-in planters are placed so that they receive no strong daylight, it is difficult to grow thriving plants. If the builder of your house left you this kind of planter, fluorescent lighting (Chapter 11) may be the answer. Or, you can adopt a rotation plan, letting plants stay in the

planter for about two weeks, then giving them a period of time in good lighting. Depth of the actual planting areas is also important. Six inches is the minimum, and depths of 12 to 18 inches are desirable for large plants.

A planter in an entranceway, accented by a soft spotlight, forms a perfect introduction to a home decorated with plants. If there isn't room for a separate entrance, let a planter-divider create the illusion of one.

Built-in planters require rust-resistant liners made of galvanized steel. However, before contacting your local metal shop, investigate the possibility of using a molded plastic liner. These are becoming available in an increasing number of sizes and colors.

Plants can go directly into the soil of a built-in planter, or they can be left in individual pots submerged in moist peat moss. To have a planter that is attractive at all times, depend on foliage plants as the mainstays—philodendron, dracaena, Norfolk Island pine, aglaonema, aralia, dwarf palm, English ivy, dieffenbachia, cissus, fatshedera, ferns, rubber plant, fiddle-leaf fig, pilea, peperomia, and schefflera. These can be set directly into the planter soil. Set off this backdrop of greenery with only one, or a few, flowering and fruiting pot plants. You might arrange to direct a small spotlight on the plant of the moment.

Other containers for indoor gardening, such as dishes, bottles, and crystal containers for indoor gardening, are discussed in Chapter 7, hanging baskets in Chapter 8.

LEFT: *"A built-in planter...can be of any size, shape, or height to fit the location." This one, recessed into the floor in front of a bay window, provides a perfect place for a collection of tropicals. Passiflora vines and Spanish moss act as draperies. Among the plants are orchids, ferns, coleus, begonias, dracaena, palm and dizygotheca.* (Photograph by Ezra Stoller Associates)

HOUSE PLANT MAINTENANCE DEPARTMENT

Potting and Transplanting. Any plant worthy of space in an indoor garden deserves to be potted correctly. Fortunately, this is not the ritual that some growers would have us think, but merely a basic step to good plant growth. The most common error made is to use a pot that is too large. There is a rule about this that says to replant in a container only one size larger than the previous one. For instance, small wax begonias, African violets, and similar plants arrive from the greenhouse in 2¼-inch pots. Probably they are ready to be shifted to 3-inch ones. This rule is not always valid. For example, consider a plant which has grown for too long a time in its present container. Perhaps it has sent hungry roots through the drainage hole into surrounding soil of a greenhouse bench or indoor planter. In such a situation, this rule of thumb is helpful: Replant in a pot or tub whose diameter at the top equals one third to one half the height of the plant. An 18-inch angel-wing begonia in a 3-inch pot might well be transplanted directly to a 6-inch container.

Repotting, or transplanting, is necessary whenever a plant fills the soil of its pot with roots. Type and age, plus time of year, determine how often repotting is needed. To inspect the rootball, invert the plant, holding its base and the soil surface with one hand, and tap the edge of the pot on a solid object. The roots and soil will slide out. If the roots have progressed to the point of filling the pot, and show outside the soil, the plant needs repotting. If the soil ball crumbles, repot in the same container.

It isn't always necessary to give a plant a larger container at repotting time. Mature bulbs of sinningia (the gloxinia of florists), and hippeastrum (common amaryllis) can be cultivated year after year in the same containers. Only the soil is changed, usually after the plants have been in dormancy and are ready to begin new growth. Many plants such as dwarf citrus can be root- and top-pruned at transplanting time and returned to the

LEFT: *Eighteen-inch angel-wing begonia, 'Corallina de Lucerna,' in 3-inch clay pot as it was purchased. Obviously this plant is completely out of proportion to its container. Even the usual shift to a pot one size larger wouldn't be enough. "In such a situation, this rule of thumb is helpful: Replant in a pot or tub whose diameter at the top equals one third to one half the height of the plant."* RIGHT: *The same begonia, transplanted to a 6-inch plastic pot whose diameter at the top is equal to a third of the plant's height.* (Photographs by Nicholson)

same container. This method works for many house plants, and makes it possible to keep them small enough for indoor culture even when they are many years old.

How To Pot a Plant. The actual potting routine begins with the placement of a piece of broken clay pot over the drainage hole. This is put concave side down, thus allowing moisture to escape but preventing the potting soil from going with it. Next comes a shallow layer of pebbles or gravel. (At this point when working with a container larger than 5 inches in diameter, it is a good idea to add a layer of unmilled sphagnum moss.) Follow this with potting soil and placement of the plant itself—usually in the center of a square or round pot. Hold the plant in position with one hand, and fill in the soil with the other. A tablespoon is a useful tool. Firm the soil in place around the roots, working carefully with your fingers. To allow for watering, leave a half

After depotting, "if roots have progressed to the point of filling the pot, and show out-side the soil (like those of this coleus which form a solid mass), the plant needs repotting. If the soil ball crumbles (as it did for this fuchsia in semi-dormancy), repot in the same container." (Photograph by Nicholson)

inch of space at the top of pots up to four inches in diameter, and an inch or more in larger ones.

After potting, settle the soil by tapping the base of the pot gently on a solid surface. Then water thoroughly, either from above, or by immersing the base of the pot in water until beads of moisture show on the surface. After draining, put the newly potted plant in a brightly lighted place for a few days, then move to its permanent location.

Label Your Plants Lest You Forget. Except in a small collection of house plants, limited to the most common kinds, a label on each makes indoor gardening more fun. I use the white plastic labels which are sold along with other gardening supplies, both locally and by mail. There is room on the label to include the name of the plant and its species, variety, or cultivar. Some examples: *Episcia cupreata, Episcia cupreata* var. 'viridifolia,' and *Episcia cupreata* cv. 'Chocolate Soldier.' In addition to the name, I usually include the date received, as well as the plant's source.

In the labeling examples above, there is a lesson to be learned from the International Code of Nomenclature for Cultivated Plants. *Episcia cupreata* is the original species of this plant as it was discovered in nature. *Episcia cupreata* var. 'viridifolia' is a spontaneous variation of the original, found either in nature or cultivation. *Episcia cupreata* cv. 'Chocolate Soldier' is the result of a hybridizing program carried on by man.

In practice, the abbreviations "var." and "cv." are seldom used except by plant breeders. The label for *Episcia cupreata* var. 'viridifolia' might even be shortened simply to *Episcia* 'viridifolia.' *Episcia cupreata* cv. 'Chocolate Soldier' is known everywhere as episcia 'Chocolate Soldier.'

Why the Latin names, which often seem forbidding? They remain the universal language of plantsmen. Some indoor gardeners call the episcia a "flame violet," but this name is known to relatively few people, and it is misleading. Not all episcias have flame-colored flowers, and none of them is a true violet. They are related to the African violet, which itself is no violet, but rather a *Saintpaulia,* and a member of the Gesneriad family. For more information on the rules that concern plant names, as adopted by the International Horticultural Congresses, send your request to the American Horticultural Society, Mount Vernon, Virginia, 22121, enclosing $1 for a copy of "The International Code of Nomenclature for Cultivated Plants."

Rejuvenating Large Planters. Extensive plantings in built-in containers and large tubs do not require complete replanting every year. In fact, if good soil is used to begin with, they can be left without any replanting for about two years. Regular feedings of a liquid house plant fertilizer such as 15-5-5 or 23-21-17 will help keep the plants in good condition. After eighteen to twenty-four months, another way to stall off replanting is to top-dress the soil. To do this, remove all of the old soil possible, taking all you can get without actually uprooting the plants. Replace with new soil.

Watering. One of the questions most often asked of me is, "How much water shall I give my plants?" There is no single answer. Hairy, thorny, or waxy-leaved plants need less water than smooth, thin-leaved kinds. Plants growing in plastic or glazed containers needn't be watered as frequently as those in clay. Plants growing on a cool sun porch need less water than those in ordinary living-room temperatures.

The general rule is to apply moisture when the topsoil feels dry to the touch. Use water of room temperature, and apply enough so that the soil of each plant is wet thoroughly from top to bottom. Do not water again until the topsoil feels dry. Never let water remain in a saucer more than an hour after moistening a plant. Plunge the pots of large plants like azaleas, hydrangeas, and palms into a bucket of water at least once a week. When soaked through and through, remove, allow to drain, then return to growing area.

Another way to determine a plant's need of water is by the use of a moisture comparator, a simple instrument comprising a glass meter atop a metal rod. When stuck into the soil, the meter registers immediately whether the soil is dry, moist, or wet.

While the convenience of letting a moisture comparator make the decision regarding when and when not to water may appeal to some people, most gardeners find it more practical to rely on sight and touch. When the top half inch of soil feels and looks moist, the plant needs no water. If water collects at the surface and stays there several hours or days without draining, the plant is in trouble. Drain off the water, then unpot the plant. Wash off its root system, and cut away any parts that appear to be diseased or rotted. Before replanting in a porous medium such as Black Magic Planter Mix, coat the roots with a fungicide such as horticultural dusting sulfur. In the future, be more careful about frequency and quantity of watering.

Wilted leaves generally mean a dry soil condition, but they can indicate also more serious troubles, such as crown rot (see instructions for culture of African violets, pp. 227–28), or nematodes (discussed later in this chapter).

What kind of water is best for potted plants? Generally speaking, any kind that is safe to drink. Chlorinated city water does not ordinarily contain enough chemicals to injure plants. If it did, you would find it completely distasteful. Rain water is satisfactory only if it has been caught in a vessel away from the eaves of a building. Water softeners of the ion-exchange type, such as Zeolite, replace the natural calcium in water with sodium, which is harmful to plants. If this is your problem, remove water for plants from the tap before it enters the softener.

Feeding House Plants. There are good chemical fertilizers on sale at most plant counters. The best kinds come as liquid concentrate to be diluted with water and applied according to package directions. In general, plants in active growth and planted in a basic potting mixture need to be fed every other week. Plants growing in a soilless mix can be fed with every watering, using fertilizer mixed at one-fourth to one-fifth the usual strength.

Organic fish emulsion fertilizers have always given good results, and now they are made by a process which removes most of the objectionable odor. Gesneriads, begonias, and all foliage plants are especially responsive to this kind of fertilizer.

House plant foods sold in sticks and tablets work well if

applied exactly according to package directions. With my large plant collection, I find them unsatisfactory because I never know which plant has had a tablet or stick, or when. My system is to fertilize every plant in active growth once every two to three weeks. Sometimes I do not have time, or the weather is cold and cloudy for several weeks, and the plants aren't fed at all. I avoid applying fertilizer to any wilted plant, or one that appears diseased or dormant.

Plant Sanitation. One of the nicest things about gardening indoors is the time spent in grooming individual plants. As often as possible (once a week is ideal), take each plant to a sink and clean the leaves with a gentle spray of tepid water. This removes dust and insect eggs, and discourages red spider mites. Keep hairy-leaved plants away from bright light until they are dry. Plants too large for moving to the kitchen can be cleaned with a soft brush, such as the kind a barber uses, with long, extra pliable bristles. It will whisk away dust on the most fragile leaves without harming them.

Large philodendrons and similar foliage plants can be cleaned by the use of a moist tissue or soft cloth. Afterwards, glossy foliage can be given an application of leaf-shining liquid. This is a common product wherever plants are sold. It gives a healthful-looking glow to naturally glossy leaves, and makes them more resistant to lint and dust.

The removal of withering leaves, stems, and flowers is a vital part of house plant sanitation. Cut these with the kitchen scissors, a razor blade, or small pruning shears. At the same time, study the plant to determine which growing tips need to be removed to induce bushiness. You can do this by pinching out the tender tip growth with your thumbnail and forefinger.

Staking. This is another facet of routine maintenance of house plants. Slender green bamboo stakes and Twist-ems are needed for this. Place stakes as inconspicuously as possible, and in any way to make a plant more attractive. Sometimes staking will help achieve a more graceful shape. Heavy flower heads often need support. The basic rule about house plant staking is this: Do it early. It's possible to keep a straight stem straight, but it may be disastrous to try to straighten a crooked one.

Many plants with aerial roots require another kind of staking, which utilizes a piece of bark-covered wood, a rectangle of pressed osmunda fiber, or a wire cylinder filled with unmilled sphagnum moss. This kind of stake is known in the trade as a "totem pole." It is vital to the proper growth of climbing philodendrons, monsteras, and syngoniums. Garden centers and florists frequently stock several kinds of totems, or you can make your own by using small-meshed poultry netting and moist sphagnum or osmunda fibers. Totems give the best support if they extend all the way to the bottom of the container, with potting soil firmed all around. Keep totems moist so that aerial roots will be encouraged.

TROUBLES TO EXPECT

Good culture averts many house plant misfortunes, but every indoor gardener needs to know the trouble signs, and how to deal with them.

Keeping house plant leaves clean helps prevent insect attacks. Spraying plants once a week with a house plant pesticide is a good trouble preventive, but it doesn't take the place of proper culture. For convenience, use a spray packaged in an aerosol container. Follow the manufacturer's directions.

Aphids cluster on new growth, causing it to be discolored and malformed. (Photograph by Nicholson)

Most insects that attack house plants are too small to be seen well with the naked eye, but sucking types such as aphids, mealybugs, white flies, and scale are detected readily. These pests leave a sticky substance, called "honey dew," which in turn acts as host to a sooty mold. A 20-power pocket microscope (about $3) will enlarge all pests for easy identification.

Aphids. There are hundreds of different kinds of aphids (plant lice). They cluster on new growth, causing it to be discolored and malformed. Eradicate them by the use of an aerosol pesticide, by spraying with Zectran according to container directions; or some growers hang a Vapona pest strip among their plants.

Cyclamen Mites. This pest is difficult to control. It is an infinitesimal creature capable of rendering horrendous damage to plants. This mite feeds on the growing tips of leaves, causing them to be deformed and stunted. Mite damage is easily detected in African violets. The center leaves become thickly furred, petioles (leaf stalks) are visibly shortened, and buds have enlarged stems so dwarfed in length that flowers seem to be opening near the soil surface. Dispose of all badly infested plants and start new ones from fresh leaves. If some of the plants are irreplaceable, clean them by cutting out the infested part, and spray the plant with a miticide. African violet specialists can supply you with the best kind. Kelthane and Dimite are currently in use and recommended. Since mites quickly build up a resistance to them, it is advisable that they be used alternately at weekly intervals. As a preventive measure, African violet authority Helen Van Pelt Wilson recommends the use of P-40, an African violet miticide designed for systemic control. Miticides sprayed on an infected plant will eradicate the mites, but leaves and buds already damaged will not grow out to natural size. While treating cyclamen-mite-infested plants, keep them isolated from others. Wash your hands well before touching other plants, for these mites are easily carried from one place to another. Other gesneriads and begonias are especially susceptible.

Earthworms. While they are welcome inhabitants of the outdoor garden, earthworms have no place indoors. Eradicate by drenching the soil with malathion (mix ½ teaspoon 50 percent emulsifiable concentrate in 1 quart of water).

Gnats. These gray to near-black insects are about one-eighth inch in length. The adults, while harmless to plants, are a nuisance to have around. Use a house plant spray pesticide to control them. They hatch from whitish maggots, about one-fourth inch in length, which are likely to be in soils containing decaying plant material. A severe infestation of the maggots can damage plant roots. Eradicate by drenching soil with malathion (mix ½ teaspoon 50 percent emulsifiable concentrate in 1 quart of water).

Mealybugs. These are soft insects covered with waxy powder. They are one of the worst, most persistent pests of house plants. They look like specks of cotton on a plant. If there are but a few, kill by touching them with a small cotton-tipped stick dipped in

LEFT: *Mealybugs look like specks of cotton on a plant; note formation on this dark-leaved fuchsia.* RIGHT: *In early stages of attack, mealybugs appear as individuals, like these on the underside of poinsettia leaves.* (Photographs by Nicholson)

LEFT: *White scale on dwarf citrus robs plant of strength.* (Photograph by Nicholson) RIGHT: *Brown scale on hibiscus, shown being flicked onto piece of paper with knife point.* (Photograph by Walker)

alcohol or nail-polish remover. House plant spray which contain malathion will eradicate more severe infestations.

Nematodes. These minute eelworms suck juice from plant roots and leaves, producing brown areas between the veins. Root nematodes cause knots or swellings on the roots. It is best to burn plants and soil infested with nematodes. There are several nematocides. VC-13 is one kind which will kill young nematodes. These chemicals are extremely poisonous and require utmost caution. Sterile soil is the best nematode preventive. Some growers claim to eradicate nematodes by applying water sweetened with a small amount of sugar. Unfortunately, the proportions for successful nematode control in house plants are not known.

Pillbugs. See *Sowbugs.*

Red Spider Mites. Too small to be seen with the naked eye, these pests spin fine webs on the undersides of leaves. They suck away plant juices until the leaves become nearly transparent. Spray firm-leaved plants such as amaryllis and English ivy repeatedly with a forceful stream of cold water. Miticides Kelthane and Dimite, used alternately, are recommended. Or try a house plant spray which indicates on the label that it includes a miticide.

Scale. Hard or soft scales are brown or black, round, slow-moving insects. If the infestation is small, and the plants are glossy-leaved ones, such as citrus, or English ivy, remove the scales by washing the leaves with a solution of strong soapsuds. Otherwise, spray with Ced-o Flora, or use a regular house plant pesticide spray. Later, wipe leaves clean of dead scale.

Slugs. These unpleasant creatures are soft, slimy, and legless. Outdoors they may grow to a length of four inches, but the indoor gardener usually has to contend with nothing longer than one inch. Wherever slugs find a home, snails may be present also. Both pests damage all plant parts, especially, it seems, the leaves of one's most prized plants. Constant vigilance in plant sanitation is the best control measure to prevent these pests from damaging a house plant collection. If this fails, use a commercially prepared bait which contains metaldehyde, following container directions.

Soft, slimy slug likes tender leaves such as one on a wax or semp florens begonia. (Photograph by Walker)

HOW TO DIAGNOSE HOUSE PLANT TROUBLES

IF YOUR PLANT LOOKS LIKE THIS . . .	THE CAUSE MAY BE THIS . . .	AND YOU CAN DO THIS . . .
Leaf edges crisp and brown; new growth may quickly wither.	Too much heat. Not enough humidity. Uneven soil moisture.	Lower temperature, preferably to plant's ideal range as given in Part II. Increase humidity for plant, following suggestions given earlier in this chapter. Avoid letting soil dry out severely, then flooding.
Lower leaves yellow, drop off.	Improper growing conditions or age.	Avoid temperature extremes. Provide more humidity, except with geraniums, where the need may be for more fresh air. Check to be sure soil is kept evenly moist. Plant may need biweekly feedings of fertilizer. Be sure there is no gas leakage in your house. After you take all these precautions, a yellow leaf probably indicates that it has matured, and is ready to be clipped off the plant.
Leaves appear lifeless, plant wilts frequently, and requires watering daily.	Temperature too high; pot too small.	Provide less torrid atmosphere. Transplant to larger container.
Yellowish brown, sometimes silvery, spots on leaves.	Too much sun.	Provide more shade. Often this occurs when plants are outdoors in summer.

How To Diagnose House Plant Troubles (cont.)

IF YOUR PLANT LOOKS LIKE THIS . . .	THE CAUSE MAY BE THIS . . .	AND YOU CAN DO THIS . . .
New foliage growth is yellow.	Lack of acidity.	Water plant with solution of 1 oz. iron sulfate dissolved in 2 gals. water. Repeat at biweekly intervals until growth is proper color. Common problem with azaleas, camellias, citrus, and gardenias.
White or yellowish rings and spots on foliage.	Cold water on roots and leaves.	Always moisten soil with water of room temperature. Don't let hot sunlight shine on foliage which has drops of water on it. Watering roots of tropical plants with icy water causes leaf spotting the same as if it were placed directly on the foliage.
No flowers.	Not enough sun. Lack of moisture. Too much fertilizer.	Provide more sunlight, or move plant closer to fluorescent tubes (Chapter 11). Increase humidity as suggested earlier in this chapter. Be careful to keep soil evenly moist at all times, or as directed in Part II for your specific plant. Feed less; don't use fertilizer with high nitrogen content at time of year when plant normally blooms.
Flower buds drop.	Improper growing conditions.	Avoid high or fluctuating temperatures. Be certain plant is not in a draft. Provide at least 40% relative humidity; misting foliage and flower buds twice daily may help.

How To Diagnose House Plant Troubles (cont.)

IF YOUR PLANT LOOKS LIKE THIS . . .	THE CAUSE MAY BE THIS . . .	AND YOU CAN DO THIS . . .
Stem gradually turns to mushy brown or black rot; leaves wilt.	Improper moisture conditions.	Don't water so much or so often; check to see if soil drains properly; root cuttings of remaining healthy growth, discard old plant. A common problem with begonias, African violets, gloxinias, and geraniums.
Growth of plant is slow, no flower buds form.	Improper growing conditions.	Study carefully the environment of your plant. Check soil, light, moisture, feeding, humidity, temperature. Be sure you are meeting the plant's cultural requirements as outlined in Part II, and that there is no insect infestation.

Sowbugs. Sowbugs and Pillbugs. These annoying pests have segmented, shell-like bodies. The sowbug is oval, up to one-half inch in length and usually gray in color. When you expose one at work (eating decaying organic matter, and sometimes tender plant parts), it runs for cover. Pillbugs roll up in a ball. Eradicate both by the use of malathion mixed according to directions given in this chapter under Gnats.

Springtails. The near-microscopic insects which scurry busily on the surface of humusy, moist potting soil are called springtails. Sometimes they damage tender seedlings. They are often confused with the harmless, though annoying, psocids that live in similar conditions, and which you may have seen between the leaves of old, slightly damp books or magazines. Both nuisances can be eradicated from indoor gardens by spraying the soil surface and lower plant parts with malathion, mixed according to directions given in this chapter under Gnats.

Thrips. These small sucking insects feed on the juices of foliage and flowers. They rasp away the plant tissue, leaving thin papery scars. In the outdoor garden they are especially prevalent on gladiolus. Indoors, thrips favor gloxinias. A house plant spray pesticide which contains malathion will eradicate them. A spray of Zectran will also get rid of thrips.

White Flies. These small insects cluster on the undersides of leaves, eventually turning them yellow; likely to attack begonias, citrus, fuchsias, geraniums, abutilons, and gardenias. Use a house plant aerosol which contains malathion.

Other House Plant Problems. Not all troubles with indoor plants stem from insects. Some of them result from improper growing conditions, described in the chart on the preceding pages.

Strictly Organic Pesticide. If you prefer not to use any chemical to control insect invasions on your house plants, this organic formulation which you make at home may be the answer: To 1 gallon water add the tobacco from 2 cigarettes, 2 cloves garlic, crushed, 1 dried chili pepper, crushed; soak overnight; strain. Pour liquid into spray bottle and thoroughly moisten all infested plant parts at weekly intervals. This preparation will remain effective for at least one month, then you should mix a fresh supply.

3. How to propagate plants indoors

Plant propagation is the most fascinating thing about gardening indoors. All the numerous methods for plant multiplication can be divided into two groups—vegetative and seed. Vegetative, or asexual, propagation includes the use of cuttings, stolons, offsets, divisions, air-layers, and grafts. Seed, or sexual, propagation utilizes seeds and spores, and gives the indoor gardener an opportunity to enter the exciting world of plant breeding.

VEGETATIVE PROPAGATION

By Cuttings. A cutting can be a single leaf from an African violet, or a terminal shoot or "slip" taken from a stem or branch of a begonia, fuchsia, geranium, or similar leafy plant. Professional gardeners often root cuttings in a sieved mixture of rich soil and sand. Beginners often root them in water. For the house plant hobbyist, I recommend rooting plant parts in a nonorganic medium such as vermiculite or Perlite, or in sphagnum moss, peat moss, or sand.

64

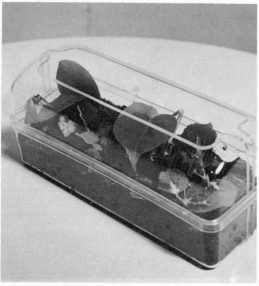

LEFT: *Drinking glass creates greenhouse-like atmosphere over coleus cutting in moist Perlite.* RIGHT: *Plastic bread box with transparent cover makes excellent propagating box.* (Photographs by Nicholson)

Cuttings root faster when given a close, humid atmosphere. This need not entail an elaborate setup. A single cutting may be covered with a drinking glass or a transparent plastic bag to create a greenhouse-like atmosphere. Similarly, to root a tray filled with cuttings, invert a large plastic bag over the entire planting to heighten humidity and promote rapid rooting. If cuttings are short, set a pane of glass over the propagator. There are numerous seed starters and miniature greenhouses on the market which work well for all kinds of plant propagation.

Plastic bread boxes with transparent covers make excellent containers for cuttings. Use a heated ice pick to force a few ventilation holes in the top. This simple kind of propagator is large enough to accommodate twelve or more leaf cuttings, and at least eight terminal cuttings from geraniums or wax begonias. Another favored propagator is an 8- or 10-inch clay or plas-

tic bulb pan (a shallow pot) with a 3-inch clay pot placed
in the center, its drainage hole closed with a cork. The pan is
filled with a rooting medium and the small center pot with
water. Moisture seeping through the clay walls of the center
pot will furnish dampness for the cuttings.

Large transparent plastic boxes, about 8 inches deep, and
12x16 inches in dimension, are sold by house plant supply
houses as propagators. This kind of box can be used to propagate an amazing quantity of material. I keep a box like this on
hand to preserve my supply of plants. Whenever I obtain a new
plant, I make a cutting from it as quickly as possible and insert
it in this propagator. If the parent plant should die, I always
have a rooted replacement.

Glass, covered Pyrex casseroles can serve as splendid leaf or
seed starters. A shallow redwood box built especially for propagating, covered with a pane of glass, also makes a practical
propagator, especially on a sun porch or under fluorescent lights.

Select a propagating container according to the size and number of cuttings to be propagated. If the container has drainage
holes in it, cover them with pieces of broken clay pot, or unmilled
sphagnum moss. Add the planting medium and set the container in a tray or sink filled with tepid water. When the planting medium shows beads of moisture on the surface, set it aside
to drain. When working with propagators having no drainage
holes, moisten the planting material before adding it to the container. Sphagnum and peat moss need to be moist enough to form
a loose ball when crushed in the hand before they are placed in
any container—pot or propagator.

Light, ventilation, moisture, and temperature are vital to
successful plant propagation. A warm, humid atmosphere and
moderate moisture induce faster rooting. The majority of house
plants root well at 70-75°F., but some tropicals such as croton
(Codiaeum) and rubber plant (Ficus) prefer a range of 75-80°F.
The heating cables included in most miniature greenhouses and
seed starters are preset at 72°F., but cables purchased separately
can be adjusted to bring up the bottom heat of the planting

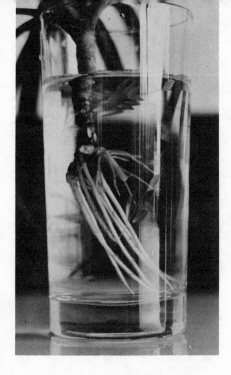

The simplest way to start cuttings is to root them in a glass of plain water. These healthy roots belong to a terminal cutting of Dracaena marginata. (Photograph by Nicholson)

medium without making the house uncomfortably warm.

Cuttings root best in a bright but not sunny area. This means keeping them away from the direct sun of eastern, southern, or western exposures. Too much light shining through the propagating case may burn cuttings or raise the temperature inside to the point of encouraging rot and mildew.

Slip the pane of glass or plastic covering away from the case at least once a day (oftener if necessary) to keep side walls and ceiling from filling with condensed moisture. Cuttings that root in two to three weeks, such as English ivy, philodendron and wax begonia, seldom need additional water. Cuttings that remain in the propagator for a longer period may need occasional watering.

The gardener who needs only one more African violet, begonia, or ivy may not want to bother with the preparation of propagators and special rooting mediums. If this is your situation, root the cutting or "slip" in water. Simply stick the end of the cutting in a glass or bottle of tap water and watch it root. The crucial part of this system lies in transplanting the water-

TOP: *Use a sharp knife to sever terminal·cuttings about ¼ inch below a node or leaf joint. Coleus is the plant shown.* LOWER LEFT: *Trim off lower leaves so that the stem can be set into the rooting medium. The flowering spike of this coleus cutting has been removed also.* LOWER RIGHT: *Insert leafy cuttings one third to one half their length in the propagating medium. Here a pencil has been used to make a hole in moist Perlite for a coleus cutting.* (Photographs by Nicholson)

rooted cutting to a pot of soil. Roots grown in water are thicker and more succulent than those produced in ordinary soil. When shifted to a soil-filled pot, this kind of cutting may take a long time to establish roots in the new growing medium.

How To Make a Cutting. Take a sharp knife and sever leafy cuttings, such as those from gardenia, geranium, and Jerusalem cherry, one-fourth inch below a node, or joint. Remove only enough of the lower leaves so that the stem can be set in the planting medium. Dip the cutting base in a hormone powder like Rootone to promote new growth.

Dry out cuttings full of sap before planting them. With cacti, the drying period may extend to several days. Before planting geranium cuttings, let the cut surface callous overnight.

Insert leafy cuttings one third to one half their length in the propagating medium. Do not let leaves touch the soil because this may cause them to rot. Make a hole in the medium with a pencil or your finger, then insert the cutting and settle it firmly in place.

The length of petiole (leaf stalk) left on African violets, gloxinias, rex begonias, and other plants propagated from leaf cuttings varies. A one-inch petiole is likely to produce better plants than a cutting with a longer stem. When little or no petiole is left on an African violet leaf, the likelihood of mutation is increased. Given optimum conditions of light, temperature, and moisture, it takes five to six months to produce a flowering plant from an African violet leaf cutting.

Rex begonia leaves can be handled exactly the same way as African violets, or it is possible to cut wedge-shaped pieces from a large rex leaf, each of which contains at least one prominent vein. When inserted in a moist rooting medium, each of these is capable of sending up one or more new plants. Gloxinia leaves with a half-inch or longer petiole can be rooted. After a time a new tuber will form at the base of the petiole. Eventually the old leaf dies, and a new plant grows from the young tuber.

The most interesting way to propagate gloxinias and rex begonias involves making small cuts through the veins on the

LEFT: *This is a mallet cutting of* Philodendron oxycardium. *Leaf forms a handle, the node and stem the head.* RIGHT: *Sansevierias can be propagated from one- to three-inch sections of leaves cut horizontally and inserted into rooting medium.* (Photographs by Nicholson)

back of a large, healthy leaf. Lay the leaf on a moist propagating medium in a covered propagator. Plantlets will form at each place where the veins were slit. When these are large enough to handle easily, remove carefully with as many roots as possible, and transplant to individual pots of moist soil. Cover the plants with glass or plastic until they are strong enough to withstand the open air.

Other plants which may be grown from leaf cuttings include sedums of all kinds, kalanchoes, and peperomias.

Leaf bud or mallet cuttings of philodendron, ivy, and rubber plant (*Ficus elastica*) are made by cutting the leaves with a node and about an inch of stem below and directly above. The leaf forms a handle, the node and stem the head, hence "mallet cutting." Insert so that the node points up, and is slightly covered by the rooting medium.

Propagate sansevierias from one- to three-inch sections of

leaves cut horizontally and inserted into a rooting medium. Such leaf cuttings usually reproduce new plants exactly like those from which they were taken. *Sansevieria trifasciata laurentii* is an exception. When this variegated plant is propagated by leaf sections, it reverts to the plain green of the species. To multiply the variegated form, divide an old plant at the base.

One way to propagate large alocasias, dieffenbachias, dracaenas, philodendrons, and Chinese evergreens is to cut the old

TOP: *Old stem of dracaena cut into four-inch pieces will yield many new plants. This section has begun to root, and several eyes are beginning to swell into growth.* (Photograph by Walker) BOTTOM: *Stolon of episcia will root quickly when pinned into a neighboring pot of moist soil like this. In a few weeks the young plant can be severed from the parent.* (Photograph by Nicholson)

stems into four-inch pieces. Coat the cutting ends with horticultural dusting sulfur, powdered charcoal, or Fermate to prevent rot. Lay them on the rooting medium in a propagator. New plants will develop from the eyes (undeveloped buds) on the cane.

Rooting Stolons. Some plants increase by sending out stolons, or runners—small plants which dangle from the mother plant. Examples include strawberry-begonia (*Saxifraga stolonifera*), episcias (African violet relatives) and spider plant (*Chlorophytum elatum*). Piggyback, or pickaback, plant (*Tolmiea menziesii*) bears new plants on the top of old leaves. The walking iris (*Neomarica northiana*) sends out plantlets at the end of the long, irislike blade which has borne the flowers.

Propagate any of these by removing the new plants and rooting them as cuttings. Roots develop quickly and the plants will be ready for potting soil in about four weeks.

Propagation by Offsets. African violets, other gesneriads, fibrous-rooted begonias, bromeliads, and haworthias are only a few of the many plants which grow offsets, or suckers. These small plants appear at the base of the old stem. They may be cut off with a sharp knife, and rooted as other cuttings. While African violets and haworthias may send out dozens of offsets, bromeliads usually send out one or two, and these only after the old plant has flowered and begun to die.

Amaryllis, fisherman's net (*Bowiea volubilis*), and many other bulbous plants increase by sending out small bulbs as offsets. Remove these when they are about two years old and replant them directly into potting soil. The sea-onion (*Urginea maritima*) sends out dozens of bulblets which cluster on the mother bulb. They are easily removed and started in any rooting medium.

Propagation by Division. Any plant with more than one stem emerging from the soil can be divided. Clivia, cane-stemmed begonias, African violets, ferns, and sansevierias are among the easily divided kinds.

There are two ways to divide a large plant: (1) Take a sharp knife and cut directly through roots and soil, removing separate divisions, or (2) knock the plant from the pot and gently pry the divisions apart. The direct cut method may seem ruthless but the plant will not suffer as great a setback as it would if roots had been pried apart. With either method, repot the divisions in sterilized soil, apply water, and shade them from direct sun until leaves are firm.

Tuber, Bulb, and Rhizome Divisions. Tubers such as gloxinias, tuberous begonias, and caladiums can be divided by cutting them into sections, each having at least one eye, or growing point. Coat the cut surfaces with Fermate or horticultural dusting sulfur, and set them in a propagator. Once rooted they can be transplanted into small pots of soil.

Bulbous plants like amaryllis, hyacinth, and lily can be propagated by removing a scale with a portion of its solid basal tissue from the parent bulb. This method requires considerable skill on the propagator's part, but it is a noble experiment. Coat the scale with horticultural dusting sulfur or Fermate and insert it into milled sphagnum moss, vermiculite, or a mixture of equal parts sand and peat moss. Give bulb scales filtered natural light or set them about four inches below a pair of 40-watt fluorescent lights. New growth will show in four to eight weeks.

A number of gesneriads, such as achimenes and smithiantha, grow from scaly rhizomes resembling pine cones. Individual scales separated from the rhizome and planted as small seeds on the surface of a moist rooting medium are capable of producing new plants.

How To Air-Layer. When large rubber plants, dracaenas, or similar specimens lose bottom leaves and become leggy, it is time to rejuvenate them. This can be accomplished by air-layering. There are two easy ways to do this: (1) remove a strip of bark directly below a node, or (2) cut a notch in the stem.

Wrap the peeled or cut portion of the stem with damp sphagnum moss and cover it with a piece of polyethylene plastic. Seal at top and bottom with electrician's tape, rubber bands, or Twistems. If the seal is good, no additional watering will be needed until the moss is full of roots and the new plant is ready for potting. If the seal isn't tight enough, the moss will have to be moistened

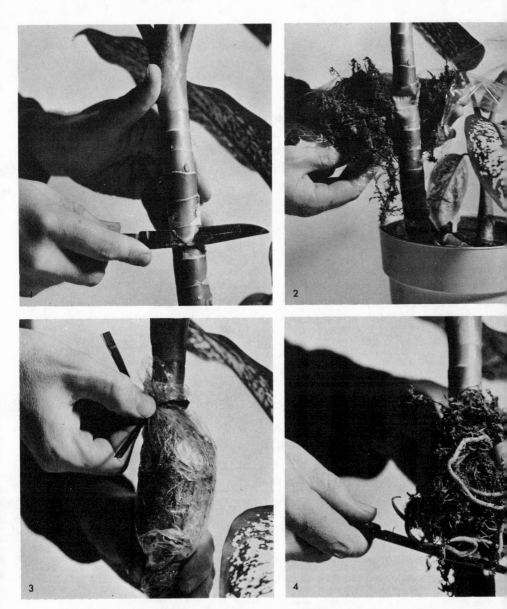

UPPER LEFT: *Step one in air-layering a dieffenbachia: Cut a notch in the stem where roots of the new plant are wanted.* UPPER RIGHT: *Step two in air-layering a dieffenbachia: Place a handful of moist sphagnum moss all around the stem, above and below the cut portion.* LOWER LEFT: *Step three in air-layering a dieffenbachia: Cover the sphagnum moss with a piece of polyethylene plastic. Seal at top and bottom with Twist-ems.* LOWER RIGHT: *Step four in air-layering a dieffenbachia: When roots show through moss, sever the new plant just below the root formation and pot it.* (Photographs by Nicholson)

occasionally. When roots show through the moss, sever the new plant just below the root formation and pot it. The old plant may send out new growth too, after having its top cut away.

Grafting. Although grafting is practiced mainly in the outdoor garden, the indoor gardener may enjoy experimenting with this form of propagation. In grafting, a potted plant is chosen for the stock, or standard. A bud, or a twig having several buds, called the cion, is inserted into the growing wood of the standard. At present, most house plant grafting is done with cacti. The Christmas cactus is often placed on an upright growing standard such as myrtillocactus, trichocereus, or pereskia. To prepare a standard like this, cut a V-shaped cleft in its center. Trim the cion of Christmas cactus to fit the standard. Pin the cion to the standard with long cactus needles, never with metal pins. Water sparingly when topsoil feels dry. If the graft is successful, the cion will show new growth within a few months.

PROPAGATING HOUSE PLANTS FROM SEEDS

Seeds are miraculous. Take, for example, the smithiantha. This plant bears seeds so small that almost two million of them placed together make only one ounce. Yet, one of these minute seeds will germinate in ten days from sowing, and will come into full bloom within eight months. The magic of a seed's sprouting, and its transformation to a mature plant, requires careful attention from the gardener. If the seeds are viable, you, as the sower, provide the conditions that will lead to their successful growth. Besides the enjoyment you will get from watching them develop, seeds will provide you with an inexpensive method of increasing house plants, and often a way of obtaining rare plants not listed by dealers.

Seeds come from species, hybrids, or fixed strains. Species are plants so nearly alike that they all might have come from a single parent. Examples are *Saintpaulia grotei* (trailing African violet), *Sinningia pusilla* (miniature gloxinia), and *Pilea involucrata* (friendship plant). Seeds from true species reproduce replicas of the

Only a sampling of the exciting house plants which can be grown from seeds—top row, left to right: chamaeranthemum, epiphyllum, smithiantha, and African violet; bottom row, left to right: angel-wing begonia, peperomia, kohleria, and billbergia. (Photograph by Brilmayer)

parent. Hybrids (discussed later in this chapter) are obtained by the cross-pollination of unlike but related plants. Fixed strains are hybrids which have been inbred through several generations until their outstanding characteristics become so stable that they can be propagated from seeds just as true species. Several named varieties of impatiens and coleus come true to type from seeds.

House plant seeds are available from many seedsmen whose names and addresses are listed under "Where To Buy Indoor Plants and Supplies for Growing Them," pages 301–05.

How To Plant Seeds. House plant seeds may be sown in any of the containers suggested earlier in this chapter for propagating cuttings. Use screened sphagnum moss, vermiculite, or a mixture of equal parts sand and peat moss for the top inch of starting medium. Bottom heat (between 70° and 75°F.) aids germination of seeds and growth of small seedlings. Small soil heating cables are available in several sizes to fit individual needs. Inexpensive models for seed flats are usually preset at 72°F. Larger ones, for greenhouse benches and outdoor hotbeds, may be thermostatically controlled.

Sow seeds sparingly and as evenly as you can. Seedlings that are bunched together will have poor air circulation. Such plants are likely to succumb to the damping-off disease. An easy way to deal with dust-size seeds is to add them to ¼ teaspoon of sterilized sand placed in a clean salt shaker. Sprinkle sand and seed evenly over the planting area.

If seeds are dustlike or powdery in size, then they are not covered, but sown on top of a moist medium. If they are larger, the rule of thumb is to cover them the depth of their own size. When I am working with seeds as large as those of coleus, impatiens, and gloxinia, I press them into the planting medium surface with the palm of my hand. No further covering is necessary.

Label each sowing, stating variety and date and any other information you may want. This is a handy reference when you want to determine how long it took certain plants to grow from seed to maturity.

Check seed sowings daily. Never allow the soil to dry out. If it shows signs of becoming dry, add water. Containers with drainage holes can be submerged in a sink or tray of water. Those without drainage can be moistened by misting the surface with tepid water. Sometimes I use a tablespoon for the careful addition of water to such a planting. If the medium should become drippy wet and stay this way for several hours, leave off the cover until the surface appears to be just nicely moist.

When seedlings show above the soil, move them to brighter light. The first two leaves that sprout from most seeds are cotyledons, which nourish the stem tip and the foliage leaves which follow. Until the foliage leaves appear, do not allow hot sunshine to reach the seedlings for more than a few minutes at a time. You can determine the amount of light seedlings need by learning the light requirements of the mature plant. For example, small geraniums need more sunlight than rex begonia seedlings. One ideal place for seedlings is 3 or 4 inches below a pair of 40-watt fluorescent lights (Chapter 11).

As soon as seedlings begin active growth, fertilize every two weeks with diluted liquid plant food. If the container does not make a strength recommendation for seedlings, mix the fertilizer at one third to one half the rate suggested for house plants.

When seedlings are started in closeness and high humidity, it is necessary for them to go through a hardening-off period. This is to accustom them to the open air. If a lid covers the container, leave it off at first for an hour or two each day. As the seedlings progress, leave the lid off all day or night, and finally entirely. If a plastic bag is used to cover a pot or small flat, it can be left open for short periods at first, then gradually longer until it is not needed. Throughout this time it is imperative that the growing medium never dry out severely.

Transplant seedlings before they begin to crowd each other. They can go into individual 2¼-inch pots, or space can be saved by transplanting several seedlings into a community pot or flat. As they grow, the largest ones are transplanted into separate containers. Use your fingers and a sharp instrument like a nail file or pencil to separate and lift tiny seedlings. Reset them at approximately the same depth as they have been growing, and firm soil gently around the roots. Water thoroughly from below.

Until transplants are established, keep them in a bright, warm

Spores on the reverses of fern fronds may be mistaken at first as a bad attack of scale. Fronds shown, starting at the top and moving clockwise, include Nephrolepis exaltata bostoniensis *(Boston fern),* Davallia fijeensis, *tip of polypodium, adiantum (maidenhair fern), and davallia (holly fern).* (Photograph by Nicholson)

place, but out of direct sunlight. They will benefit from a few days spent inside a propagator, where the air is moist.

FERNS GROW FROM SPORES

In addition to being propagated by division, ferns are grown from spores which are borne in masses of precise design, generally on the backs of their fronds, or leaves. (Some grow on separate branches.) Professional growers sometimes sow the spores in an agar solution such as that used for growing orchid seeds. I plant them successfully in sterilized potting soil. Spores are available from specialists, or you can pick them from your own ferns. When the powdery spores are maturing, clip the whole frond and place it in a paper bag. As the spores ripen, they become brown and even more powdery.

As quickly as possible after they ripen, sow the spores on a mixture of equal parts garden loam, sand (or Perlite), peat moss, and leaf mold (or vermiculite). I run this through a sieve, sterilize it in the oven (page 40), and add it to a 4-inch clay pot that has an inch of drainage material in it. The spores are scattered on top of the soil and a pane of glass is placed over the pot. I set the pot in a saucer of water, as it is vital that spore plantings be kept moist, and the plantings are placed

After fern spores are planted in a covered container, it may take them many months to attain the size of these young plants. (Photograph by Nicholson)

in a north window or near the end zones of a pair of 40-watt fluorescent lights. When the ferns have grown large enough to be handled on the point of a knife or nail file, I transplant them into 2-inch pots of sandy leaf mold and keep them in the same location. Later, as they mature, I use the young ferns in planters, hanging baskets, and dish and bottle gardens.

HOMEMADE HOUSE PLANT HYBRIDS

Having mastered the art of growing plants from seeds, you need very little more knowledge to make your plants produce seeds that will develop into interesting variations of the parents. Start with easy ones such as amaryllis, geranium, or gloxinia. Cross plants of the same kind, as one amaryllis with another amaryllis. To make most plants produce seeds, place pollen (yellow powder) from the anthers of one flower onto the tip of the pistil (this is called the stigma) of another flower. When the stigma is ready for pollination it generally widens, breaking into parts as in an amaryllis; or it may show an opening as in a gloxinia; or a feathery tip as in a geranium. If the pollination has been successful, the flower usually wilts within a few hours. Soon a swelling occurs in the ovaries located at the base of the flower. It takes a month to six weeks for amaryllis, geranium, and gloxinia seeds to ripen. The seed capsule or pod is ripe when it becomes brown, or shows openings. Shell the seeds into an envelope and store in a cool, dry place.

Seed vitality diminishes with age, but I have had five-year-old gloxinia seeds show 25 per cent germination. It takes about two years for amaryllis seedlings to reach blooming size. Gloxinias and geraniums bloom when less than a year old. If your cross was made on hybrid plants, or between a species and a hybrid, there may be some plants among the seedlings that will rival the beauty of the parents. There is always a chance that at least one seedling will be an improvement over the parent plants.

LEFT: *Pollinating a sinningia (the gloxinia of florists): Powdery yellow pollen is placed onto the tip, or stigma, of the pistil.* RIGHT: *The pollination was successful! Two pods have ripened and split open; they are ready to be harvested. The other will mature within a few days.* (Photographs by Schulz)

HOW TO START FLOWER AND VEGETABLE SEEDS INDOORS

If you have a sunny window, there are some flowers and vegetables for the outdoor garden which will benefit from an early start indoors. Twelve to sixteen weeks before the average date of your last killing frost in the spring, start any of these seeds: wax begonia, heliotrope, impatiens, snapdragon, torenia, and vinca. Eight to twelve weeks before the average date of your last killing frost in the spring, start any of these seeds: ageratum, browallia, calliopsis, coleus, dahlia, dusty miller, globe amaranth, gloriosa daisy, lobelia, marigold, nicotiana, petunia, phlox, salvia, verbena, and eggplant. Six to eight weeks before planting-out time, you can start quick-maturing annuals such as sweet alyssum, balsam, calendula, cockscomb, dianthus, zinnia, pepper, cabbage, and tomato. Start annual asters about six weeks before your frost-free date; they resent being root- or pot-bound at any time.

The easiest way to start bedding plants and vegetables indoors is to purchase pre-seeded planters. Most of them could be called "instant gardens." All you add is water.

If you plant your own seeds, they may be sown in pots or flats (shallow boxes) of sterilized potting soil. In the absence of seed packet directions, follow these general rules: Do not plant seeds deeper than their own thickness. Water the planting by submersing it in water, and afterward cover the surface with a pane of glass, a sheet of plastic, or several thicknesses of newspaper. A temperature near 72°F. speeds germination.

As soon as seedlings appear, set the container where it will get good light from an east or south window. Within a day or two the seedlings can take full sunlight, as they are sturdier than most house plants. Seedlings under fluorescent lights need to be three or four inches directly underneath the tubes. As they expand, gradually lower them away from the light.

Keep the soil moist at all times, and begin feedings of fertilizer when seedlings are about two weeks old. Transplant to individual containers, such as peat pots, before plants crowd each other. Cool temperatures help seedlings develop sturdily; a range of 50-65°F. is desirable.

PERENNIALS FROM SEED

One special pleasure I derive from gardening indoors is the starting of hardy perennial seedlings for the outdoor border. If planted by March, some kinds bloom the first year. These include anthemis, coreopsis, dianthus, gaillardia, lychnis, delphinium, hesperis, matricaria, catananche, Formosa lily, flax, platycodon, chrysanthemum, and Michaelmas daisy.

Frequently I save some of the seeds which bees set on the irises, day lilies (Hemerocallis), and roses that grow in our garden. Day lilies and irises started indoors in early spring reach flowering age in two or three years. Day lily seeds are large and easily handled. I plant them about ½ inch deep in moist potting soil. Germination occurs within six weeks. Iris and rose seeds are slower. To encourage rapid sprouting, I put these seeds in an ice tray filled with water and place it in the refrigerator. After a few days I plant the ice cubes in a flat of moist soil, being careful to locate each so that its seed is about ½ inch deep. Roses often germinate within a week or two after planting this way, and it is not unusual for the first flower to open two or three months later.

4. House plants outdoors

MANY house plants benefit from a summer spent outdoors. Move them into open air when the weather is thoroughly warm in spring or early summer, and bring indoors well ahead of frost time in autumn. They need the same care as other plants in the garden. Provide routine pruning, regular spraying to prevent insect damage, watering in the absence of sufficient rainfall, and biweekly or more frequent feedings of soluble fertilizer. It is easier to care for potted plants being summered outdoors if they are grouped together in one or two places rather than scattered over the garden.

Any location that receives protection from whipping winds and hard rains can be decorated with container plants. They are especially enjoyable near entranceways, on steps, terraces, patios, porches, walks, landing strips by driveways, tops of walls, sun decks, and rooftop gardens. Many house plants thrive in the summer under large trees, heavy-foliaged shrubs, or beneath groups of perennials such as day lilies and hostas. Some of them do well in hanging baskets, window boxes, and large planters.

For the ultimate in summer care of house plants, use a lath house, shaded cold frame, or air-conditioned greenhouse. When plants growing in containers outdoors are kept moist and protected from searing winds, they are more tolerant of sunlight. Kinds that prefer sunny locations indoors (see list, pp. 33–34) usually do well outdoors in sun-drenched places, but partial shade will also give pleasing results. House plants that prefer semi-sunny and semi-shady locations indoors (see lists, pp. 31–33, 34–35) thrive outdoors in the dapply shadows cast by majestic trees, or on the north side of a building. True shade-loving plants (see list, p. 35), can be summered outdoors in a shady, moist nook which receives little or no direct sun.

HOW TO MOVE PLANTS OUTDOORS

Moving day for house plants may be scheduled for any convenient time after the average date of last frost in a given area. If you do not know this date for your community, ask a neighbor who gardens successfully, or your County Agricultural Agent. He represents the United States Department of Agriculture, and generally has an office in the county courthouse.

In the Northeast I begin to move cool-loving house plants (see list, p. 35) outdoors in late April or early May. By the third weekend of May, most of the tropicals are situated for the season. All plants growing in built-in planters and in the large tubs, which play a part in our interior decoration, are left inside all year. In addition, from late April until early November, we keep the fireplace filled with ferns, caladiums, episcias, small angel-wing begonias, African violets, and gloxinias. A portable fluorescent light with two 20-watt daylight tubes keeps the plants in good condition. The light unit itself extends far enough into the chimney so that the reflector cannot be seen.

The house plants I put outdoors spend most of the summer on shelves placed along the north side of the house. This area receives bright light all day, and direct sun in the early morning and late afternoon. When the soil is kept evenly moist, I find that all of my house plants do well in this location, regardless of light preferences. When this summering area is filled, I place other container plants on a bricked surface in the shade of a six-foot redwood fence. From these two groupings and the plants in a small lath shelter described later in this chapter, I choose whatever is needed to decorate the house or outdoor living area on special occasions.

House plants sunk to the pot rim in the garden require less watering than those set in the open. Wax begonias, impatiens, and coleus can be planted directly in the garden. Geraniums also can be handled this way, but they bloom more when the roots are contained by pots buried in the soil.

Before setting plants into garden areas, they need to be hardened off for a few days. Do this by placing them on a cool porch, under trees and shrubs, or beneath overhanging eaves. This gives them time to harden or stiffen stems, and to firm up foliage. These are necessary adjustments plants must make to a change from the artificial warmth of indoor living quarters to the natural elements outdoors.

Do not move choice or irreplaceable plants outdoors unless you have insurance in the form of rooted cuttings, seedlings, or small bulbs or tubers of the same kind. Plants outdoors can offer no resistance to hail, exceedingly strong winds, or an onslaught of grasshoppers and caterpillars.

When house plants are placed directly in garden soil, keep their lower parts clean and the area free of weeds by mulching with a generous layer of buckwheat hulls, ground corncobs, cocoa-bean shells, pebbles, or small water-polished stones.

Orchids and bromeliads do well hung from tree limbs or the roof of a lath house during warm weather. These locations closely duplicate the way they grow in nature.

While African violets, when handled carefully, can benefit from a vacation spent outdoors, they should not be set directly into garden soil. I summer part of my collection in hanging baskets (Chapter 8). Others are placed on shelves at the north side of the house. One of my friends summers a large number

A lath house makes an ideal place to summer house plants outdoors. It is excellent also for a propagating case (shown at left), a potting bench, and pails of potting mix. (Photograph by California Redwood Association)

of African violets in a shaded cold frame. The pots are set on sand kept constantly damp from drops of water seeping through a perforated copper tube centered within the area. A wooden frame covered with muslin is slipped over the cold frame to keep sun off the plants. One-inch wooden blocks spaced along the cold-frame wall raise the muslin cover enough to allow the necessary fresh air to circulate for ideal growing conditions.

A LATH HOUSE FOR SUN CONTROL

A lath house can provide ideal summer conditions for all house plants. Such structures are made of narrow wooden slats placed closely enough to keep direct sun off the plants below them. They can be of any size, free standing, attached to a building, or even portable. To create a shadier atmosphere, inexpensive reed screening is sometimes used instead of the typical laths or slats.

My portable lath house was designed for utility, but when it holds plants, there is beauty too. This small shelter is 33 inches high, 36 inches wide, and 10 feet long. It is made of ¼-inch strips ripped from a 10-foot redwood plank 1¾ inches thick and 6 inches wide. The strips are spaced three quarters of an inch apart on the top and three sides. I cut the legs from redwood two-by-fours, the cross members from one-by-fours. This structure is easily moved and will supply ample shade for even the most delicate plants.

A larger lath house might include an exciting collection of plants, including aeschynanthus, achimenes, columnea, plectranthus, hoya, *Campanula isophylla,* orchids, anthuriums, caladiums, all kinds of begonias, gloxinias, and rechsteinerias. Baskets of pendulous tuberous begonias, fuchsias, ferns, and species African violets could hang from the ceiling.

THE RETURN TRIP FOR VACATIONING HOUSE PLANTS

Start bringing house plants indoors by late August. Many of them can be left outside until early October, but in some areas frost may come by the middle of September. When plants have been placed directly in garden soil, it is usually better to make root cuttings of them instead of trying to save the old plants. If you want the old plants, dig them with as little root disturbance as possible. Repot in a container whose circumference measures one third to one half the height of the plant. Moisten thoroughly and place in a sheltered area, like a porch, for about a week. Before returning plants to the house, groom them carefully to remove damaged leaves and dried flowers. Scrub pots clean, then spray foliage, stems, and topsoil with an aerosol pesticide designed for house plants.

5. Spring-flowering bulbs for indoor bloom

SPRING-FLOWERING bulbs make a spectacular display of color in a winter window garden. The dormant bulbs, purchased in September or October, already contain the perfectly formed flower buds. These await only warmth, moisture, and light to be brought into full bloom, but the period from early fall until around January 1 is an important one. During that time the bulbs need coolness and evenly moist soil. These conditions promote the formation of a sturdy root system.

SOIL FOR POTTED BULBS

Any good garden soil that contains a reasonable amount of humus and sand is satisfactory for forcing bulbs. One good mixture is made by combining equal parts of soil, peat moss, and sand. Commercially prepared potting soils offered for African violets and other house plants are usually satisfactory for forcing bulbs. Paperwhite narcissi are frequently planted in bowls of pebbles and water. Hyacinths also may be planted this way, but no other spring bulbs do well without soil.

Bone meal, a slow-acting organic fertilizer, is an excellent ingredient of soil mixtures used for bulbs. It is especially desirable for potting those which eventually will be moved to the outdoor garden. Add bone meal at the rate of one heaping teaspoonful for each 5- to 7-inch pot of soil.

WHEN TO PLANT BULBS FOR FORCING

Pot spring-flowering bulbs for forcing in early fall. If you can get healthy, firm bulbs up to the middle of November, they will still force satisfactorily. Some bulb varieties force better than others. The list at the end of this chapter can be your guide, or, study fall bulb catalogues to find varieties suggested as superior for forcing. It is important that the bulbs be of top (jumbo), or first, size, firm, and otherwise in perfect condition.

A 4- or 5-inch pot will accommodate one hyacinth; one or possibly two daffodils; two or three tulips; or four to eight of the small bulbs like grape hyacinths (Muscari), crocuses, and miniature daffodils.

A 6- or 7-inch pot can be planted to three or four hyacinths; three or four daffodils; four to six tulips; or six to twelve of the small bulbs. Plant larger containers accordingly, allowing about a half inch of space between bulbs. When forcing tulips, try planting one bulb to a 3- or 4-inch pot. Planting several to a large container is fine, but where space is limited, one tulip blooming each week for a month in late winter may be more appreciated than a large pot of them blooming all at one time.

Position forcing bulbs with the necks protruding slightly above the planting medium. Moisten the soil thoroughly after potting. Then, place the pots outdoors in a trench or cold frame

FT: *Spring-flowering bulbs planted in pots and forced to bloom early loors make a delightful picture window. Hyacinths, paperwhite narcis-;, crocuses, and double tulips are shown with episcias, African violets, d Christmas cactus.* (Photograph by Genereux)

and cover with a 6-inch layer of sand, peat moss, or cinders. Instead of putting them outdoors, for the formation of roots it may be more convenient to place the potted bulbs in a cool attic, a closet, an attached garage, or in the cool part of a basement. Constant temperatures below freezing and above 50°F. should be avoided. If possible, keep the potted bulbs in darkness while the roots are forming. Bulbs put outdoors need protection from mice. Do this by leaving some poison rodent bait in the trench or cold frame when the bulbs are put there.

Constant moisture during the period when roots are forming, and after growth begins, is vitally necessary for bulbs. When leaves and flowers start into growth, severe drought, either in the soil or in the air around them, may cause buds to wither and die without ever opening.

HOW BULBS ARE FORCED

Six to ten weeks are required for spring-flowering bulbs to form a good root system. For example, bulbs planted October 1 could be brought out of storage in late November for blooming in late December or January. However, only very early-blooming varieties should be chosen for this kind of treatment. The time required from the beginning of forcing (when you bring bulbs into a warm, sunny atmosphere) to blooms varies according to temperatures, amount of light, varieties, and time of year. At a temperature of 65-75°F., forcing early in the season requires about four weeks. The colder the temperature, the slower the blooms will develop and the higher will be their quality. Also, as the season advances toward spring, bulbs come into bloom more quickly than they do in early winter.

PLAN FOR SUCCESSION OF BLOOM

To have a constant succession of bulb bloom, a schedule will be helpful. For example, to force one pot of six tulips, daffodils, or hyacinths into bloom every ten days to two weeks from late

BULBS RECOMMENDED FOR FORCING

DAFFODILS (*Narcissus*)	*Early*	*Midseason*	*Late*
	'Bartizan'	'Bartizan'	'Beersheba'
	'February Gold'	'Fortune'	'Fortune'
	'Forerunner'	'Golden Harvest'	'John Evelyn'
	'Golden Harvest'	'King Alfred'	'King Alfred'
	'Orange Queen'	'Orangeglow'	'Orangeglow'
	'Rembrandt'	'Pres. Lebrun'	'Pres. Lebrun'
	'W. P. Milner'	'Rembrandt'	'Scarlet Leader'
		'Scarlet Leader'	'Texas'
		'Texas'	'Tunis'
		'Tunis'	

HYACINTHS	*Early*	*Midseason*	*Late*
	'Anne Marie'	'City of Haarlem'	'Carnegie'
	'Bismarck'	'Delft Blue'	'King of Blues'
	'Delight'	'Gertrude'	'Marconi'
	'Dr. Lieber'	'Grand Maitre'	'Queen of Pinks'
	'Jan Bos'	'Lady Derby'	
	'La Victoire'	'Ostara'	
	'L'Innocence'	'Perle Brilliante'	
	'Pink Pearl'		

TULIPS	*Early*	*Midseason*	*Late*
	'Brilliant Star'	'Albino'	'Albino'
	'Crown Imperial'	'All Bright'	'All Bright'
	'Delice'	'Bartigon'	'Bartigon'
	'Demeter'	'Dante'	'Discovery'
	'Mon Tresor'	'Edith Eddy'	'Fantasy'
	'Pierson Parrot'	'Golden Harvest'	'Kantara'
	'Rose Copland'	'Her Grace'	'Mothersday'
	'Scarlet Cardinal'	'Ibis'	'Murillo'
		'Murillo'	'Niphetos'
		'Prince of Austria'	'Rising Sun'
		'Triumphator'	'Scarlet Admiral'
		'Willemsoord'	'Telescopium'
		'William Pitt'	'Triumphator'
			'Willemsoord'

January to April 1, plant approximately forty-eight bulbs of each. For bulbs planted October 15:

forcing could begin	*for blooms approximately*
December 17	January 28
December 31	February 7
January 14	February 18
January 28	February 28
February 11	March 11
February 25	March 21
March 11	April 1

WHEN THE BLOOMS FADE

Forced blooms will last for several days, even to two weeks if they have constant moisture and coolness (70°F. or less). If you have no outdoor garden, then discard bulbs, plants, and all when flowers fade, or when foliage is no longer useful as greenery. If you have an outdoor garden, these forced bulbs can be a nice addition to it in years to come. When the petals wither, cut off the flower stems with a sharp knife and discard them. Set the pots outdoors in a cold frame, or keep them in a cool, light place indoors, until the weather permits planting them in the garden. They may not bloom well the following season, but will thereafter.

It is almost useless to try to force the same bulbs again, but the miniature daffodils (Narcissus) may be an exception to this rule. Species such as *Narcissus juncifolius, N. bulbocodium citrinus* and *N. watieri,* have done well for me when cultivated year after year in pots. Here is a seasonal schedule for them:

AUTUMN   Plant bulbs and prepare to force as for regular daffodils.

WINTER   After good root system forms, force slowly (60°F. maximum). When buds show, begin feeding biweekly with applications of half-strength house plant fertilizer, continuing until early summer.

SPRING   After blooms fade, continue to give good care to plants: cool temperatures (55-70°F.), sunlight, and moist soil. When danger of hard freezing is past, sink pots outdoors in garden or window box.

SUMMER   Continue regular care and watering until foliage ripens and turns yellow of its own accord. Then, leave pots alone, even forgetting about them, until autumn. (They like to be baked by the warmth of summer sun.) Repot in autumn and start a new forcing cycle.

COMMON TROUBLES OF FORCED BULBS

THE SYMPTOMS	THE CAUSE	WHAT YOU CAN DO
Foliage is stunted and yellowish.	May be botrytis blight, basal rot, smoulder, or bulb mite.	Discard plant and soil; inspect bulbs at planting time and discard any that show signs of diseases (sponginess or dark specks that may be sclerotia, the resting form of a fungus).
New leaf growth and flower buds covered with white, gray, or green insects.	Aphids.	Spray weekly for as long as necessary with malathion or pyrethrum.
Buds dry up before opening.	Bud Blast.	Next year, provide cooler temperatures; keep soil uniformly moist at all times; be sure bulbs have good root system before forcing is begun.

OTHER BULBS FOR FORCING

In addition to daffodils, hyacinths, and tulips, many other hardy spring-flowering bulbs do well when forced indoors. These include chionodoxa, ixia, ixiolirion, crocus, Dutch iris, *Iris reticulate,* grape hyacinth (Muscari), ornithogalum, puschkinia, sparaxis, and triteleia.

With the exception of paperwhite narcissus and amaryllis, the tender winter- and spring-flowering bulbs (freesias and zantedeschias, for example), are discussed in Part II of this book.

BULBS EVERYONE CAN FORCE

The apartment dweller or anyone else who lacks proper facilities for forcing hardy spring bulbs can find equal enjoyment in forcing fragrant and beautiful paperwhites (and the similar 'Soleil d'Or' with golden flowers), lilies-of-the-valley, colchicums, and amaryllis. These bulbs do not need a period of cold before they bloom.

To force paperwhite narcissus, all you need is water, pebbles, the bulbs, and a bowl at least three inches deep and large enough to hold three to twelve of them. Fill the bowl half full of pebbles. Set the bulbs on this surface, allowing about a half inch of space between them. Pour in more pebbles until a third of each bulb is in the gravel. Pour water into the bowl until it touches the bulbs and place the planting in a cool (50-60°F.), dark place for about two weeks. By that time root growth will be active, and the planter may be brought to a sunny, warm place. Except in the South, where the bulbs are planted outside after forcing, they are discarded after one season.

Paperwhites may fail to bloom if they dry out severely during the rooting period; if they are not allowed a cool period during which to form a root system; or, if they are forced in a hot, dry, poorly lighted location. If paperwhites have a good root system, a supply of fresh water at all times, and a sunny window in which to complete their growth, success with them is a certainty.

A pot of fragrant lily-of-the-valley bells makes an exciting addition to a midwinter window garden. Even the most inexperienced gardener can expect a perfect performance from them. Specialists prepare the pips or rootstocks in such a manner that it is necessary only to set them and their moist packing fiber into a planter and wait for flowers to appear. However, if plants are destined for later use in the outdoor garden, the pips are better planted in a mixture of equal parts soil, sand, and peat moss.

Fall-flowering *Colchicum autumnale* grows from a corm rather than a bulb, but it can be flowered by merely planting it in a pot of moist soil in midsummer. Indeed, the colchicum is so easily flowered that it is often advertised as "the magic bulb that blooms without soil or water." And this it does, with inferior results. I have seen unplanted corms flowering on shelves in seed stores. Occasionally, when lack of time has prevented me from potting up all of my colchicum corms, I have discovered some of them flowering in their storage quarters!

Dutch hybrid amaryllis in white, pink, or red, or patterned reds and whites, are among the showiest plants cultivated indoors. If good bulbs are planted in fall or winter, flowers will appear four to eight weeks later. It is almost impossible to fail with amaryllis bulbs obtained from a reliable grower. Only moisture, warmth, and light are needed to bring out their magnificent flowers. Blooming-size hybrid amaryllis bulbs sold by colors cost from $1.50 to $3.50. Named varieties start at $2.50, range upward to $7.50 and more. Any good hybrid amaryllis is a long-paying investment. With proper care, individual bulbs will last a lifetime.

Plant amaryllis bulbs in a 6-inch pot into which has been placed an inch of broken pot chips or pebbles. Add an inch or two of a mixture of equal parts soil, sand, and peat moss, and spread the root tips into this. If bulbs have short roots or none at all, place a handful of moistened sphagnum moss at the bulb base. Adjust finished planting so that about one half to three fourths of the bulb shows above the soil line, with one to two inches of space between it and the pot rim.

Water the planting and bring it into an eastern, southern, or southwestern window garden. Turn the pot frequently so the bud scape or stalk will not lean toward the light. Large hybrid amaryllis usually send up a flowering scape before the leaves appear. Remove the scape after flowering, unless you intend to

ripen seed pods. Fertilize every second week with any good
house plant fertilizer. The bulb needs to grow a heavy crop of
leaves to form buds for future flowers. Plunge the pot in the
garden during summer or keep it on a window sill. In fall,
withhold water so that the leaves turn yellow, then set it in a
cool basement or closet to rest. Give the pot an occasional
sprinkling of water. When new growth shows, water the planting thoroughly and bring it to the light to produce its new crop
of flowers. Repot at this time at least every second year.

6. An herb garden in your window

THE WONDERFUL scent of herbs can be a part of most window gardens. These plants need a sunny location which has a temperature range of 50-75°F. with 30-60 per cent relative humidity. Potted herbs need a well-drained moist soil composed of equal parts garden loam, sand, well-rotted and pulverized manure, and peat moss or leaf mold. If you do not have access to these ingredients, use a medium that is packaged commercially for African violets and other potted plants.

If these basic requirements are met, container-grown herbs will be a constant source of pleasure, to the grower and to anyone else who has the privilege of seeing, smelling, and perhaps, using them in food.

FIVE STEPS TO SUCCESS WITH HERBS

Before starting an herb garden in your window, read Chapter 2 of this book. After you have a collection of potted herbs, the information in Chapters 3 and 4 may be useful from time to

A WINDOW GARDEN OF HERBS. *Left to right, beginning with the hanging basket:* Mentha requienii, *sage, basil, lemon verbena, spearmint, parsley, chives, rosemary, sweet bay, and mint geranium* (Pelargonium tomentosum) *in the basket at right.*

time. Also, putting these suggestions into practice will help you have a thriving window herb garden:

(1) Set the pots in trays or other containers filled with an inch or two of moist sand or pebbles.

(2) Group the plants together, as shown in the accompanying illustration. Several plants together on a window sill create their own atmosphere—a microclimate which is moist and conducive to vigorous growth.

(3) At least once a week, wash off the foliage of potted herbs in water of room temperature. The plants, besides thus being kept fresh and clean, will respond by growing more lushly—just as if they had been revived by a summer shower.

(4) Turn pots and baskets of herbs in a window about once a week so that the plants will be more shapely. Frequent pinching out of the growing tips will encourage potted herbs to be bushier.

(5) Give herbs fresh air. During cold weather, provide this indirectly by opening a window or door in another room for a few minutes each day. As the warmth of spring comes on, more direct fresh air will be beneficial.

HERBS IN THE SUMMER

During the summer, potted herbs do well outdoors in a window box, or in the garden. There they are valuable for foliage, fragrance, and occasionally for flowers. The leaves and stems may be cut back severely at the time herbs are put out in the late spring; healthy new growth will appear quickly. In late August or early September, repot in new soil, trim back the summer growth, and bring the herbs back to the window garden. It is important to do this early so that they are thriving indoors before heating units are turned on.

If you plan to use herbs for culinary purposes, be careful with pest control measures. Rotenone, pyrethrum, and methoxychlor are safest; *avoid* DDT, dieldrin, chlordane, lead arsenate, lindane, malathion, and nicotine sulfate.

A SELECTION OF
HERBS TO GROW INDOORS

NAME	GROWTH HABIT AND LIFE SPAN	HOW AND WHEN TO START	CULTURE
Allium schoenoprasum (chives)	Upright hardy perennial.	Buy small clump at grocery store any time, or obtain by mail.	This bulbous herb is more easily grown indoors than most of the others. Provide some sun, warmth, and moisture; clip and use leaves as desired.

A Selection of Herbs To Grow Indoors (cont.)

NAME	GROWTH HABIT AND LIFE SPAN	HOW AND WHEN TO START	CULTURE
Anethum graveolens (dill)	Upright annual.	Plant seeds in late summer or early fall indoors.	Provide sunlight, a cool to warm temp., and moisture. Clip and use leaves as desired. Discard plants at end of one season.
Anise (see *Pimpinella anisum*)			
Anthemis nobilis (chamomile)	Upright hardy perennial.	Buy young plant in late summer, or pot one from the garden.	Provide sunlight, moisture, and a cool to moderate temp. A medicinal herb.
Anthriscus cerefolium (chervil)	Upright annual.	Plant seeds in pots indoors where they are to grow in early fall.	Same as anethum.
Basil, Sweet (see *Ocimum basilicum*)			
Bay, Sweet (see *Laurus nobilis*)			
Borage (see *Borago officinalis*)			
Borago officinalis (borage)	Upright annual.	Same as anthriscus.	Provide full sun, a cool to warm temp., and moisture. Nice for baskets or pots; plant several seeds to a pot, thin to two or three. Discard at end of one season.
Brassica hirta (white mustard)	Upright annual.	Sow seeds in darkness, warmth, and moisture at any time.	Provide sunlight, cool to warm temp., and moisture. Use leaves as desired; discard when plants are no longer productive.

A Selection of Herbs To Grow Indoors (cont.)

NAME	GROWTH HABIT AND LIFE SPAN	HOW AND WHEN TO START	CULTURE
Caraway (see *Carum carvi*)			
Carum carvi (caraway)	Upright hardy biennial.	Start seeds in spring or fall.	Provide sunlight, cool to moderate temp., and moisture. Use dried seeds for flavoring.
Catnip (see *Nepeta cataria*)			
Chamomile (see *Anthemis nobilis*)			
Chervil (see *Anthriscus cerefolium*)			
Chives (see *Allium schoenoprasum*)			
Coriander (see *Coriandrum sativum*)			
Coriandrum sativum (coriander)	Upright annual.	Start seeds in summer or fall.	Provide sunlight, cool to moderate temp., and moisture. Use dried seeds for flavoring.
Corsican Mint (see *Mentha requienii*)			
Cress, Garden (see *Lepidium sativum*)			
Dill (see *Anethum graveolens*)			
Dittany of Crete (see *Origanum dictamnus*)			
Fennel (see *Foeniculum vulgare*)			
Foeniculum vulgare (fennel)	Upright hardy perennial.	Start seeds in summer or fall.	Provide sunlight, cool to warm temp., and moisture. May be cut back in spring and fall, or started each year from seeds. Use young leaves and seeds to flavor salads and fish.
Geranium, Scented (see *Pelargonium*)			

A Selection of Herbs To Grow Indoors (cont.)

NAME	GROWTH HABIT AND LIFE SPAN	HOW AND WHEN TO START	CULTURE
Horehound (see *Marrubium vulgare*)			
Laurus nobilis (sweet bay)	Tree, nearly hardy outdoors in the North.	Buy young potted plant in early fall.	Provide sunlight, cool to moderate temp., and moisture. Prune as necessary to keep as small tree or bush. Use leaves as desired for flavoring.
Lavandula officinalis (lavender)	Upright hardy perennial.	Buy young potted plant in the fall.	Provide sunlight, cool to moderate temp., and moisture. Tender species *L. multifida*, *L. stoechas*, and *L. dentata* are also desirable for indoor herb gardens.
Lavender (see *Lavandula officinalis*)			
Lavender-Cotton (see *Santolina chamaecyparissus*)			
Lemon Balm (see *Melissa officinalis*)			
Lemon Verbena (see *Lippia citriodora*)			
Lepidium sativum (garden cress)	Low, upright annual.	As for brassica.	As for brassica.
Lippia citriodora (lemon verbena)	Upright tender perennial.	Buy young potted plant in fall.	Provide sunlight, cool to warm temp., and moisture. Prune back severely in the fall, and again as necessary to keep compact.
Majorana hortensis (sweet marjoram)	Upright tender perennial.	Start seeds in warmth and moisture any time.	Provide sunlight, cool to warm temp., and moisture. Fragrant leaves are used for seasoning foods. May be discarded after one season, or pruned back and grown again.

A Selection of Herbs To Grow Indoors (cont.)

NAME	GROWTH HABIT AND LIFE SPAN	HOW AND WHEN TO START	CULTURE
Marjoram, Sweet (see *Majorana hortensis*)			
Marrubium vulgare (horehound)	Upright tender perennial.	Start seeds in spring.	Provide sunlight, cool to warm temp., and soil that is allowed to dry out occasionally for short periods.
Melissa officinalis (lemon balm)	Upright hardy perennial.	Start seeds any time, or buy young plant in fall.	Provide sunlight, cool to warm temp., and moisture. Fragrant leaves useful in cool drinks and for arrangements.
Mentha citrata *M. piperita officinalis* *M. requienii* *M. spicata viridis* (mints)	Upright hardy perennials, except *M. requienii,* which is tender.	Buy young potted plants in spring or fall.	Provide sunlight, cool to warm temp., and moisture. *M. requienii* is nice for a hanging basket. Leaves of all are used for flavoring.
Mustard, White (see *Brassica hirta*)			
Nepeta cataria (catnip)	Upright hardy perennial.	Start seeds any time in warmth; or buy young potted plant in spring or fall.	Provide sunlight, cool to warm temp., and moisture. Cut back severely in fall, and again as necessary to keep small enough for indoors.
Ocimum basilicum (sweet basil)	Upright annual.	Start seeds in fall or spring.	Provide sunlight, cool to warm temp., and moisture. Leaves used fresh or dried in salads; also with cheese, eggs, tomatoes. Discard when plants cease to be productive.
Orange Mint (see *Mentha citrata*)			

A Selection of Herbs To Grow Indoors (cont.)

NAME	GROWTH HABIT AND LIFE SPAN	HOW AND WHEN TO START	CULTURE
Origanum dictamnus (dittany of Crete)	Upright tender perennial.	Buy young potted plants in spring or fall.	Provide sunlight, cool to moderate temp., and moisture. Cut back in fall, and again as necessary to keep compact. Use leaves for seasoning.

Parsley (see *Petroselinum crispum*)

| *Pelargonium crispum* P. denticulatum P. fragrans P. fulgidum P. graveolens P. odoratissimum P. quercifolium P. tomentosum (scented geraniums) | Upright tender perennials. | Buy young potted plants in spring or fall. | Provide sunlight, cool to warm temp., and moisture. Leaves fragrant. Cut back as necessary to keep compact. |

Peppermint (see *Mentha piperita officinalis*)

| *Petroselinum crispum* (parsley) | Upright hardy biennial. | Buy young potted plant in fall, or sow seeds any time, first soaking them in water for 24 hours. | Provide sunlight, cool to warm temp., and moisture. Use leaves as desired for garnishing foods. Discard when plants cease to be productive. |
| *Pimpinella anisum* (anise) | Upright annual. | Start seeds in spring or fall in pots where they are to grow. | Provide sunlight, cool to warm temp., and moisture. Use young leaves to garnish salads; seeds are used for flavoring cookies. |

Rosemary (see *Rosmarinus officinalis*)

A Selection of Herbs To Grow Indoors (cont.)

NAME	GROWTH HABIT AND LIFE SPAN	HOW AND WHEN TO START	CULTURE
Rosmarinus officinalis (rosemary)	Upright tender perennial.	Buy young potted plant in fall or spring.	Provide sunlight, cool to warm temp., and moist, alkaline soil. If soil is acid, add a tsp. of pulverized limestone to each five-inch pot of planting medium. Prune as necessary to keep in bounds; use for seasoning.
R. officinalis prostratus	Trailing tender perennial.	Buy young potted plant in fall or spring.	Culture as for the species. Nice for a hanging basket.
Sage (see *Salvia officinalis*)			
Salvia officinalis (sage)	Upright hardy perennial.	Buy young potted plant in fall or spring.	Provide sunlight, cool to warm temp., and moisture. Prune as necessary to keep in bounds. Tender variety *tricolor* has gray-green leaves variegated with pink and cream-white. Pineapple sage, *S. rutilans,* also tender, is desirable for indoors.
Santolina chamaecyparissus (lavender-cotton)	Semi-upright or trailing hardy perennial.	Buy young potted plant in spring or fall.	Provide sunlight, cool to warm temp., and moisture. Nice for a hanging basket. Prune as necessary to keep in bounds.
Satureja montana (winter savory)	Upright hardy perennial.	Buy young potted plant in fall or spring.	Provide sunlight, cool to warm temp., and moisture. Prune as necessary to keep in bounds. Leaves used for seasoning.

A Selection of Herbs To Grow Indoors (cont.)

NAME	GROWTH HABIT AND LIFE SPAN	HOW AND WHEN TO START	CULTURE
Savory, Winter (see *Satureja montana*)			
Spearmint (see *Mentha spicata viridis*)			
Thyme (see *Thymus*)			
Thymus serpyllum and its varieties *T. vulgaris* and its varieties (thyme)	Trailing hardy perennials.	Buy young potted plant in spring or fall.	Provide sunlight, cool to warm temp., and moisture. Nice for hanging basket. Trim as necessary to keep compact. Leaves used for seasoning.

7. Terrariums—
under-glass gardens

A TERRARIUM can be reminiscent of a specially loved land-scape, or planted so that it recalls the lushness of a tropical garden. This kind of miniature garden might also rival the charm of a cactus-studded desert, capture the essence of a ferny wooded dell, or be a midget replica of some other favored out-door scene. Also, a terrarium can be a Lilliputian dream gar-den—representing one that is impossible to create under exist-ing indoor growing conditions.

A glass or plastic container filled with growing plants is called a terrarium. Its size is limited only by display space and plant choice. There are two requisites for terrariums. They need to be transparent and colorless in order to admit light to plants, and waterproof so as to keep moisture from seeping onto the display area.

Make terrariums in empty fish tanks, rose bowls, brandy snifters, goblets, large drinking glasses, tobacco humidors, glass casseroles, or bottles. Glass jars of all kinds—battery, candy, apothecary, preserve, or pickle—make first-rate containers for under-glass gardens.

Cover the terrarium opening for humidity-loving plants such as small-growing orchids, saintpaulias (African violets), and the diminutive *Sinningia pusilla* (miniature gloxinia). Do not use a cover for desert plants such as cacti and other succulents. Have a glazier cut glass or Lucite (a heavy, rigid plastic) to fit large terrariums. Cover smaller bowls with glass plates or clear plastic.

Making terrariums is one of the most rewarding aspects of my indoor gardening. I have a bottle garden in my study which fascinates visitors, and gives me much pleasure. It is a narrow-mouthed glass jug in which spring water was delivered. It protects a wide-spreading African violet that is always covered with bright blue flowers. Friends cast questioning looks at this terrarium wondering how I managed to squeeze a mammoth African violet into the bottle. The answer is simple: I didn't. I added drainage material and planting soil to the bottle, then sprinkled in some African violet seeds. As the seedlings grew, I used long, slender tongs to pull out the smaller ones. Finally, some five months after planting, I removed all but the strongest one. It began to bloom when seven months old. Today, some five years later, it still blooms steadily.

HOW TO PLANT TERRARIUMS

Envision the terrain in the garden you are re-creating. Shape the soil into a corresponding landscape, complete with hills, valleys, or plains. A good planting medium for terrariums may be composed by mixing together equal parts of soil, sand, and peat moss. For cacti and other succulents, use equal parts of soil and peat moss with a double portion of sand and Perlite.

Select compatible plants for the terrarium. Miniature orchids, small anthuriums, filmy ferns, small gesneriads, and dwarf rex begonias all thrive under the same humid, filtered-light conditions. As a rule, it is a mistake to include rampant-growing plants in these small gardens. I make an exception to this sometimes with newly rooted cuttings of coleus, artillery-fern (*Pilea microphylla*), and other plants which can be cut back severely, as necessary, without harm.

Tropical paradise within a brandy snifter; plants include miniature caladium, at left, carpeting and upright forms of selaginella, and a miniature gloxinia (Sinningia pusilla) *blooming in the center.* (Photograph by Brilmayer)

The old-fashioned sweat jar or bottle garden makes a delightful addition to any room. Choose plants which grow small or slowly, and kinds which require humidity and shade. Interior by Sermon-Anderson. (Photograph by Nicholson)

Cacti and other succulents of all kinds can be planted together, in an open-topped terrarium. A similar planter makes a good showcase for a collection of small rosette- or star-shaped bromeliads like *Cryptanthus acaulis* with its wavy green leaves, and its striped variety, *zebrinus.*

When planting a woodland scene, carpet the bottom of the terrarium with moss and lichen-covered wood found in the woods. If you can't take a stroll in the woods, purchase some green sheet moss and use it for ground cover.

A number of small creeping plants will also provide suitable ground covering: mossy-leaved selaginella, hairy-leaved *Pilea repens,* and cup-leaved *P. depressa,* for example. Bronze and chartreuse *Pellionia daveauana* or gray-blue *P. pulchra* lend interesting form and color. For fragrance, plant the smallest of mints, lavender-flowered *Mentha requienii.* Baby's-tears (*Helxine soleirolii*) with its round, apple-green leaves is a rampant, easily cultivated terrarium creeper.

Saucer for large clay pot makes an appropriate container for a dish garden of succulents. Neat rosettes of sempervivum grow in the foreground; toward the back, left to right, small-leaved sedum, striped leaves of aloe, upright whorls of a crassula, and cluster of echeveria hybrid. (Photograph by Nicholson)

Favorite terrarium for New Englanders, or anyone who has access to plants of the woodland. Keep evenly moist, in bright light and moderate coolness (60-72° F.) during the wintertime. (Photograph by Genereux)

Inside a terrarium, or in a dish garden, you'll find these creepers have many decorative uses. One terrarium might be planted entirely of creepers by building terraces at different levels so they can creep, cascade, and show off. They can be made to swing down a small-scaled wall, or creep up a soft piece of rotted bark. They'll carpet the soil around and between larger, upright plants. One of the smallest can border a small "pool," and appear to dip some of its leaves delicately into the water.

TECHNIQUES FOR PLANTING A BOTTLE GARDEN

Before planting a bottle garden, remove smears or smudges inside the bottle by spraying the inside with a window-cleaning spray. Let it remain inside a minute, then wipe it off using a lintless cloth on a bent stick or wire. Do not fill the bottle the same day you have used the cleaning spray, for the fumes might harm sensitive plants.

Make a funnel of aluminum foil, inserting it so that the narrow end is at the bottom of the bottle. Pour an inch of drainage material down the funnel, then a half inch of crushed charcoal. Tap the bottle on a hard surface. Then add spoonfuls of pasteurized soil that is just moist enough to cling together when squeezed lightly in your hand. Use a long bent stick, wire, slender tongs, or chopsticks to pack the soil firmly against the sides of the bottle. Fill the bottle about one-fourth way with soil. Use the wire or stick to make planting holes. Remove plants from pots, wash the earth from the roots, then drop one into each planting hole. Press earth firmly around the roots of the plants. Trailing strawberry-begonias (*Saxifraga stolonifera* and its variegated variety *tricolor*) and dainty ferns like *Pteris tremula* are choice for bottle plantings. The umbrella-plant (*Cyperus alternifolius*), or feathery-fern (*Asparagus plumosus*) provide height-giving centers for bottle plantings. Add a miniature African violet or begonia for extra color and for flowers. For other bottle plants, see list of "Plants That Like the High Humidity of a Closed Container," at the end of this chapter.

LIGHT IS IMPORTANT FOR TERRARIUM PLANTINGS

Providing just the right amount of light for terrariums is the key to successful culture. Newly made terrarium plantings set in moist friable soil, given correct light and a cover to hold in humidity, can go on for days, weeks, months—yes, even years—

without water. Recently I saw a stoppered bottle planted with ferns and saxifragas that had not been watered since it was made some seven years before. But this is not standard procedure. Check terrariums at least once a week to see if the plants have enough moisture.

The location of the planter will greatly influence just how often water is needed. Naturally, a terrarium placed in a sunny spot will dry out faster than one in filtered light or shade. Indeed, it is never a good practice to place terrariums, other than those planted entirely with cacti and other succulents, in a bright window. The sun creates a steamy junglelike atmosphere inside the terrarium, and covers the plants with beads of moisture. Sun, shining on these, turns them into veritable burning glasses which disfigure the tender foliage. Place all newly planted terrariums in a shaded area—near a northern window, for instance, or atop a piece of furniture out of the direct sun for a week to ten days. When the inside fogs over with condensation, remove the cover for an hour or so to allow the excess moisture to evaporate.

After a new terrarium has full shade for a week to ten days, begin to give it more light. Move it into better light, and wait a few days to see how the plants are doing. If they appear to be losing color and leaning in an ungainly position, move them still closer to strong light. Once the lighting requirements are established, you can move this garden under glass to any similarly lighted spot in your home.

Providing just the right moisture for terrarium-grown plants is important, but if you have followed the initial directions and have found a good growing site, watering will be no problem. As with other plantings, too much water encourages rot; too little causes thin leaves to shrivel.

If plantings appear dry, water them with a pitcher or one of the new bottle and tube watering devices. They will benefit also from a mist with a fogger or atomizer filled with clean water. Siphoning water through a small tube makes it easy to add moisture precisely where it is needed in a terrarium. Covered terrariums growing in filtered light seldom need watering more often than once every four to six weeks. Use a half-strength solution of fertilizer for every other watering.

TERRARIUM PLANTS GROUPED BY PREFERRED GROWING CONDITIONS

PLANTS THAT LIKE THE HIGH HUMIDITY OF A CLOSED CONTAINER:

Begonias 'Baby Rainbow,' 'Berry's Autumn,' 'Calico,' *imperialis* var. 'Smaragdina,' 'It,' 'Red Berry,' and 'Winter Jewel'
Bertolonia species
Calathea species
Chamaeranthemum species
Cissus striata
Dionaea muscipula
Erythroides nobilis argyroneurus

Ficus repens and *F. radicans variegata*
Fittonia species
Kohleria lindeniana and *K. amabilis*
Maranta species
Nertera depressa
Polystichum tsus-simense
Pteris ensiformis victoriae
Selaginella species
Sinningia pusilla
Stenandrium species

PLANTS THAT LIKE OPEN AIR INDOORS THAT CIRCULATES FREELY:

Adromischus species
Aglaonema species
Aloe aristata
Bambusa nana
Bryophyllum species
Carissa grandiflora nana compacta
Ceropegia species
Chlorophytum bichetii
Conophytum species
Crassula species
Cryptanthus species
Cyanotis somaliensis
Cyperus species
Dracaena 'Florida Beauty' and *D. marginata*
Echeveria species
Echinopsis species
Euonymus japonicus microphyllus
Euphorbia 'Bojeri'

Faucaria species
Gasteria liliputana
Gymnocalycium species
Hatiora salicornioides
Haworthia species
Kalanchoe species
Lithops species
Lobivia species
Mammillaria species
Monanthes species
Notocactus species
Opuntia 'Maverick'
Osmanthus fragrans
Pachyveria species
Pelargonium hortorum (miniature varieties)
Portulacaria afra variegata
Punica granatum nana
Rebutia species

Terrarium Plants Grouped by Preferred Growing Conditions (cont.)

PLANTS THAT LIKE OPEN AIR INDOORS THAT CIRCULATES FREELY:

Rhipsalidopsis species
Rhipsalis species
Rosa rouletii and other miniature
   roses

Scindapsus species
Sedum species
Syngonium species
Tillandsia ionantha

PLANTS THAT AREN'T PARTICULAR; MAY BE COVERED, OR GROWN IN AIR
THAT CIRCULATES FREELY:

Acorus gramineus pusillus
Adiantum species
Allophyton mexicanum
Alternanthera species
Caladium humboldtii
Begonia species and varieties:
   'Bowerii,' 'China Doll,' 'Foliosa,'
   hydrocotylifolia, 'Medora,' and
   dwarf *semperflorens* varieties
Episcia species and varieties
Hedera helix varieties
Helxine soleirolii
Hypoestes sanguineus
Impatiens species and varieties

Malpighia coccigera
Mentha requienii
Neanthe bella
Pellionia species
Peperomia species and varieties
Philodendron species and varieties
Pilea species
Plectranthus coleiodes
Saintpaulia (miniature varieties)
Saxifraga stolonifera and var.
   tricolor
Scilla violacea
Siderasis species
Tradescantia species

8. Plants for hanging baskets

THE ATMOSPHERE of an indoor garden, terrace, patio, lath house, or home greenhouse can be enhanced by the addition of hanging baskets filled with a profusion of flowers and foliage. Baskets create eye-level gardens. They add color and interest to bare walls, and afford extended planting space—a real boon to gardeners whose plantings are limited to a small area. The imaginative gardener will discover unusual containers and countless ways to use them around the house and garden.

I use the word "basket" to designate any container which will hold living plants, and which can be suspended from a support. It could be a purchased or homemade wire basket filled with pendulous tuberous begonias, achimenes, and English ivy, to be hung from the roof of a porch. It might be a bucket of blue-flowered browallia, a slatted wooden box planted with sedum, a pail of cascading fuchsias, or a pendent ivy in a coconut shell.

SITES FOR HANGING BASKETS

Suspend hanging baskets from terrace or patio standards, porch ceilings, awning frames, wooden or metal tripods, overhanging eaves, or from tree branches. Hang them from brackets on walls, fences, posts, or from ornamental grillwork. Hang them from wire hooks in greenhouses, lath houses, and sun porches. Suspend small baskets such as raffia-wound jugs, cans, or pots from screw eyes or brackets in any room. Paint a bird cage to harmonize with interior décor, and plant it with greenery or flowers to match or contrast with the color scheme.

When you make plans to decorate with any kind of hanging basket, remember that when it is filled with moist soil and plants, strong support will be needed. Use screw eyes, eyebolts, clothesline hooks, brackets, or some type of pulley arrangement for holding the baskets. The specific kind of hardware is a matter of personal preference, as long as requirements of the location are met.

HOW TO PLANT A BASKET

Attach an aluminum tray or a plastic pot saucer to the bottom of each hanging basket indoors. Otherwise water will drip onto floors, woodwork, and furnishings.

Wire baskets or open-spaced wooden ones can be lined with sheet moss, placed green side out. If this is not immediately available, ask your florist to order some for you. A 2-inch layer

PER LEFT: *In planting a hanging basket, line wire frame with sheet
ss or unshredded sphagnum moss; after adding soil mixture, place upright
nt in center.* LOWER LEFT: *The final step in planting a hanging bas-
is to fill in with a row of lower plants, and add trailers at the edge. This
uping for a shaded location includes several pink and green caladiums
th the creamy foliage of* Dracaena godseffiana *'Florida Beauty.'*
hotographs by Philpott)

of unshredded sphagnum moss also makes a good liner. Moisten the moss and press it firmly against the sides of the container. A layer of aluminum foil or sheet plastic will keep soil from shifting through the moss and will also help the planting retain moisture. To facilitate drainage, punch holes in the foil or plastic near the bottom of the basket. The aluminum or plastic lining is not necessary where random water seepage from the basket creates no problem, as on the lawn or on a cement, brick, or stone patio surface.

Use a moisture-retentive soil that consists of at least one third of peat moss. Equal parts of garden soil, sand, and peat moss is my preference, though sometimes I use pure, unshredded sphagnum moss for baskets of house plants. Moisten the soil before putting it in the basket, and keep the soil level about an inch below the top of the basket. Set roots directly in the soil, or sink potted plants to the pot rims in it. Plants grown in peat pots are excellent for these plantings. Their roots will grow directly through the pot walls and into the planting medium. Plants set directly into the soil do not dry out as rapidly as those left in clay pots. It is easier to develop a planting design when you do not have to reckon with solid pots. However, some gardeners find it cuts down planting time to insert clay pots into the planting medium. Then, if the basket needs refurbishing, it is easy to remove individual pots and insert new material.

Plants that are uncrowded will develop more gracefully and will enjoy better health than those in thickly planted baskets. If color is wanted in a hurry, many blooming plants may be massed together in a basket, but the planting will not have the season-long beauty of a more sparsely furnished basket.

When new plants are needed around the sides of a basket, remove them from their pots, and make small openings in the moss. Insert the plants, inclining them slightly upward. Work slowly and carefully when moving foliage and stems around wires or slats. Slip small pads of moistened moss against the wire parts touching the plants.

MAINTAINING BASKET PLANTINGS

Check baskets daily to see that soil is moist. During hot weather, baskets growing in sunny places may need twice-a-day watering. Those in shaded or wind-sheltered areas, like porches or lath houses, may need watering only every other day. If drippings are no problem, or cold water does not harm tender leaves, use the garden hose to moisten baskets. Otherwise, remove each basket and submerge it in a bucket of water. Leave it until the soil is thoroughly moistened. Then drain the basket until dripping ceases and return to its elevation.

Fertilize hanging gardens about a month after planting, then follow with biweekly feedings. Nip off any seed pods that form. Prune or pinch back plants to make them grow sturdier and to give the hanging garden a more pleasing contour. Outdoors in the summer, and indoors in a sun-drenched window in winter, petunias make showy baskets. The key to having them continue blooming is to shear them periodically. For example, if they are cut back several inches in late July or early August, they will produce an abundant floral display all through autumn.

SUGGESTED BASKET PLANTINGS

The container's size and location together determine the kind and size of plants that will do well in it. An angel-wing begonia like 'Helen W. King' will put on a magnificent show of flowers in a 4-inch pot, placed inside a 5- or 6-inch hanger. Larger baskets may be planted to as many as four plants of the same variety, for balance. Episcias start well this way; and they can be encouraged to cover the basket by hairpinning the stolons to the soil or into the sphagnum moss, where they will take root.

A mixture of plants can be effective, but in one container mix only those kinds which like similar growing conditions. Dry-growing peperomias, for example, will rot in a basket kept

A SELECTION OF BASKET PLANTS GROUPED BY PREFERRED GROWING CONDITIONS

FULL SUN

Abutilon megapotamicum variegatum
(flowering-maple)
Campanula isophylla (star-of-
Bethlehem)
Hoya carnosa variegata (wax plant)
Kalanchoe uniflora
Lobularia maritima (sweet alyssum)
Lotus bertholetii (winged pea)

Mahernia verticillata (honey bells)
*Passiflora caerulea, P. caerulea
trifasciata,* and other passion-
flowers
Sedum morganianum (burro's-tail)
Streptosolen jamesonii (orange
browallia)

TROPICAL WARMTH, HUMIDITY

Achimenes, all varieties
Begonia bowerii and its hybrids
  B. digswelliana
  B. foliosa
  B. fuchsioides
Cissus adenopodus
  C. discolor
Columnea arguta
  C. banksii
  C. gloriosa, and many others
Episcia, all varieties
Ferns, many varieties, particularly
  Nephrolepis

Helxine soleirolii (baby's-tears)
Manettia bicolor (firecracker-vine)
Maranta massangeana
Pellionia dauveauana
  P. pulchra
Philodendron micans, and many others
Pilea depressa
  P. involucrata
  P. repens
Schizocentron elegans (Spanish shawl)
Selaginella, almost all kinds
Smilax mexicana
Syngonium, many varieties

FOR COOL SUN PORCH

Cymbalaria muralis (Kenilworth-ivy)
Fuchsia, many varieties
Hedera helix (English ivy), almost
all varieties
Lantana montevidensis (trailing
lantana)
Lobelia, and other small, trailing
annuals
Nepeta hederacea variegata
(variegated gill-over-the-ground)
Oxalis, many varieties

Pelargonium peltatum (ivy-geranium),
all varieties
  P. tomentosum (peppermint
geranium)
Saxifraga stolonifera and var.
  tricolor (strawberry-begonia)
Senecio mikanioides (German or
parlor ivy)
Tolmiea menziesii (piggyback plant)
Vinca major variegata (variegated
periwinkle)

A *Selection of Basket Plants Grouped by Preferred Growing Conditions (cont.)*

AVERAGE HOUSE

Begonia varieties
  Angel-wing types
  Rhizomatous (star) types:
   'Black Magic'
   'Cleopatra'
   'Bow-Nigra,'
   and many others
Browallia speciosa major
Ceropegia debilis (devil's tongue)
  C. woodii (rosary vine) .
Chlorophytum elatum vittatum (spider
  or airplane plant)
Ficus pumila (creeping fig)
Peperomia prostrata

P. fosteriana
P. cubensis, and
  many others
Plectranthus australis
  P. oertendahlii
Scindapsus aureus ("pothos" of
  florists)
  S. pictus
Senecio confusus (orangeglow vine)
Serjania communis glabra
Setcreasea, Callisia, Tradescantia,
  and *Zebrina*
  (inch-plants or wandering Jew),
  many varieties

moist enough for ivy; shade-loving ferns will blister in the sunlight that pleases sedums. A selection of tropical plants—all of which like moisture, humus, and humidity—can be a delight, and can thrive. A general planting rule for mixed baskets is to place an upright accent plant in the center. Edge the basket with vines and trailers. Place low-growing flowering and foliage plants between the vines and the accent plant.

For a sunny site outdoors in the summer, center a large basket with *Aloe serrulata,* add dwarf geraniums, and edge with variegated *Vinca major.* For a shady nook use a fern in the center, upright tuberous begonias for color, and Hahn's English ivy to cascade over the edge. Before incorporating window-grown plants into outdoor basket plantings, set them in a sheltered part of the garden for a few days to harden off. Otherwise the sun and wind may damage them.

Although I have made and enjoyed many kinds of hanging baskets, one of my favorites is planted with African violets. In the winter I suspend it from the ceiling in front of a sunny window; in summer it decorates the lath house, and sometimes the terrace. Some growers like to plant African violet baskets with an assortment of varieties and colors. I prefer those planted with a single color of free-blooming plants. An established basket appears to be a ball of flowers and leaves.

While common philodendrons, grape-ivies, and pothos are easy to obtain for hanging baskets, many other plants will give more interesting effects. The accompanying lists will suggest some of the less usual kinds. Certain ones are large plants, others are small; some grow fast, others slowly; some bloom attractively, many are primarily foliage plants. For more complete descriptions of unfamiliar ones, see Part II of this book.

9. House plants grown to tree form

House plants which usually grow as bushes or shrubs take on a new dimension of beauty when they are trained into tree shapes. The standard or tree rose is a good example of this gardening concept. House plant trees give distinction to any setting, whether indoors during cold weather, or outdoors in the summer in a protected place. Geraniums, angel-wing begonias, fuchsias, calamondins, heliotropes, chrysanthemums, tibouchinas, miniature roses, ornamental peppers, rivinas, lantanas, acacias, royal poincianas, abutilons, gardenias, and avocados, also hypoestes and coleus are some of the tender plants that lend themselves to this kind of training.

HOW TO GROW A HOUSE PLANT TREE

The basic rules for training a tree hold true for all the plants suggested above. Late winter or early spring is a good time to begin. Select a young plant which has strong tip growth, and be sure that the main growing tip is not harmed. A rooted

127

cutting or seedling which is growing as one stem makes a good choice. Work toward a finished shape which will show a bare trunk topped by a ball, pyramid, cone, or umbrella of leaves and flowers.

Remove all side shoots as soon as they form on the young tree. This encourages the trunk to increase rapidly in height. Leaves, however, that grow along the trunk should be allowed to remain until the tree has begun to form a terminal framework of branches.

By the time a new tree is twelve inches tall, it will need to be in a 6- to 8-inch container. This allows room for a bamboo stake of sufficient height and diameter to accommodate the mature tree. Use Twist-ems to attach the trunk to the stake. If strings are used, there is always the possibility that they may scar the trunk, or cut it so deeply that the entire top of the tree topples over.

Repot whenever roots begin to fill the container. Give good culture in regard to light, temperature, water, and food. A sunny location is necessary in order to develop a straight trunk.

Remove the main growing tip when the trunk has reached the height at which you desire branches to form. Later, pinch out the branch tips to improve the tree's shape. From the time branches begin, turn the tree slightly every day so that it can develop symmetrically.

Chrysanthemum Trees. It takes about ten months to grow a tree chrysanthemum. Varieties 'April Showers,' 'Gyokuhai,' 'Magic Carpet,' and 'Magic Light' have been recommended by one grower. Start with a well-rooted, compact, straight-stemmed cutting in March or April. Follow the basic rules for training a house plant tree. A cutting started in early spring can be finished at twelve to twenty-four inches in an 8- to 10-inch pot the following autumn. When flowers fade, keep plant through the winter as described on page 207.

Fuchsia Trees. Most fuchsias can be trained as standards. Some especially good kinds include 'American Beauty,' 'Bluebird,' 'Cardinal,' 'Cascade,' 'Checkerboard,' 'Flamboyant,'

Chrysanthemum tree reaches maturity in autumn following the rooting of a cutting the preceding March or April. (Photograph by Nicholson)

LEFT: *Pelargonium (common garden geranium) trained to tree form makes an elegant accent indoors, as in the author's sunny, west-facing living-room window, or outdoors during warm weather (if completely protected from the wind). This tree of the variety 'Inferno' was developed in less than one year from a rooted cutting.* RIGHT: *'Inferno' tree geranium three months after training began. Note frequent placement of Twist-ems to keep a straight stem. When desired height is reached, the growing tip is pinched out to induce branching.* (Photographs by Nicholson)

'Marinka,' 'Muriel,' 'Red Spider,' and 'Trailblazer.' One of the easiest is red-flowered 'Gartenmeister Bohnstedt,' the honeysuckle fuchsia. Its leaves are lovely too—metallic green with purplish undersides. Fuchsia standards are usually four to six feet tall. Start with a straight-stemmed, vigorous plant in a gallon-sized tub. At nearly every node along the stem, attach it to the stake with a Twist-em. When it reaches three feet, transplant it to a permanent 5-gallon tub, and change to an inch-square redwood stake, long enough to protrude above the soil at the height you want the full-grown tree to reach. Keep removing side branches and tying up the trunk until the growing tip reaches the top of the stake; then nip out the top. When the two new shoots that form have four leaves each, nip out their growing tips. Keep up this routine until the tree top attains the size you desire. To support and protect fuchsia standards, Tru Peterson of the California National Fuchsia Society recommends this procedure: At the time you place the permanent redwood stake, fasten a circular wire frame eighteen inches in diameter at the top. This frame needs two horizontal cross braces or spokes. As the branches of the tree form, drape them over the wire frame until it is covered completely.

Geranium Trees. Any geranium (*Pelargonium*) that grows strongly upward can be grown as a tree. I suggest 'Inferno,' 'Vérité,' 'Canadian Pink and White,' 'New Phlox,' 'Flare,' 'Monterey,' 'Fantasy,' 'Monsieur Emile David,' 'Tango,' 'Radiance,' 'Alphonse Ricard,' 'Gypsy,' 'Will Rogers,' 'Bonanza,' 'Masure's Beauty,' 'Wilhelm Langguth,' 'Jubilee,' 'Mrs. Cox,' 'Cerise Carnation,' 'Pink Rosebud,' and 'Mr. Wren.' To grow a geranium standard, follow the basic rules for training a house plant tree, outlined at the beginning of this chapter. With careful culture it is possible to keep geranium trees in good condition for eight years or more.

Heliotrope Trees. Start seeds of this fragrant-flowered plant in late winter or early spring. Follow the basic rules for training a house plant tree as outlined at the beginning of this chapter. Sometimes a heliotrope being trained as a tree will stop leaf

*Ornamental peppers ma
interesting tree forms,
especially appropriate for
holiday decorations beca
of the abundant crop of
bright-red fruit. This vari
'Purzel' has long, slende
pods of edible, but very ho
peppers.* (Photograph
Nicholson)

growth and start blooming. When this occurs, enjoy the flowers while they last. Then clip them away carefully and select one or two new growing tips to continue training upward until the desired height is reached.

Miniature Rose Trees. The tree rose seen in outdoor gardens is actually made up of two different varieties—a hardy species for the rootstock, with a hybrid type grafted to it. Miniature roses can be trained into decorative standards without grafting. These make prized pieces for sunny window gardens, greenhouses, or summering out-of-doors. If you have grown the miniature from seed or from a cutting, keep it growing upward as one stem. Pinch out all side growths. At a height of eighteen to twenty inches, remove the growing point and allow the top to develop. It takes about two years to develop miniature rose standards. If you purchase a miniature rose to train, remove all extra canes except the one chosen to be the trunk. Then train the tree as outlined above.

Rest the miniature rose standard in a light, 50-degree room from November until February. Water it often enough to make the trunk and branches stay plump. Bring to sunlight and warmth in February. After that, water and fertilize it at least twice a month. Prune carefully to maintain a desirable shape. Red spider mites (pp. 58–59) and aphids (p. 56) may attack.

Ornamental Pepper Trees. Plants of *Capsicum annuum* make delightful standards about eighteen inches tall. Grow them from seeds or cuttings. With judicious pruning they can easily be shaped into balls, squares, or cones. They grow so rapidly that a crop of shining fruit within six months after planting is not unusual. Ornamental peppers summered outdoors in a sunny to semi-shady place set more fruit than those kept inside.

TOPIARY TREES

Topiary work is the training or pruning of plant material into unnatural shapes. Practiced in gardens since the Middle Ages, it has made a comeback today. Such trained plants are at their best in a formal garden, but a fantastically shaped ivy or creeping fig lends an amusing note to an indoor garden.

Small-leaved shrubs such as boxwood can be clipped to produce topiary. I once had dinner at a home where the centerpiece was a rectangle of eight 3-inch pots of box (*Buxus microphylla japonica*), each plant trimmed to a tidy square.

When given good culture, trimmed trees become bushier than those left untrimmed. Clipping out the growing points of branches forces heavy new growth. Use the same procedure in clipping a potted plant as practiced on a hedge. Choose a contour for a tree, use sharp shears and nip away a little at a time until the desired shape is produced. Start on boxwood or *Euonymus japonicus microphyllus,* for they are reasonably priced and obtainable from nurserymen everywhere. Once the art of establishing the basic shape has been mastered, the gardener with a flair for the unusual may want to clip some of his small-leaved shrubs into spirals, cubes, balls, or pillars.

Other topiary designs can be fashioned by tying small-leaved vines or creepers to wire frames. Make these by bending 12-gauge wire or a wire coat hanger into a rectangle, a loop, a wreath, a bow, or the outline of a bird. Center the wire frame firmly in a pot of small-leaved ivy or creeping fig (*Ficus pumila*)

Malpighia coccigera *is a tropical house plant that makes an excellent bonsai, either to be grown in a bright window or under fluorescent lights. Plant shown is many years old.*
(Photograph by Arthur Norman Orans)

that has grown several long branches. Or make one by setting three or four plants in one pot. Tie the branches to the frame with green thread. Keep the thread handy to tie all subsequent growth in place until the frame is entirely covered. Rotate the plant a little every day so that the design will not become lopsided. Remove all faded leaves and straggly offshoots which might ruin the artistic effect of this living ornament.

English ivy and creeping fig can be used for another, similar artistic garden project. This consists of training them to cover entirely a pyramid, ball, or cone made of inch-mesh poultry netting. I use the green-painted kind which florists stock. After molding the wire to the shape desired, fill it with moist, unmilled sphagnum moss. Secure the base in a container of good soil and plant English ivy or creeping fig all around. If the moss is kept nicely moist, the ivy or fig will quickly cover it. Hairpins can be used to secure the stems into the moss until their aerial roots take hold.

FAKE BONSAI

Bonsai is a Japanese expression used to denote an artificially dwarfed potted plant, or plants, which has been painstakingly trained to suggest a natural scene. A bonsai twelve inches tall with an outcropping of thickened roots may appear to be an ancient tree clinging to the edge of a cliff. Conversely, a symmetrical miniature atop a straight trunk might evoke the vision of a stately old shade tree. There are miniature trees in Japan which are centuries old. These living heirlooms are passed on from one generation to the next.

It is virtually impossible for Americans to purchase ready-grown bonsai of old age. However, many gardeners who are devoted to the art of bonsai grow their own miniature trees. Information about helpful books and sources for supplies is listed in Part III. Hardy trees and shrubs whose foliage changes with the seasons make up traditional Japanese bonsai. Such plants often weaken and die in the arid winter climate of an artificially heated window garden. Summertime care requires constant vigilance in keeping the soil moist, and protecting them from drying winds.

Because my own schedule does not allow time for such an exacting procedure, I have developed some bonsai adaptations which are useful to the average window gardener. I call them "pseudo" or "fake" bonsai. Rapid-growing tropical trees with medium to small leaves and flowers are the most appropriate. Their placement in containers, pruning, and training procedures are the same as for traditional bonsai, except on an accelerated schedule as they grow throughout the year. They need warmth, sunlight, and a moist atmosphere at all times. Here are some of the plants I have enjoyed growing as fake bonsai (they will also do well in fluorescent-light gardens):

Acacia species
Calliandra surinamensis
Carissa grandiflora
Cassia grandis (pink shower)
Citrus species
Ficus benjamina (weeping fig)
Gardenia species
Harpephyllum caffrum (Kaffir-plum)
Jacaranda acutifolia
Poinciana regia
Schinus terebinthifolius (Brazilian pepper)

10. Indoor gardening
for children

Iᖴ ʏᴏᴜ have no children or grandchildren, then find some child in your community with whom you can share the joys of indoor gardening. In doing this you will be taking advantage of a golden opportunity to guide a child in learning some of the miracles of nature.

Children want to know the why of everything about gardening. When it comes to specific plants and projects, remember that they are inspired by the quick, the easy, the extra big, the miniature, and even the grotesque. They like botanical names, and a five-year-old may be better able than you to learn and remember that he has a *Streptosolen jamesonii*.

While the snow flies, or a bitter wind blows, you can spend an evening, or a Saturday morning, teaching a youngster something of what makes plants grow. One lesson could be about how plants multiply—how to take a leaf cutting of an African violet; show your student how an inch-long piece of sansevieria will root when its base is inserted in moist sand, and how a new plant will grow from it. Another time you could show him how to take tip cuttings of geraniums, Christmas cactus, chrysanthemums, and coleus.

Seed planting is a magic world to children—to all of us, in fact—and, at the outset, they are pleased most with the seeds that germinate quickly. Good choices to begin with are pots or small flats of radishes, lettuce, beans, and midget tomatoes. At the same time the child plants these, have him sow one or two bean seeds against the side of a drinking glass or small jar filled with moist soil. He can then watch these seeds swell, form roots, and push forth sprouts, and in so doing he will be able to visualize what the other seeds he has planted are doing beneath the soil.

Help your young gardener sow a packet of hybrid coleus seeds. They grow quickly, sprouting within a few days in warmth and moisture. Every seedling will have different foliage and all children are entranced by such a Persian carpet of leaf colors and designs. After the seedlings are big enough to transplant, help your beginner move them to individual small pots or to even rows in a small flat. Show the beginner how to lift the seedlings carefully out of the starting medium; how to separate the roots, and how to firm them with care into a new place. Explain about watering them after transplanting, and how they need shade from hot, burning sunlight for a few days until the roots have a chance to become established.

PLANTS FOR CHILDREN

In choosing plants for children, keep in mind that they may be more impressed by a plant with a picturesque name or with an odd growth habit than by something that is beautiful to your eye. For example, the sensitive plant, *Mimosa pudica,* has miniature locustlike leaflets, and would not be cultivated except for the fact that when one of these is touched, it responds immediately by folding up tightly. The voodoo plant, or sacred lily of India, *Hydrosme rivieri,* sends up its carrion-scented flower spathe in the winter without accompanying foliage, and although it has a revolting odor, the plant appeals to children.

Carnivorous, or meat-eating, plants are not the easiest to grow, but if you offer a helpful hand, your child may be successful with *Dionaea muscipula,* the Venus flytrap. One way to grow this plant is to pot it in humus-rich soil combined with an equal part of sphagnum moss. Place it in high humidity, as inside a miniature plastic greenhouse or other terrarium.

Cacti and succulents are ideal plants for children. Such common names as rainbow bush (*Portulacaria afra* var. *tricolor*), velvet leaf (*Kalanchoe beharensis*), painted lady (*Echeveria derenbergii*), crown of thorns (*Euphorbia splendens*), tiger jaws (*Faucaria tigrina*), burro's-tail (*Sedum morganianum*), necklace vine (*Crassula perforata*), heart vine (*Ceropegia woodii*), old lady cactus (*Mammillaria hahniana*), old man cactus (*Cephalocereus senilis*), golden stars (*Mammillaria elongata*), and bishop's cap (*Astrophytum myriostigma*) are appealing to children and may be the beginning of a lifelong interest for them.

Christmas cactus, *Schlumbergera bridgesii,* seems to be set apart in our thinking from other cacti and succulents because its culture is more like that of other house plants. It is a plant that forms flower buds only when the days are short in the fall. If it receives artificial light during the period between sundown and sunrise for any length of time in the fall, then buds may not form at the proper time, if at all. Chrysanthemums also are plants that bloom when the days are short in the fall.

The shrimp plant, *Beloperone guttata,* has salmon bracts that are shaped and colored in such a way as to remind us of shrimp. It is a favorite of children and not difficult for them to grow. The pickaback plant, *Tolmiea menziesii,* has leaves of bright green and, as these mature, small perfectly formed new plants grow on top of each. Wax, angel-wing, and beefsteak (rhizomatous) begonias are good choices for a child's indoor garden. Since coleus roots easily from cuttings placed either in water or in moist soil, it will provide plenty of material with which a child may experiment to learn how plants can be increased vegetatively.

A good project for a child who has a sunny window is to grow a pot of morning-glories. A few seeds may be planted at any time in a 5- or 6-inch pot. After they have some growth, they should be thinned to leave the three strongest. Keep the soil moist, the pot in a sunny warm place, and the plants will begin to bloom when they are about three months old. After one season the plant should be discarded.

The spider plant, *Chlorophytum elatum,* has thick white tuberous roots, similar to a white icicle radish, and its rosette-forming grasslike foliage grows easily under all sorts of conditions. It propagates itself naturally by sending out slender branches, the end of each tipped by a young rosette. As this grows and attains weight it is lowered to the ground. If it finds moist soil, the new plant will form its own roots. Children like to help a young plant get started on its own by pinning it into a neighboring pot of moist soil. As soon as roots form, the plant may be severed from its parent.

Children find fun in starting an avocado seed in a glass of water. Insert three toothpicks at intervals around the seed so that the larger, lower third is in the water, but the rest is held above. After a root forms and top growth begins, transplant to regular potting soil. Avocados may be trained as small trees or bushes and kept inside the year round, or they can be put outdoors during warm weather, and brought indoors in the winter.

As your young gardener progresses, and his interest grows, he or she will find gardening full of unlimited possibilities. The plants and activities suggested here are a mere beginning. As additional reading and resource material, I suggest these books: *How Plants Travel,* by Joan Elma Rahn (Atheneum Publishers, New York City; $4.95), *Learning About Nature Through Indoor Gardening,* by Virginia W. Musselman (Stackpole Books, Harrisburg, Pa.; $3.95), *50 Easy Garden Projects,* by Jacqueline Heriteau (Popular Library, New York City; $1.50), and *Growing Up Green* (Parents & Children Gardening Together), by Alice Skelsey and Gloria Huckaby (Workman Publishing Company, Inc., New York City; $8.95 hardcover, $4.95 paper).

11. Space-makers for indoor gardening— fluorescent lights and home greenhouses

Whether you need an extra four feet of indoor gardening area, or an entire room, it can be acquired by installing fluorescent lights. Another way of adding space is to invest in a home greenhouse. Some preliminary pointers on a greenhouse setup are given later in this chapter.

FLUORESCENT LIGHTS

Artificially lighted indoor gardens can be devised in closets, attics, and basements; in cabinets, bookcases, and planters; and in various kinds of lighted plant carts.

With the possible exception of some orchids, geraniums, cacti, and other succulents, all house plants thrive and bloom under fluorescent lights. Bulbs, tubers, and cuttings root quickly. Seedlings too are easy to grow with this kind of illumination, which knows no short, cloudy, or rainy day.

Plants placed directly under the lights grow symmetrically with never a turn, for they receive evenly balanced light from

TABLE OF ILLUMINATION IN FOOT-CANDLES

Illumination of plants at various distances from two or four 40-watt standard cool white fluorescent lamps mounted approximately two inches below a white-painted reflecting surface.

DISTANCE FROM LAMPS	ILLUMINATION TWO LAMPS* USED**	FOUR LAMPS* USED**	NEW
(inches)	(f-c)	(f-c)	(f-c)
1	1100	1600	1800
2	860	1400	1600
3	680	1300	1400
4	570	1100	1300
5	500	940	1150
6	420	820	1000
7	360	720	900
8	330	660	830
9	300	600	780
10	280	560	720
11	260	510	660
12	240	480	600
18	130	320	420
24	100	190	260

* Center-to-center distance between the lamps was two inches.
** These lamps had been used for approximately 200 hours.

overhead. Incandescents (ordinary light bulbs) too can be useful, especially for giving green foliage plants some extra light.

Plants need properly balanced red and blue light rays to promote good growth and flowering. An initial light setup can be made from a pair of 40-watt, 48-inch fluorescent tubes, one cool white, the other warm white, in a standard industrial reflector. Do not use supplementary incandescent with fluorescent light; they give off too much heat and burn too much electricity.

A pair of ordinary 40-watt fluorescents, with starters and a reflector, will cost less than $30. A reflector is necessary to throw the light onto the plants. The tubes and reflector should be suspended about eighteen inches from the plant table. Chain, rope, or wire may be used. Lights may be left on twelve to eighteen hours a day, the time depending on the type of plants being grown. Those that flower need more light than foliage kinds. Energy-conscious under-light gardeners report no adverse effects from 12-hour days. Certainly 14-hour days will grow almost any common house plant or herb under lights.

Lights may be switched on and off manually, but it's best to let a timer do the job. Do not leave lights on continuously. In fact, if you do not have an automatic timer, it is better to leave the lights off when you go away for a weekend.

Fluorescent light is the most efficient user of electrical energy —much better than incandescent. The cost of operating lighted shelves, tables, or even multilevel carts for plants is negligible considering the pleasure they give. Tubes last approximately a year, but quantity of light diminishes with age.

The amount of bloom given by house plants depends in large part on the foot-candles of light they receive. A foot-candle is a measure of illumination. The accompanying table prepared at the United States Department of Agriculture gives an idea of the light output at the center of a pair of tubes. The light decreases somewhat as it nears the ends of the tubes.

African violets, for instance, need 300 to 600 foot-candles of light. Their requirements vary with age. Seedlings need more light than older plants. Pink- and white-flowered varieties require less light than blue-flowered types. For a guide, measure the distance from the center of the tube to the pot rim. Generally speaking, mature blue-flowered varieties grow into fine specimens when placed with eleven inches between the light tube and the pot rim. If window-grown plants show tall upright growth, they will become shorter and more compact in a fluorescent-lighted garden. If leaves of plants under fluorescents look yellow and bleached, they may be receiving too much light. Either cut down on the total hours of illumination per day, or move them farther from the lights. When petioles (leaf stalks) are too long and blooming is poor, plants are not receiving enough light. Move them closer to the tubes.

Set cuttings and seedlings as close as three to four inches from the tubes to promote rapid, compact growth. Use lights to hasten growth on newly planted gloxinias, other gesneriads, tuberous begonias and caladiums. Dwarf geraniums grow beautifully when given eighteen hours of light per day and spaced so there are six to eight inches between tubes and pot rims. Begonias of all types flourish under lights. And to help forced bulbs develop perfectly, place them under lights while flower buds and stems are lengthening.

The author's fluorescent-lighted Tubecraft FloraCart decorates a basement recreation room that might otherwise be dark and lifeless. Plants on upper shelf include rex begonias—'Her Majesty' and others—African violets, temple bells (Smithiantha multiflora nana), *African hybrid amaryllis, Christmas begonia 'Lady Mac,' walking iris* (Neomarica northiana), *and* Chamaeranthemum igneum. *Plants on lower deck include African hybrid amaryllis, angel-wing begonia 'Corallina de Lucerna' and* Dieffenbachia picta. (Photograph by Nicholson)

My first light setup, made several years ago, was a pair of light tubes suspended by a chain over a collection of gesneriads. Since then I have had many different arrangements of light. My current favorite is a three-tiered portable cart manufactured for the purpose. It gives twenty-four square feet of ideal growing space. Another unit I like is a bookcase with lights above the top shelf, and books on the under shelf. This combination case is 51 inches long, 32 inches high, and 18 inches wide. It is equipped with sliding glass doors to maintain humidity. I use it as a display area for specimen African violets, rex begonias, gloxinias, and episcias.

An entire plant room can be made in a cellar or heated attic. Some enthusiasts grow hundreds of plants in areas such as these, and it is not unusual for fluorescent light-grown plants to win top prizes at flower shows.

Incandescent bulbs give off red rays that are beneficial to plants. Although they also give off more heat than fluores-

Fluorescent-lighted bookcase provides an ideal place for episcias at either end with seedling African violets between. (Photograph by Schulz)

cents, they are the answer to maintaining large foliage plants, hanging baskets, and trees where natural light is not bright enough. Use standard Cool Beam (General Electric) or Cool-Lux (Sylvania) spotlights in ceramic sockets. These can be mounted on inexpensive light stands (the kind used by photographers), or in a ceiling track system. The bulbs are available in sizes from 75 to 300 watts. Smaller ones can be as close as 12 to 18 inches from the leaves, larger ones may need to be 3 or 4 feet away so that the foliage is not burned. Give plants 6 to 12 hours of illumination out of every 24. Spindly new growth indicates not enough light; increase wattage or hours of illumination. Burned foliage indicates light is too close. Wilting may be caused by light too close, or the plant may need more water.

GREENHOUSES TO BUY OR BUILD

A home greenhouse of any size offers indescribable pleasure to an indoor gardener. Here, tropicals can be grown which may be too large or too difficult to handle in the window garden. A greenhouse gives the hybridizer, the propagator, and the ardent collector extra space for an always expanding hobby.

A window greenhouse is a small luxury which will fit into almost any gardener's space and budget. A heated window greenhouse makes a delightful display area for such plants as begonias, geraniums, orchids, and cacti. Prefabricated models are available (pp. 301–05); otherwise, anyone looking for a small building project will find a window greenhouse easy to construct.

These small greenhouses have glass or heavy-gauge transparent plastic on the top and three outer sides. The fourth side can be left open to the room, or it may be formed by the window of the house. In building such a greenhouse, use rot-resistant wood for the framework. In size it should not be so large that it

RIGHT: *Exterior view of window greenhouse. Note remarkable number plants which one of these structures will hold.* (Photograph by Br: mayer)

will look ungainly. Mine, which accommodates about thirty plants in 4-inch pots, is 20 inches deep, 32 inches wide, and 22 inches high. It is situated on the east side of our house. The top slopes so rain and snow can drain off.

Inside my window greenhouse, potted plants are set atop moistened pebbles in a galvanized tray. A thermometer and humidity combination inside the unit tells me whether the area needs added heat, ventilation, or moisture. In severely cold weather, an electric soil cable, obtainable from seed stores and mail order houses, warms the air. Vents on the top and bottom of the end panels serve to admit fresh air. These openings, 1½x16 inches, have window screen tacked to the outside to keep out insects. Four wooden strips ¼x2x17 inches, fastened over the inside of the openings, cover the ventilators. These covers, or shutters, are secured with a single screw and can be pushed open to admit air. Humidity can be increased by spraying plants with water, and by adding water to the pebble tray.

Building a greenhouse or putting together one of the prefabricated ones is not a tremendous project. The greenhouse can be attached to a dwelling, or it can be a free-standing unit.

I built my first small lean-to greenhouse when I was twelve years old. This 6x9-foot plastic-covered structure cost only $70, but it housed many plant treasures—begonias, geraniums, gloxinias, oxalis, and amaryllis. Today it continues to give pleasure to my parents.

My present greenhouse is attached to an east-facing bedroom window of our home. It has an even-span roof, is 10 feet wide, and extends out 20 feet from the house. I spent about a week putting together this greenhouse, a prefabricated model which came complete with cooling, heating, and humidifying equipment. I supplied the foundation, a pebble-surfaced concrete floor, and redwood benches.

The first step in acquiring a home greenhouse is to check local building restrictions. Write for catalogues of home greenhouse manufacturers (pp. 301–05). After placing an order, you will receive a blueprint of the greenhouse. With this informa-

The author, with sons Steven and Mark, in his 10 x 20 greenhouse. It is a prefabri-cated model which came complete with heating, cooling, and humidifying equipment. Protection from too much sun is provided by Lumite Saran Shading Cloth. (Photo-graph by Nicholson)

tion, it is possible to proceed with foundation construction. Some greenhouses have glass extending to the top of the foundation at ground level; others have glass to the top of a wall that extends three or four feet above the foundation.

If possible, locate an attached greenhouse so that it has an eastern and a southern exposure to admit maximum light. Too much light can be controlled, but the only way to bring additional illumination to heavily shaded greenhouse areas is by adding fluorescent lights.

Once completed, the greenhouse will need utilities such as electric wiring, a heating unit, and plumbing. A cooling system is not absolutely essential but it makes for easier greenhouse gardening during warm seasons. A floor of concrete, brick, or gravel will be necessary, as well as benches to hold the plants. Shading to keep light from burning the plants is part of maintenance from spring to late fall. This can be regular greenhouse whiting powder stirred into water and brushed on the outside of the glass, or wooden slats, or roll-up reed screening. I use Lumite Saran shade cloth because it is inexpensive, long-lasting, and comes in several types of weaves to comply with various lighting problems. It eliminates hot spots and heavily shaded areas, and is rot-, rust-, and mildew-proof. This shading comes as a slip cover tailored to fit your greenhouse; you attach it on the outside, and cut out places for doors and ventilators.

A greenhouse's temperature, humidity, and light are governed by the plants grown in it. Greenhouses are referred to as cold or alpine houses (unheated), cool houses (45-50°F. at night), moderate houses (50-60°F. at night) and warm houses (60-70°F. at night).

If you live where night temperatures seldom drop much below 32°F., you can grow such plants as spring-flowering bulbs, primroses of all kinds, and winter-flowering pansies in an unheated greenhouse. You'll find this a good place, too, for wintering miniature roses, hardy bonsai, and container-grown citrus trees.

Cool and moderate greenhouses require less frequent attention given to watering, but the routine maintenance of any hobby greenhouse requires a surprisingly small amount of time. My greenhouse has automatic heating, cooling, and ventilating equipment. In the master bedroom of our home there is a bell which warns if the greenhouse temperature drops below the minimum being maintained (usually 50°F.). I have warm and cold water in the greenhouse, with a mixing faucet. To control insects and diseases, I use a hose-end sprayer once every two weeks. Although the greenhouse is lighted with incandescent bulbs, I do most of the work in an hour or two each Saturday morning.

part II

AN ILLUSTRATED ENCYCLOPEDIA OF INDOOR PLANTS

Arranged alphabetically according to plant families. For example, philodendrons are discussed with the Arum Family. To find a plant whose family name you do not know, refer to the index. If you have only a plant's common name, the index will guide you to its botanical name and family. Unless noted otherwise, fertilize plants according to the general directions given in Chapter 2.

ACANTHUS FAMILY

Tender perennials with simple, opposite leaves. Spikes of irregular, one- or two-lipped flowers.

Acanthus

DESCRIPTION: *A. mollis*, 3 to 4 ft., from southern Europe. Handsome, large foliage; showy spikes of white, rose, or lilac flowers. Special uses: for accent in tub or planter.
CULTURE: Light, semi-sunny. Temperature, 50-70°F. Humidity, 30-60%. Soil, equal parts sand, loam, peat moss; keep evenly moist. Propagate by seeds in spring; division spring or fall.

Aphelandra

DESCRIPTION: *A. squarrosa louisae*, 3 ft., from Brazil. Although classified as a flowering plant, its spectacular terminal spike of waxy flowers is fully matched in beauty by shiny emerald-green leaves, strikingly veined in white. Most of the Aphelandras have white or pale veins; most flower in terminal four-sided bracted spikes, and flower colors are predominantly orange-scarlet or yellow. Of them all, *A. squarrosa louisae* is undoubtedly the

Aphelandra squarrosa louisae

showiest, and has recently joined the ranks of flowering plants offered by florists.

CULTURE: Light, semi-sunny. Temperature, average house. Humidity, 30% or more. Soil, 1 part loam, 1 part sand or Perlite, 2 parts peat moss or leaf mold; keep evenly moist. Propagate by tip cuttings in spring at 70-80°F.

Beloperone

DESCRIPTION: *B. guttata,* 1½ ft., from Mexico, the popular shrimp plant. A wiry-stemmed plant that needs frequent pruning to prevent its becom-

Beloperone guttata

ing scraggly. The brick-red, overlapping, and drooping bracts which surround the flowers resemble a shrimp. The true flowers, small and white, are barely visible except on close inspection. The cultivar 'Yellow Queen' has chartreuse bracts and is also called shrimp plant. *B. comosa* 'Red King' has bracts of solid, bright red.

CULTURE: Light, sunny, or semi-sunny. Temperature, average house. Humidity, 30% or more. Soil, equal parts loam, sand, and peat moss;

allow to be dry on surface, then moisten thoroughly. Propagate by cuttings any time.

Chamaeranthemum

DESCRIPTION: *C. gaudichaudii,* small creeper from Brazil. An attractive plant with silver-centered dark-green leaves that are small and oval. *C. igneum* from Peru has more pointed leaves colored brownish green with a soft suedelike appearance, and veined in shades of red and yellow. *C. venosum* from Brazil differs in having small, hard leaves netted with silver. All bear small but showy clusters of bracted flowers. Special uses: for terrarium gardens.

CULTURE: Light, semi-shady. Temperature, average house. Humidity, 30% or more. Soil, equal parts loam, sand, and peat moss; keep evenly moist. Propagate by cuttings rooted in high humidity.

Crossandra

DESCRIPTION: *C. infundibuliformis* (formerly *C. undulaefolia*), 1 to 3 ft., from India. The tubular blossoms, expanded at the top, are borne on fairly long, thick, four-sided spikes

Crossandra infundibuliformis

and are heavily bracted in green. Their color is rich salmon-orange, and a well-grown plant is nearly everblooming. Exceedingly showy in terra-cotta pots.

CULTURE: Light, semi-sunny. Temperature, average house. Humidity, 30% or more. Soil, 1 part loam, 1 part sand or Perlite, 2 parts peat moss or leaf mold; keep evenly moist. Propagate by sowing fresh seeds, or by tip cuttings; provide warmth (70-80°F.).

Eranthemum

DESCRIPTION: *E. nervosum,* 1 to 4 ft., from India. A rare but worth-while plant bearing small, ovate, rough leaves. Its bracts of one-inch gentian-blue flowers create a breath-taking sight when they appear in midwinter.
CULTURE: Same as Crossandra.

Fittonia verschaffeltii

Fittonia

DESCRIPTION: *F. verschaffeltii,* 8 in., from Peru. Semi-upright or trailing plant with pink-veined leaves. Variety *argyroneura* has white-veined leaves; variety *pearcei* has papery, thin, olive-green leaves with carmine veins. Special uses: for terrarium gardens.
CULTURE: Light, semi-sunny to semi-shady. Temperature, average house.

Humidity, 30% or more. Soil, 1 part loam, 1 part sand or Perlite, 2 parts peat moss or leaf mold; keep evenly moist. Propagate by tip cuttings rooted in warmth and high humidity.

Hemigraphis

DESCRIPTION: ` *H. colorata,* creeper, from Java. Sometimes called red or flame ivy. Smooth, glossy leaves are reddish purple in semi-sun, silver in shade. Pleasant clusters of white flowers.
CULTURE: Same as Fittonia, except hemigraphis grows too rampantly for terrarium culture. Grow it in a pot or hanging basket.

Hypoestes

DESCRIPTION: *H. sanguinolenta,* 1 to 2 ft., from Malagasy (Madagascar). Pointed, oval, dark-green leaves spattered with pink to rose markings give this plant such common names as freckle-face and pink polka-dot. It produces terminal spikes of lavender flowers. A cultivar named 'Splash' has larger leaves more clearly variegated with rose. New growth of hypoestes is covered with fine white hairs which disappear as the leaves mature. Frequent pinching of the growing tips is necessary to keep plants compact. When given abundant sunlight, the spots take on a deeper color and the entire leaf surface will be flushed red. If grown in too much shade, hypoestes will have few "freckles."
CULTURE: Light, sunny to semi-sunny. Temperature, average house. Humidity, 30% or more. Soil, 1 part loam, 1 part sand or Perlite, 2 parts peat moss or leaf mold; keep evenly moist. Propagate by seeds or cuttings any time. After flowering the plant may die back to the soil; keep barely

Hypoestes sanguinolenta

other jacobinias, and orange blossoms in the summer.

It is the tendency of jacobinias to become scraggly unless they are properly cultivated. In their native habitat, they become shrubby perennials, but when pot-grown, they generally do better if treated as annuals. After the flowering season ends, take tip cuttings and discard the old plant. CULTURE: Light, semi-sunny. Temperature, average house. Humidity, 30% or more. Soil, equal parts loam, sand, and peat moss; keep evenly moist. Propagate by cuttings at any time, but especially at the close of a flowering period.

moist until new growth begins. May be grown in pots, planters, baskets, or as a standard (Chapter 8).

Jacobinia

DESCRIPTION: *J. carnea*, 3 to 4 ft., from Brazil. Large, dark-green leaves topped with a huge, bracted head of clear pink, arched, two-lipped blossoms give this plant the names Brazilian plume and king's crown. It blooms in the spring and summer. *J. chrysostephana*, 3 to 4 ft., from Mexico, has yellow flowers in the winter. *J. ghiesbreghtiana*, 1 to 2 ft., from Mexico, begins to bear its orange-red flowers in early winter and continues until summer; attractive, light-green foliage. *J. suberecta*, 1 ft., from Uruguay, has softly hairy leaves, a less erect manner of growth than

Jacobinia carnea

Pseuderanthemum

DESCRIPTION: *P. alatum*, 1 ft., from Mexico, has coppery brown leaves blotched with silver-gray near the main rib. Often called "chocolate plant." *P. atropurpureum tricolor,* a small shrub from Polynesia, is more beautifully variegated. It has heavier-textured, almost leathery leaves of metallic purple irregularly splashed with green, rose, and white.

CULTURE: Light, semi-sunny to semi-shady. Temperature, average house. Humidity, 30% or more; moist atmosphere increases leaf size, although pseuderanthemums will grow satisfactorily under normal indoor conditions. Soil, equal parts loam, sand, and peat moss; keep evenly moist. Propagate by cuttings in spring or summer.

Ruellia

DESCRIPTION: *R. amoena,* 1 to 2 ft., from South America, is noted for bright red, pouched blossoms borne in sprays from the leaf axils. It has green, papery leaves narrowed at both ends. *R. makoyana,* a low, spreading plant from Brazil, is valued chiefly for its foliage. The leaves are small, satiny, olive-green with purple-red shadings and silvery veins. The funnel-shaped flowers are rosy carmine.

CULTURE: Same as Pseuderanthemum.

Stenandrium

DESCRIPTION: *S. lindenii,* 6 to 12 in., from Peru, is a trailing plant with broadly oval, dark-green, velvety

Stenandrium lindenii

leaves. These have a feathering of creamy white along the veins, and purplish reverses. The flowers are yellow, in 3-inch spikes arising from the axils.

CULTURE: Light, semi-sunny to semi-shady. Temperature, average house. Humidity, 30% or more. Soil, 1 part loam, 1 part sand or Perlite, 2 parts peat moss or leaf mold; keep evenly moist. Propagate by cuttings rooted March to July in high humidity and warmth (75-80°F.). Excellent for terrariums.

Ruellia makoyana

Strobilanthes

DESCRIPTION: *S. dyerianus,* 3 ft., from Burma, has attractive leaves, iridescent silver-blue and lavender above, and rosy purple beneath. It has pale-violet flowers in autumn. *S. isophyllus,* 2 to 3 ft., from India, has willowy leaves, and funnel-shaped, blue and white flowers in the winter.

CULTURE: Same as Pseuderanthemum.

Thunbergia

DESCRIPTION: *T. alata,* a 4- to 6-ft. vine from tropical Africa, has apricot or white flowers with purple center, hence "black-eyed-susan vine." It is a tender perennial usually cultivated as an annual from seeds sown in winter or spring. After a period of heavy bloom, cut back nearly to soil. This promotes new growth and more flowers. This cutting-back procedure, combined with regular feeding and yearly repotting, can be used to keep *T. alata* as a perennial. Or, at the end of one flowering season, discard the plant and start anew with seeds. *T. grandiflora,* 10 to 15 ft., from India, is a shrubby vine with showy blue flowers in late summer. It is sometimes called "blue-sky vine." Nice for a large sun porch; trim back as necessary after flowering.

CULTURE: Light, sunny. Temperature, average house. Humidity, 30% or more. Soil, equal parts loam, sand, and peat moss; keep evenly moist. Propagate by seeds or firm young cuttings in winter or spring.

FIG-MARIGOLD FAMILY   Aizoaceae

Subtropical tender succulents with single, daisylike flowers. In addition to those described, these genera may be grown indoors with the same general culture: Argyroderma, Cheiridopsis, Delosperma, Dinteranthus, Erepsia, Gibbaeum, Glottiphyllum, Hymenocyclus, Mesembryanthemum, Nananthus, Ophthalmophyllum, Pleiospilos, Rhombophyllum, Titanopsis, and Trichodiadema. On the whole, they have no common names.

Aptenia

DESCRIPTION: *A. cordifolia,* a creeper or trailer from South Africa, has small, mealy, light-green, heart-shaped leaves. Tiny purple flowers come in spring and summer. When allowed to cascade from a hanging basket, it will reach a length of 1 to 2 ft. in one season. Sometimes called "ice plant."

CULTURE: Light, sunny. Temperature, average house. Humidity, average house. Soil, equal parts loam, sand, and peat moss; keep evenly moist,

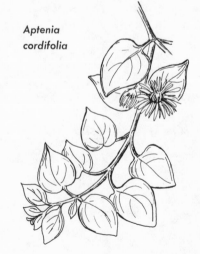

*Aptenia
cordifolia*

but more so in sunny, warm weather. Propagate by stem cuttings in spring.

Conophytum

DESCRIPTION: Species *C. aureum, C. elishae, C. giftbergensis, C. griseum, C. minutum, C. muscosipapillatum, C. truncatellum, C. wiggettae,* and many others, all from South Africa, are called "living stones," "stone faces,"

Faucaria tigrina

Conophytum aureum

or "cone plants." Some are pebblelike miniatures less than 1 in. tall and ¼ in. across. They seldom exceed 4 in. Treasures for collections of individual pots, or in Lilliputian landscapes created with other succulents.
CULTURE: As for the related Lithops.

Faucaria

DESCRIPTION: *F. tigrina,* 3 in., from South Africa, has a low rosette of fleshy, triangular leaves, paired, and with teethlike structures along the edges, hence "tiger jaws." The gray-green leaves are heavily spotted with white. Flat, large, daisylike yellow flowers appear in the fall. *F. tuberculosa* is similar, but has dark-green, warty leaves and may be called "knobby tiger jaws."
CULTURE: Light, sunny. Temperature,

average house. Humidity, average house. Soil, 1 part peat, 1 part loam, 2 parts sand; or, 6 parts sand, 3 parts loam, 2 parts leaf mold, 1 part crushed brick; water thoroughly, and not again until growing medium is dry. Propagate by seeds sown in spring or fall; by cuttings taken in May or June, first dried, then rooted in barely moist sand.

Fenestraria

DESCRIPTION: *F. aurantiaca* (yellow flowers) and *F. rhopalophylla* (white flowers), are miniature succulents 1 to 2 in. tall from South Africa. They form clusters of toelike leaves, hence "baby toes." The translucent area at the top of each is called a "window."
CULTURE: As for Faucaria.

Lampranthus

DESCRIPTION: *L. emarginatus,* 1 ft., from South Africa, has very narrow leaves, attractively set off in summer with many purple, daisylike flowers. Often called "ice plant." *L. multiradiatus,* also from South Africa, is more trailing in habit, to 2 ft. when allowed to cascade from a basket or shelf. It has 2-in. pink flowers.

CULTURE: Light, sunny. Temperature, average house. Humidity, average house. Soil, equal parts crushed bricks or broken clay pots, loam, leaf mold, and sand; keep evenly moist in summer, on the dry side in winter. Propagate by seeds or cuttings from March to September. Lampranthus may be used outdoors in warm weather as a bedding plant in sun.

Lithops

DESCRIPTION: This is a large genus of small South African plants which consist of a pair of close-set, fleshy leaves separated by a cleft. The common names "stone face" and "living stone" come from their uncanny resemblance to a small, split rock. In autumn they may produce yellow, white, or orange blossoms larger than the leaves. After flowering the plants become dormant, looking quite dead until they break open to show two new leaves.

Lithops julii-reticulata

CULTURE: Light, sunny. Temperature, average house. Humidity, average house. Soil, 6 parts sand, 4 parts loam, 1 part finely crushed brick; keep evenly moist May to November, dry balance of year. Propagate by seeds sown in moist atmosphere at 55-60°F. in spring. When transplanting lithops, bury one fourth of the plant body.

AMARANTH FAMILY   Amaranthaceae

Tender annuals and perennials, often with highly colored foliage, or showy flower heads. Two perennials are of interest to the indoor gardener, Alternanthera and Iresine.

Alternanthera

DESCRIPTION: *A. bettzickiana*, 2 to 3 in., from Brazil, has twisted narrow leaves irregularly marked with colors from creamy yellow to salmon-red. Sometimes called "miniature Joseph's coat." *A. ramosissima*, 8 to 12 in., from Brazil, has broad, pointed leaves of metallic wine-red, purple beneath, and flowers like small, stiff, white clover blooms, hence "indoor clover." *A. versicolor*, 3 in., from Brazil, is a compact plant with almost round leaves, crisped and corrugated, of dark-green or coppery red with purplish veining and pink and white edging. It is the popular "Joseph's coat," a name also applied to its large, outdoor garden relative, *Amaranthus tricolor*.

CULTURE: Light, sunny to semi-sunny. Temperature, average house. Humidity, average house. Soil, equal

Alternanthera bettzickiana

veins, make these foliage plants attractive.

CULTURE: Light, sunny. Temperature, cool to average house. Humidity, average house. Soil, equal parts loam, sand, and peat moss; keep evenly moist. Propagate by cuttings at any time, but especially in the winter and early spring, because iresines are useful outdoors in the summer in sunny to shady places for bedding, also for planting in boxes, tubs, urns, and baskets.

parts loam, sand, and peat moss; keep evenly moist. Propagate by cuttings at any time.

Iresine

DESCRIPTION: *I. herbstii*, 1 ft., from Brazil, and its varieties, such as *aureoreticulata*, have rounded leaves noticeably notched or "dimpled" at the tip. It is from this shape that an absurd common name, "chicken gizzard plant," arises. *I. lindenii*, 1 ft., from Ecuador, and its varieties such as *formosa*, have pointed leaves. Foliage of all iresines is highly colored, predominantly deep crimson red, hence "bloodleaf." Yellow and green areas in the leaves, especially along the

Iresine herbstii var. aureo-reticulata

AMARYLLIS FAMILY   **Amaryllidaceae**

Mostly tropical bulbous plants that differ only slightly from members of the lily family. Amaryllid flowers have six segments, and are usually borne in umbels above the foliage.

Agave

DESCRIPTION: *A. miradorensis*, from Mexico, is called the "dwarf century plant." It has short, broad, gray-green leaves arranged in a symmetri-

Agave miradorensis

cal rosette. While this species is slightly pliable, another dwarf, *A. pumila,* also from Mexico, has very stiff dark-green leaves which are attractively striped with silver and tipped with black. There are many other Agaves, but their formidable armament and huge size prevent frequent use indoors. They are often confused with Aloes (members of the lily family). The spine-tipped leaves of agaves are tough, fibrous, with hard, sharp teeth, while those of the aloes are soft, fleshy, almost pulpy.

CULTURE: Light, sunny. Temperature, average house. Humidity, average house. Soil, 2 parts loam, 1 part sand; water sparingly when soil is bone-dry on the surface. Propagate by removing small offsets at any time.

Amarcrinum

DESCRIPTION: Amarcrinums are inter-generic hybrids between *Amaryllis belladonna* and *Crinum moorei. A. howardii* (called *Crinodonna corsii* in Italy), has beautiful, fragrant pink flowers borne in clusters atop 3-ft. stems in autumn. 'Delkin's Find' is similar in all respects, except that it

is smaller and bears more perfectly formed flowers. 'Dorothy Hannibal,' also pink-flowered, may bloom at any season.

CULTURE: Same as Crinum.

Clivia

DESCRIPTION: *C. miniata,* 1 to 2 ft., from Natal, is a tender, evergreen, bulbous plant with thick, fleshy roots. It is noted for clusters of yellow to scarlet, trumpet-shaped blossoms. Unlike hippeastrum (common amaryllis), clivias should never be dried off completely. Throughout the year they need to be watered enough to keep the large strap-shaped leaves in good condition. During semi-dormancy in late fall, the bulbs may be given less water,

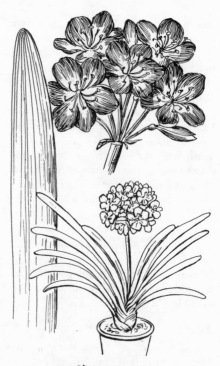

Clivia miniata

but never so little that the leaves wilt.

CULTURE: Light, semi-sunny to semi-shady. Temperature, cool to average house. Humidity, 30% or more. Soil, equal parts loam, sand, and peat moss. Propagate by division, but remember that better flowering will result if clivias are left undivided as long as possible. When a clump begins to increase in size, shift it to a larger pot without disturbing the roots. Divide only when the plant becomes so large that it can no longer be accommodated conveniently.

Crinum

DESCRIPTION: *C. kirkii,* 2 to 4 ft., from Zanzibar, has white blossoms with a red center stripe, in summer. *C. moorei,* 2 ft., from South Africa, has large pink to rosy-red flowers in late summer or fall. 'Ellen Bosanquet,' 2 to 4 ft., a well-known hybrid crinum has deep wine-red blossoms in September. *C. powellii alba,* 3 ft., is a choice variety with pure white flowers.

Crinums are evergreen plants arising from very large bulbs which need to be potted half in and half out of rich soil. Although inclined to grow too large for use in a window garden, crinums can be grown in tubs which are held in semi-dormancy in a cool place during the winter, then brought into full growth outdoors at the beginning of warm weather.

CULTURE: Light, sunny to semi-sunny. Temperature, average house, except that coolness (50-65°F.) is preferable in winter. Humidity, average house. Soil, equal parts loam, sand, and peat moss; water copiously and provide liquid plant food in the sum-

mer, but keep on the dry side and withhold fertilizer through fall and winter. Propagate by removing offsets at repotting time, which is necessary every three or four years.

Cyrtanthus

DESCRIPTION: *C. flanaganii,* 9 in., from South Africa, has fragrant, yellow flowers. *C. mackenii,* 12 in., from Natal, has fragrant, pure white flowers. *C. sanguineus,* 12 in., from South Africa, has orange-red flowers. The cyrtanthuses are relatively unknown. Their flowers are more tubular than lilylike, and the foliage is like that of a miniature hippeastrum (common amaryllis).

CULTURE: Same as Hippeastrum.

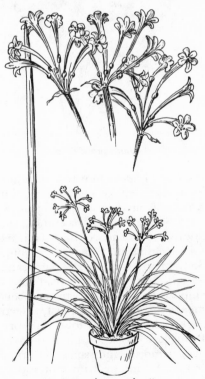

Cyrtanthus mackenii

Eucharis

DESCRIPTION: *E. grandiflora*, 1 to 2 ft., from the Andes of Colombia, is a bulbous plant of great beauty, bearing umbels of showy white, fragrant, narcissuslike flowers in late winter, spring, or early summer. With careful attention to watering, and to the diminishing of it after flowering, eucharis may be brought into bloom several times a year.

Eucharis grandiflora

CULTURE: Light, sunny to semi-sunny. Temperature, average house, but preferably on the cool side (55-65°F.) from September to December. Humidity, 30% or more. In dry air, red spider mites may be troublesome. Soil, 3 parts leaf mold, 3 parts sand, and 1 part each of peat moss, chipped charcoal, and steamed bone meal. Keep evenly moist, except slightly less from October to April. Propagate by seeds planted ½ in. deep in moist, sandy soil and warmth (80-85°F.) in late winter or spring; by offsets at transplanting time. Pot new bulbs, or transplant in late spring or early summer. Ten-inch pots or tubs will hold six bulbs. Remove some topsoil and replace with a fresh mixture every March. Division and complete repotting is necessary every third or fourth year.

Habranthus

DESCRIPTION: *H. brachyandrus*, 12 in., from Brazil, has lavender-pink blossoms with a crimson throat. *H. robustus*, 9 in., from Argentina, has larger, purplish pink flowers. *H. texanus*, 12 in., from Texas, which has only recently entered the market, has deep-yellow flowers stained reddish gold outside. By allowing habranthus bulbs to go completely dry occasionally, then soaking, they can be made to flower several times a year, hence the name "rain lily." CULTURE: Light, sunny. Temperature, cool to about 70°F. in winter. Humidity, average house. Soil, equal parts loam, peat moss, and sand; moisten thoroughly and not again until soil is quite dry. Propagate by offsets at any time.

Haemanthus

DESCRIPTION: *H. albiflos*, 1 ft., from South Africa, bears up to 100 or more white flowers in each closely packed umbel during June. Its stiff foliage is green. *H. coccineus*, 1 ft., from South Africa, dies down in autumn, then sends up umbels of dark-red flowers. *H. katherinae*, 1 to 2 ft., from Natal, bears spectacular salmon-red flowers clustered in umbels to 10 in. across in May or June. Its leaves are nearly evergreen. *H. multiflorus*, 1 ft., from South Africa has 6-in. heads of light- to dark-crimson flowers in late spring, fol-

Haemanthus multiflorus

Peru, is the plant from which most of today's popular forms of amaryllis originated. These are the easiest, the showiest, and probably the most favored of all pot-grown bulbs. Hybrids of Dutch, American, or South African strains are available. Good cultivars sell for around five dollars. Flowers of all tend toward lily shape, and are composed of three outer and three inner segments which are nearly equal in size and equidistant

Hippeastrum vittatum hybrid

lowed by attractive foliage that grows until water is withheld in September to rest the bulb. Highly recommended for indoor gardens. This and the other red-flowered species are called "blood-lilies."

CULTURE: Light, sunny to semi-sunny (except semi-shady during actual blooming period to prolong flowers). Temperature, average house. Humidity, 30% or more. Soil, equal parts loam, sand, and peat moss; when potting, allow only 1 in. between the haemanthus bulb and the pot wall. Do not repot every year. Instead, after the plant begins to grow strongly, give regular feedings. Keep soil evenly moist except nearly dry during rest period in fall and winter. Propagate by removing offsets whenever bulbs are being repotted.

Hippeastrum

DESCRIPTION: *H. vittatum*, 2 ft., from

from each other, though often not identically marked. They are borne atop stout scapes, usually in clusters of from two to five. In color the flowers may be pure white or of pink or red tones, including salmon, wine-red and violet-rose; they may have throats of lighter or deeper tones, or they may be banded, striped, or bordered in contrasting color. Many times a single bulb will send up as many as three scapes, resulting in a magnificent, long-lasting display.

When amaryllis bulbs are first received, usually late fall, winter, or early spring, remove any dead roots, but leave all the live ones. When selecting a container, allow 2 inches of space between its walls and the amaryllis bulb. Set the bulb so that about half of it extends above the soil. Water when first potted, and add little if any moisture until growth starts. During the growing period, late fall or winter until late summer for most amaryllis, keep plants in a warm, sunny place, and water copiously. Make biweekly applications of a liquid house plant fertilizer. About September, allow the bulbs to dry off gradually by withholding water from the soil, and store them in their containers in a cool place (50-60°F.). Watch for signs of a flower bud, and when one appears, renew the top inch of soil and top-dress with a fresh mixture before placing the amaryllis in good light and moisture. Complete repotting is necessary every three or four years.

Hybrid amaryllis may fail to bloom if growing conditions do not promote at least four to six healthy new leaves during the spring and summer.

CULTURE: Light, sunny to semi-sunny, except that plants in flower can be enjoyed anywhere in the house without permanent harm to the amaryllis. Temperature, average house, except that dry heat shortens flower life. Humidity, average house. Soil, equal parts loam, sand, and peat moss or leaf mold; see above for water requirements. Propagate by removing offsets at repotting time; by sowing fresh seeds in spring or summer. Seedlings reach maturity in two to three years.

Nerine

DESCRIPTION: *N. bowdenii*, 1½ ft., has pink flowers. *N. curvifolia*, 1 to 1½ ft., has brilliant scarlet flowers. Its variety *fothergillii* has 2½-in. crimson or salmon-red flowers. *N. sarniensis*, 2 ft., the "Guernsey lily," has salmon or orange-scarlet flowers. Nerines, all from South Africa, are some of the most beautiful of all flowering bulbs. Bloom from them is possible from late summer into winter. A prominent feature of the blossoms is the manner in which the stamens (usu-

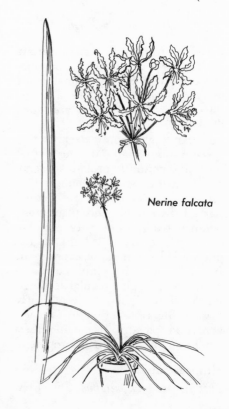

Nerine falcata

ally straight) protrude past the recurving petals.
CULTURE: Light, sunny. Temperature, coolness, not exceeding 65°F. in the winter. Humidity, 50% or more. Soil, equal parts loam, sand, peat moss, and leaf mold. Pot any time from August to November, allowing half of bulb to extend above the soil. Plant one to a 4- or 5-in. pot; three in a 6- or 7-in. container. Do not apply water until flower bud or foliage is visible; then keep soil evenly moist and make biweekly applications of house plant food, usually September to May; keep dry and do not fertilize from May to September. In August remove some of the old topsoil and replace with mixture of equal parts of loam, dehydrated manure, and sand. Propagate by removing offsets at repotting time, which is necessary every three or four years.

Sprekelia formosissima

Sprekelia

DESCRIPTION: *S. formosissima* (sometimes called *Amaryllis formosissima*), 2 ft., from Mexico and Guatemala, bears handsome crimson flowers that remotely resemble a cattleya, hence "orchid-lily." Other popular names are "Jacobean lily" and "St. James lily." Blooms may appear from March to June, usually preceding the attractive, small, linear leaves which grow 8 to 12 in. long.
CULTURE: Light, sunny. Temperature, average house February to September; 50-60°F. September to February. Humidity, 50% or more, especially after flower bud pushes out of bulb, and until it begins to open. Soil, equal parts loam, sand, and peat moss. Pot in late winter or spring, covering two thirds of the bulb. Keep soil evenly moist from the time growth appears (usually February) until September. Keep dry from September to February. Propagation, top-dressing and repotting as for Nerine.

Vallota

DESCRIPTION: *V. speciosa* or "Scarborough lily," 2 to 3 ft., from South Africa, has showy crimson flowers in late summer and autumn. There is also a white form. The flowers are borne in clusters of five to ten above straplike evergreen leaves, 1¼ in. wide and 1½ to 2 ft. long. The lower leaves have a purple cast which makes them especially attractive on a sun porch, or in a cool room with other plants in winter.
CULTURE: Light, sunny. Temperature, cool (40-65°F.) from September to March; 55-70°F. until warm weather. Humidity, 30% or more. Soil, equal

parts loam, sand, and peat moss. Keep barely moist September to March, apply plant food and more water March to June, and hold on the dry side June to September. Pot up new bulbs in fall or spring, almost covering them with soil. Propagate by removing offsets at repotting time. This is necessary every three or four years, and is best done in June or July. If vallota fails to do well, and other conditions seem in order, check to be sure soil acidity has a pH rating near 6.0.

DOGBANE FAMILY   Apocynaceae

Tender perennials with milky juice and smooth-edged leaves. Flowers are regular, either solitary or in clusters.

Allamanda

DESCRIPTION: *A. cathartica hendersoni,* 5 to 10 ft., from Brazil, has leathery, dark-green leaves set on stems which are pliable when young but brittle and shrublike at maturity. The trumpet-shaped flowers are golden yellow, and reach a diameter of 3 in. This is a showy tub plant, especially for porch, terrace, or patio in summer. Prune stems back in spring to keep plant at convenient size.

CULTURE: Light, sunny. Temperature, average house, preferably never less than 55°F. Humidity, 50% or more. Soil, equal parts loam, sand, or Perlite, and peat moss or leaf mold; keep evenly moist and provide biweekly feedings April to September. Withhold fertilizer and keep soil on dry side through fall and winter. Propagate by rooting cuttings of half-ripened stems in spring; keep in high humidity and warmth (75-80°F.) until roots form.

Carissa

DESCRIPTION: *C. grandiflora,* 5 to 7 ft., from South Africa, is the Natal plum. It is a fast-growing, sprawly, spiny shrub with glossy, dark-green leaves. White flowers, 2 in. across, are followed by delectable red fruits 1 to 2 in. long. *C. grandiflora* 'Boxwood Beauty' is more desirable than the species as a house plant. Its oval leaves, arranged in pairs along the stems, overlap like shingles. The large, five-pointed, fragrant white

Allamanda cathartica hendersoni

Carissa grandiflora 'Boxwood Beauty'

blossoms are borne singly or in clusters at the tips of branches. *C. grandiflora nana compacta,* sometimes called "bonsai carissa," is similar to 'Boxwood Beauty' and, like it, is an ideal plant for bonsai work (Chapter 9). CULTURE: Light, sunny to semi-sunny. Temperature, average house. Humidity, average house. Soil, equal parts loam, sand, and peat moss; keep evenly moist. Frequent overhead showering with plain water helps maintain the glossy appearance of the leaves. Propagate by cuttings of mature wood, or by sowing seeds, at any time.

Dipladenia

DESCRIPTION: *D. splendens,* climbing to 8 ft. or more, from Brazil, is one of the showiest of all vines for the sunny window garden. It has leathery leaves to 8 in. long, and clusters of rosy pink, 3-in., funnel-shaped flowers in summer and autumn. Often listed as Mandevilla.
CULTURE: Light, sunny to semi-sunny. Temperature, average house. Humidity, 50% or more. Soil, equal parts loam, peat moss, sand or Perlite, and

chipped charcoal. Keep evenly moist and apply biweekly feedings except in winter; then keep on the dry side and withhold fertilizer. Propagate by stem cuttings or seeds in spring. As a house plant, dipladenia may be planted in a 10- to 15-in. pot or tub, and trained to cover a wire frame 3 to 5 ft. high. Any pruning deemed necessary may be done at the beginning of the growing season in spring.

Dipladenia splendens

Ervatamia

DESCRIPTION: *E. coronaria,* 6 to 8 ft., from the Old World tropics, has many common names, including crepe jasmine, fleur d'amour, butterfly gardenia, East Indian rose-bay, Adam's-apple, and Nero's crown. In addition, it is sometimes classified as *Tabernaemontana coronaria.* By any name, ervatamia is a delightful evergreen shrub which may be cultivated in a 12- to 15-in. pot or tub, and kept pruned back as necessary in February or March. In the summer it bears clusters of 1½- to 2-in. waxy,

Ervatamia coronaria

white, funnel-shaped, fragrant flowers.

CULTURE: Same as for Allamanda, except keep soil evenly moist all year.

Nerium

DESCRIPTION: *N. oleander,* to 20 ft., from the Mediterranean, is the common oleander which has been a favorite house plant for many years. It has rosy red flowers at the tip of willowy branches which are set with leathery lance leaves. Variations of the type include *album* (single white flowers), *atropurpureum* (single carmine), *carneum flore pleno* or 'Mrs. Roeding' (double salmon-pink) and *variegatum* (single carmine-rose flowers with gray-green leaves edged creamy white). 'Compte Barthelemy' is cultivated for its double red flowers.

Oleanders are easily kept to an appropriate size for indoors by pruning, either after flowering or in autumn. English references advise the prompt removal of any young shoots which issue from the base of the flowers. The juice in the stems is poisonous, however, and clippings need to be discarded carefully, where children or pets cannot get to them. CULTURE: Light, sunny to semi-sunny. Temperature, cool in winter, average house at other times. Humidity, 30% or more. Soil, equal parts loam, sand, and peat moss; keep evenly moist, except on the dry side in late fall and early winter. Feed biweekly in spring and summer. Propagate by rooting cuttings of firm tip growth in spring or summer.

Plumeria

DESCRIPTION: *P. rubra,* 10 to 15 ft., from Mexico to Venezuela, is known as "frangipani" and "red jasmine." It has large leaves, to 16 in. long and 4 in. wide. The highly fragrant summer flowers vary in color from pink to rosy purple. They are about 2 in. long and flare at the top to an equal width. Plant in a 12- to 15-in.

Plumeria rubra

pot or tub and prune to convenient size each year immediately after the flowering season.

CULTURE: Light, sunny. Temperature, average house. Humidity, 50% or more. Soil, equal parts loam, sand, and peat moss. Keep evenly moist March to September; on the dry side, but never completely so, in fall and winter. Apply biweekly feedings in spring and summer. Propagate by cuttings in the spring.

Trachelospermum

DESCRIPTION: *T. jasminoides,* a twining Chinese vine. Leaves small, shiny, dark green. Wonderfully fragrant, star-shaped flowers, white or yellow most of the year excepting the dead of winter. Keep the growing tips pinched back and it will stay a fairly tidy small bush. Commonly called Confederate or star jasmine; a very popular plant outdoors in the South.

CULTURE: Light, sunny to semi-sunny. Temperature, preferably cool in winter, but not particular at other times. Temperatures below 50 degrees cause yellowing of the leaves. Humidity, 30% or more. Soil, equal parts loam, sand, and peat moss; keep evenly moist. Apply biweekly feedings except in winter. Propagate by cuttings, spring or summer.

Vinca

DESCRIPTION: *V. major,* trailing to 2 ft. or more, from Europe, is one of our country's most popular window-box and hanging-basket plants. It bears bright-blue, periwinkle flowers from May to October. *V. major variegata* has leaves attractively splashed and margined with creamy yellow.

CULTURE: Light, sunny to semi-sunny. Temperature, preferably cool in winter, but not particular at other times. Humidity, 30% or more. Soil, equal parts loam, sand, and peat moss; keep evenly moist. Whenever growing conditions are good, usually spring and summer, apply biweekly feedings. Propagate by cuttings or division in spring.

Vinca major variegata

ARUM or CALLA FAMILY   Araceae

Mostly tropical plants with bitter, sometimes poisonous juice, and smooth-edged leaves which are often lobed attractively. The tiny flowers are clustered on a fingerlike spadix which protrudes out of, or is shielded by, a leaf- or funnel-shaped spathe. While the true flowers are not showy, the spathe in many genera is large, colorful, and long-lasting.

Acorus

DESCRIPTION: *A. gramineus pusillus*, 2 to 3 in., from Japan, has tufts of iris-like leaves. *A. gramineus variegatus*, 6 to 9 in., also from Japan, is similar, but attractively marked with creamy white. Both may be called "miniature sweet flag." They are small, slow-growing, grassy perennials of greatest interest when used in terrariums and dish gardens.

CULTURE: Light, semi-shady. Temperature, cool. Humidity, high. Soil, 2 parts loam, 1 part leaf mold, and 1 part sand; keep wet at all times.

Acorus gramineus variegatus

Propagate by division of the clumps in spring or fall.

Aglaonema

DESCRIPTION: *A. commutatum*, 1 ft., from Ceylon and the Philippines, has silver markings on deep-green leaves. *A. modestum*, to 2 ft., from Kwangtung, is the popular "Chinese evergreen." It has durable, waxy green leaves, oblong, moderately narrow, tapering to a thin tip, and closely set along thin canes. *A pictum*, 1½ ft., from Malaya, has dark-green leaves mottled with metallic gray and white. *A. pseudo-bracteatum*, 1 to 2 ft., from Malaysia, has brightly variegated leaves splashed with creamy white to yellow. Its stems also are cream-colored. *A. roebelinii*, 2 ft. or more, from Borneo and Malaya, makes a wonderful house plant, very similar in appearance to a dieffenbachia (dumb-cane). This aglaonema is often called schismatoglottis. Its leaves are almost entirely silver except for the dark-green edges and midrib area. *A. simplex*, 1½ ft. or more, from Java, is similar to *A. modestum*, and may also be called "Chinese evergreen." *A. treubii*, 1½ ft., from the Celebes, has narrow, lance-shaped leaves of light-green with cream to chartreuse variegation.

CULTURE: Light, semi-shady to shady. Temperature, average house. Humidity, average house, but preferably 30% or more. Soil, equal parts loam, sand, and peat moss; keep moist at all times. *A. modestum* and *A. simplex* may be cultivated for long periods in water. Occasionally, sponge the leaves of aglaonemas with clear water to keep them glossy. Propagate by cutting the canelike stems into 2-in. lengths, and inserting them to half their length in damp sand, Perlite, soil, or water. It is best to do this in the spring or early summer.

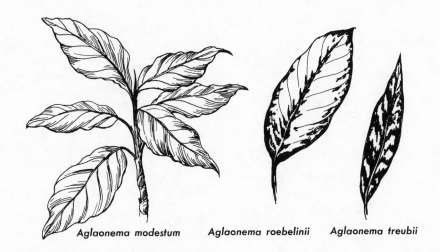

Aglaonema modestum   Aglaonema roebelinii   Aglaonema treubii

Alocasia

DESCRIPTION: *A. cuprea,* 1 ft., from Borneo, has heavy, wavy, prominently veined leaves, dark metallic green above, and maroon-purple

Alocasia cuprea

beneath. *A. watsoniana,* to 5 ft. or more, from Sumatra, is a magnificent plant with huge, corrugated, leathery, blue-green leaves veined and edged in silver-white, with purple on the reverses.

These and the many other Alocasias are truly exotic plants with heart-shaped leaves of large size, usually displaying striking vein patterns.

CULTURE: Light, semi-sunny to semi-shady. Temperature, warm. Humidity, 50% or more. Soil, 2 parts peat moss, 1 part chipped charcoal or Perlite; keep evenly moist. Feed regularly. Protect from drafts, or the leaf edges may turn brown. Propagate by removing offsets from mother plant when they are large enough to handle.

Amorphophallus

DESCRIPTION: *A. bulbifer,* 1 ft., from India, is grown primarily as a curiosity, and like the related Hydrosme, may be called "voodoo lily," "devil's-tongue," or "sacred lily of India." The "flower" rises on a leafless stalk, and has a green spathe with rose and yellow outside, yellow-green inside, surrounding a green and pink spadix. The spadix emits such an unpleasant odor that it is often removed. It should be cut out carefully with a sharp knife.

CULTURE: Same as Hydrosme.

Anthurium

DESCRIPTION: This genus may be divided roughly into two groups— those species grown primarily for their showy, flowerlike spathes, and those grown for foliage.

In the first group, *A. andreanum,* from Colombia, as well as its many varieties and hybrids, has patent-leather-like spathes in white, pink, coral, and red. These flowers appear to have been varnished or highly waxed, and last for several weeks. *A. scherzerianum,* from Costa Rica, is known as flamingo-flower and pigtail-plant. It has bright scarlet spathes, and spirally twisted spadixes. One variety of this species has a spathe of red dotted with white, and another has a double spathe of white dotted with red. One other form of note is 'Gold Charm' which has white spathes followed by golden fruits.

In the second group, the velvet-leaved foliage types include *A. clarinervum,* from Mexico, *A. crystallinum,* from Colombia and Peru, *A.*

warocqueanum, from Colombia. *A. pictamayo,* called "begonia-leaf," and *A. pentaphyllum,* palmately lobed with fingerlike segments, are examples of the anthuriums grown for oddly cut foliage. Others are cultivated for highly attractive leaves which are neither velvety nor cut. These include *A. caribaeum,* waxy bluish green, from the West Indies; *A. recusatum,* dark green, wavy-edged with prominent pale veins, from eastern Cuba; and *A. veitchii,* quilted, rich metallic green, from Colombia.

Anthuriums differ widely in their habits, and may be vining, self-heading, treelike or shrubby. They may cling to trees, grow on rocks, or be content to have their roots in a pot of soil.

CULTURE: Light, semi-shady. Temperature, warm. Humidity, 50% or more. Soil, a very loose medium such as osmunda, leaf mold, or unmilled sphagnum moss; keep evenly moist. Feed biweekly to monthly with liquid fertilizer to assure maximum growth and good health. If plant develops aerial roots,

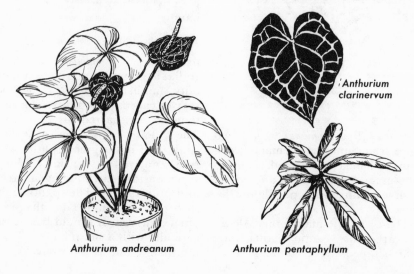

Anthurium andreanum   Anthurium pentaphyllum

Anthurium clarinervum

these may be covered with sphagnum moss as for Philodendron. Propagate the vining types by cuttings. Self-headers will throw out offsets which may be severed from the parent plant when they are large enough to handle.

Caladium

DESCRIPTION: There are almost countless named varieties of hybrid caladiums. Most of the outstanding kinds on the market today originated with a Florida hybridizer, Frank M. Joyner. Apart from the jewel-colored hybrids, one species is sometimes cultivated. It is the miniature *C. humboldtii*, from Pará in Brazil. All caladiums are prized for their showy foliage during the warm months of the year.

CULTURE: Light, semi-sunny to semi-shady. Temperature, warm. Humidity, 30% or more. Soil, equal parts loam, peat moss, and sand; keep evenly moist through the growing season, spring to fall, but nearly dry during the balance of the year. Pot caladium tubers from February to April, and provide moisture and warmth (70-80°F.) to promote growth. Fertilize biweekly until the first cool days of September, then withhold food and allow tubers to ripen. Withhold water gradually beginning in October until foliage dies down. Store caladiums where the temperature will not fall below 55°F. Propagate by dividing clumps of tubers at potting time in the spring.

Colocasia

DESCRIPTION: *C. esculenta,* from Hawaii and Fiji, produces large, heart-shaped leaves which are predominantly green. They may reach 3 feet or more in length, hence the popular name, "elephant's-ears." Ideal indoors or outdoors, where there is ample space for the enormous leaves to unfurl.

CULTURE: As for Caladium.

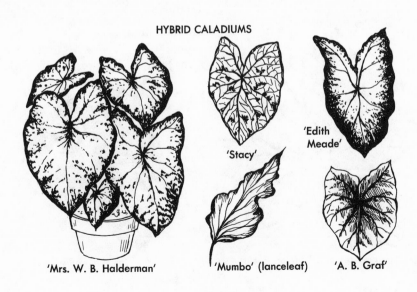

HYBRID CALADIUMS

'Stacy'

'Edith Meade'

'Mrs. W. B. Halderman'

'Mumbo' (lanceleaf)

'A. B. Graf'

Dieffenbachia

DESCRIPTION: Names of the species, mutants, and hybrids of Dieffenbachia have given us a long list of handsome foliage plants. Eighteen or more are easily available, and more appear each year. The best known is *D. picta,* 4 ft., from South America, the leaves white-spotted on a green background. Its variety 'Rudolph Roehrs' has creamy white or pale-chartreuse leaves with dark-green midrib and border.

Dieffenbachias, known as dumb-canes because the acrid juice will cause partial paralysis of the tongue if placed in contact with it, are shrubby, thick-stemmed plants with long, pointed, oblong leaves ascending spirally around the canes. Too much sun will burn the leaves, but too much shade will cause them to be poorly colored. Too much water may drown the fleshy roots, or cause rank, weak growth. Well-grown plants have stout stems, completely hidden by the bases of the leaf petioles where they clasp, but exposed below, where older leaves have fallen.

The only frequent complaint about dieffenbachias is that they have bare stems with only a small tuft of leaves at the top. After a certain age, this is more or less normal, and the resulting treelike form is not unattractive. However, to shorten a plant, or simply to eliminate the bare stem, air-layer it (Chapter 3). Or, sever the top portion just below the leaves and root it in water, provided that the foliage can be syringed frequently until new roots form.

CULTURE: Light, semi-sunny to shady. Temperature, average house. Humidity, 30% or more to promote luxurious growth. Soil, equal parts loam, sand, and peat moss; moisten this thoroughly, then not again until it is approaching dryness. Propagate by stem cuttings, usually about 4 in. long, inserted vertically to half their length in moist peat moss and sand, or in damp, loose potting soil. If possible, do this in spring or early summer.

Homalomena

DESCRIPTION: *H. humilis,* under 1 ft., from Java, makes a rosette of slender,

Dieffenbachia picta 'Rudolph Roehrs'

Homalomena wallisii

pointed, dark-green leaves. *H. wallisii,* under 1 ft., from Colombia, is a showy, low plant with reflexed, oval leaves. Their dark olive-green coloring makes a perfect foil for the generous blotches of creamy silver. CULTURE: Light, semi- sunny to semi-shady. Temperature, average house. Humidity, 30% or more. Soil, equal parts loam, sand, and peat moss; keep evenly moist. Propagate by stem cuttings of old plants whenever warmth (70-80°F.) and high humidity can be provided.

Hydrosme

DESCRIPTION: *H. rivieri,* 3 ft. or more, from Indochina, has been promoted in commerce by such names as "voodoo lily," "sacred lily of India," and "devil's-tongue." It has sometimes been called amorphophallus. During warm weather, hydrosme

Hydrosme rivieri

does well outdoors in a shady, protected place. There it forms a leafy umbrella 3 to 4 ft. tall, and as wide, atop a single stem. In autumn, this leaf growth is ripened and dried off as for Caladium, and the tuber is stored dry at not less than 50°F. Large tubers planted in February, kept warm and moist in a well-lighted location, will bloom within six weeks. The bizarre, calla-like spathe is an intense maroon color. A 9- to 10-inch spadix of white and dark purple arises out of the center of the spathe, and it yields an evil odor. This "flower" perches atop a marbled green stem which may reach a height of 3 ft. or more.

CULTURE: Light, sunny to semi-sunny in winter; partial shade outdoors in summer. Temperature, average house. Humidity, average house. Soil, equal parts loam, sand, and peat moss; keep this moist from February until autumn, and provide biweekly feedings. Keep soil dry and withhold fertilizer in late fall and winter. Propagate by removing the offsets which grow from the parent tuber. When a new plant is 5 or 6 in. tall, remove from the parent tuber with a sharp knife. Cover the cut with horticultural dusting sulfur, or other fungicide, to prevent rot. Plant in a 3-in. pot of soil.

Monstera

DESCRIPTION: *M. acuminata,* from Guatemala, is called the "shingle plant" because its stiff oval leaves, when young, overlap each other. Thus, in nature they may "shingle" the bark of a tree, and in cultivation a moss-covered totem pole. When mature, the leaves have characteristic perforations. *M. deliciosa,* from southern Mexico and Guatemala, is errone-

Monstera deliciosa

ously known in its juvenile stage as *Philodendron pertusum*. It is a vining plant with large leathery leaves variously cut and perforated. Thick aerial roots give the plant a means by which to climb. Sometimes these reach down to the soil, or a moss-covered totem pole may be provided. CULTURE: Light, semi-sunny to shady. Temperature, average house. Humidity, average house, but preferably 30% or more. Soil, equal parts loam, sand, and peat moss; keep this evenly moist and provide biweekly feedings. Syringe the foliage frequently; as often as possible, sponge it clean. Propagate by cuttings of the stems, inserting a node with leaf attached into the rooting medium. Provide warmth (70-80°F.) and high humidity until new growth is well along.

Nephthytis

DESCRIPTION: *N. afzelii,* from Liberia and Sierra Leone in Africa, has large, papery, green leaves. The "nephthytis" of florists is *Syngonium podophyllum,* which see.

CULTURE: Light, semi-shady. Temperature, average house. Humidity 30% or more. Soil, equal parts loam sand, and peat moss; keep evenly moist. Propagate by stem cuttings or division of the rhizomes.

Philodendron

DESCRIPTION: Nature must have designed the philodendrons with contemporary interior decoration in mind —their lines are so right for today's architecture. And yet, no plants could possibly have more practical reasons for being the way they are. They are adapted to growing in the jungles of Central and South America, where shade is more plentiful than bright sunshine, and protracted moist periods can be followed by sudden droughts. And the giant types, which often grow on trees, are equipped with holes all over their leaves so tropical hurricanes cannot whip them to shreds.

All of this means that the philodendrons are also adapted to growing in our homes; that they will accept the light in hot sun or dim corner; and that we can forget to water them from time to time and get away with it. They will endure dry air or humid, high temperatures or low—even chilly air conditioning— with agreeable aplomb. Some will live, often grow a little, with their stems in a glass of water.

But who needs to extoll the virtues of *Philodendron oxycardium,* better known as *P. cordatum?* This is one of the sturdiest plants in captivity and, consequently, the most popular and widely grown. What is needed, instead, is to introduce interior decoraors—amateur and professional—to more of the incredibly varied but equally rugged species and varieties that number well into the hundreds, with more new types being introduced every year.

There are two ways to classify philodendrons. There are long-stemmed types that climb and cover jungle trees or indoor totem poles, or hang from baskets or wall brackets; and there are the non-climbing, "self-heading" plants with all the leaves emerging from one crown near the soil. These become wider as they grow, instead of higher. For both types, there are species and varieties with solid leaves of varying shapes and colors, and others with leaves cut into holes in the center or along the edge. So you can select philodendrons according to whether you want them to grow up, down, or out—and whether you want foliage that is heavy and solid, or light and airy.

Here are a few of the many exotic philodendrons from which you may choose:

SOLID-LEAVED CLIMBERS: *P. hastatum,* medium-sized arrow-shaped leaves, strikingly streaked with cream in the variegated variety; *P. sodiroi,* deep-green leaves of perfect heart shape, mottled with lustrous silver; *P. verrucosum,* shimmering, velvety bronze-green heart-shaped leaves with lighter veins, pure emerald on the edge and purplish underneath. The ubiquitous *P. oxycardium* also belongs here, but there are two more appealing species of similar size and habit—silky-iridescent *P. micans,* and the more delicate, humidity-loving *P. andreanum,* called "black gold" for its near-ebony leaves and yellow veins.

CUT-LEAVED CLIMBERS: *P. radiatum* (or *P. dubium*), heavy leaves cut many times, nearly to the midvein; *P. panduraeforme,* olive-green leaves of irregular shape, but similar enough for the plant to be called "fiddleleaf" philodendron; *P. squamiferum,* deeply lobed leaves looking like two pairs of wings. The plant called *P. pertusum* is described under *Monstera deliciosa.*

CLIMBING PHILODENDRONS   **SELF-HEADING PHILODENDRONS**

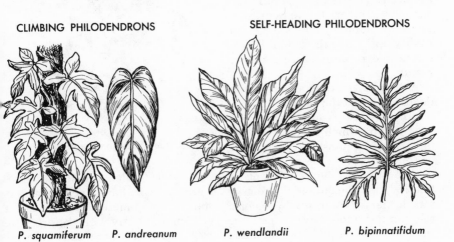

P. squamiferum   *P. andreanum*   *P. wendlandii*   *P. bipinnatifidum*

SOLID-LEAVED SELF-HEADING PHIL-
ODENDRONS: *P. cannifolium,* sword-
shaped leaves on swollen stems; *P.
wendlandii,* nestlike rosette of long
oval leaves with thick midrib; *P.
undulatum,* smaller type with arrowhead leaves wavy on the edge; and
the hybrid 'Burgundy' with red
stems and leaves maroon to dark
reddish green.

CUT-LEAVED SELF-HEADING TYPES:
P. selloum, leaves deeply lobed when
young, feather-cut when mature;
and *P. bipinnatifidum,* large leaves cut
into a dozen segments on each side,
each segment cut again.
CULTURE: Light, semi-sunny to shady.
Temperature, average house. Humidity, average house suits most, but
30% or more will encourage more
luxurious growth. Syringe the leaves
as often as possible to keep them
fresh and clean. Soil, equal parts
loam, sand, and peat moss; keep this
evenly moist. Fertilize at biweekly to
monthly intervals, and repot only
when roots have completely filled
the pot and begun to emerge through
the drainage hole in bottom. Propagate the climbers by stem cuttings;
the self-headers by offsets. High humidity and warmth (70-80°F.) will
encourage prompt rooting of new
plants.
A frequent problem with philodendrons is that the cut-leaf climbers
retain solid leaves unless they have
a support on which to climb. Pressed
fir bark, sphagnum-filled totem poles,
or rough-barked slabs of tree trunk
are suitable for the aerial roots to
find lodging. Encourage the roots to
attach themselves firmly by keeping
the support moist, even upending
the pot and soaking both totem and
plant in water for five to ten minutes.

Pothos

DESCRIPTION: True species of pothos
are seldom available in commerce.
Plants sold as such are actually
Scindapsus.

Scindapsus

DESCRIPTION: *S. aureus* and its varieties are the plants called "pothos"
by florists, which are known also as
"devil's-ivy." *S. aureus* has waxy,
dark-green leaves splashed with yellow. In juvenile form, the leaves are
broad pointed ovals, normally less
than 6 in. long. At maturity, plants
in satisfactory growing conditions
have leaves 2 ft. long, cut and perforated like those of Monstera. 'Marble Queen' is the most popular variety; its foliage may be more white
than green. 'Orange Moon,' 'Silver
Moon,' and 'Yellow Moon' are newer
varieties with coloration varying
from apricot through creamy yellow

Scindapsus aureus 'Marble Queen'

to pewter. 'Wilcoxi' is similar to *S.
aureus,* except that its yellow streaks
start and stop more abruptly instead
of blending softly with the green. *S.
pictus* has larger, more leathery leaves
than the other Scindapsus in culti-

vation. The dark-green leaves display large areas of silver variegation. *S. pictus argyraeus* is similar, but has smaller, more delicate leaves of iridescent blue-green, spotted with silver. CULTURE: Almost the same as for Philodendron, except that scindapsus plants need to become nearly dry between waterings. In addition, they show a marked preference for tropical warmth. Abundant light tends to increase foliage variegation.

Spathiphyllum

DESCRIPTION: *S. cannaefolium,* 1½ to 2 ft., from British Guiana and Venezuela, is a choice plant of pale-green foliage and large, fragrant, white flowers. *S. clevelandii,* 1½ to 2 ft., is the most popular variety of spathiphyllum. It has narrow leaves and glistening-white blossoms; a very free-branching and floriferous plant. *S. wallisii,* from Colombia and Venezuela, is similar but smaller. *S. floribundum,* 1 ft., from Colombia, has velvety green leaves and white spathes which are smaller than in the others described.

Spathiphyllums are outstanding plants for container culture, yet they have never achieved much popularity. They are short-stemmed or stemless plants with calla-like spathes or "flowers." CULTURE: Light, semi-sunny to semi-shady. Temperature, average house. Humidity, 30% or more. Soil, equal parts loam, sand, peat moss, and leaf mold; keep moist at all times. Propagate by division of the thickened rootstocks, preferably in the spring or early summer, but at any time when high humidity and warmth (70-80° F.) can be provided for the young plants.

Syngonium

DESCRIPTION: *S. podophyllum* and its many varieties, including 'Dot Mae,' 'Ruth Fraser,' 'Emerald Gem,' 'Imperial White,' and 'Trileaf Wonder,' are among the most useful of all foliage plants for indoors. They are sold by most growers as nephthytis, to which they are closely related. Most syngoniums have arrowhead

Spathiphyllum clevelandii

Syngonium 'Trileaf Wonder'

or shield-shaped leaves, many are colorfully variegated with chartreuse, yellow, white, or silver, and all have long leaf stalks (petioles). At maturity syngoniums bear leaves which are cut into fingerlike lobes. CULTURE: Light, semi-sunny to shady. Temperature, average house. Humidity, average house. Soil, equal parts loam, sand, and peat moss; keep moist. Propagate by cuttings at any time.

Zantedeschia elliottiana

Zantedeschia

DESCRIPTION: Z. aethiopica, 2 to 4 ft., from South Africa, is the florists' white calla lily. Its best flowering season is in the winter and spring. Abundant sunlight, water, fertilizer, and warmth (65-70°F.) encourage luxurious leaf growth and large flowers. Z. elliottiana, 2 to 3 ft., from South Africa, is a lovely calla with deep yellow spathes (commonly called "flowers"), and attractive foliage spotted with translucent silver. It blooms in summer. Z. rehmannii, 2 ft., from Natal, has rosy pink spathes in summer, and long, slender, lance-shaped leaves.

The rhizomes of Z. aethiopica are planted in late summer or early autumn; those of the summer-flowering species are potted in late winter or spring.

CULTURE: Light, sunny. Temperature, average house. Humidity, 30% or more. Soil, equal parts loam, sand, and peat; keep barely moist until growth is evident, then water freely. When potting, cover the rhizomes with about 2 in. of soil; a 12-in. pot is sufficient for three to six callas. Propagate by removing offsets at potting time, or by sowing seeds in warmth (70-80°F.) and moisture. Seeds of the Apricot Sunrise Hybrids yield spathes in shades of apricot, pink, red, yellow, gold, and cream.

GINSENG FAMILY   Araliaceae

Members of this family that are cultivated indoors for their foliage represent tropical as well as temperate parts of the world. Leaves may be simple or compound, and the insignificant flowers are greenish white, in clusters, racemes, or panicles.

Dizygotheca

DESCRIPTION: D. elegantissima, from the New Hebrides, has palmately compound, leathery leaves of dark greenish brown with lighter veins, the leaf stalks mottled with white. It is known as "false aralia." D. veitchii,

Dizygotheca elegantissima

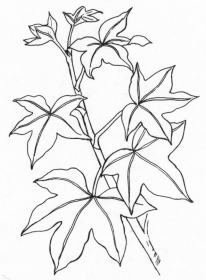

Fatshedera lizei

from New Caledonia, has leaves of similar shape, coppery green above, reddish beneath, and with light-red veins. Both of these plants are slender, graceful shrubs which tend to grow with a single, bark-covered trunk.

CULTURE: Light, semi-sunny to semi-shady. Temperature, average house. Humidity, 30% or more; frequent showerings encourage more luxuriant growth. Soil, equal parts loam, sand, peat moss, and leaf mold; keep evenly moist. Propagate by cuttings in warmth (70-80°F.) and high humidity; or by root cuttings in the spring.

Fatshedera

DESCRIPTION: *F. lizei* is a bigeneric hybrid between *Fatsia japonica* and *Hedera helix* (English ivy), both of the same family. Crosses of this type, however, are not common. The original fatshedera is an erect, weak-

stemmed shrub, with glossy dark-green leaves very much like those of its ivy parent. It is often called "tree ivy." A horticultural form, *F. lizei variegata,* has creamy white markings along the leaf edges. It is an attractive plant, but may be a little more difficult to grow than the all-green kind.

CULTURE: Light, sunny to semi-shady. Temperature, on the cool side, preferably not over 70°F. in winter. Humidity, 30% or more. Soil, equal parts loam, sand, and peat moss; keep this evenly moist. Propagate by cuttings at any time.

Fatsia

DESCRIPTION: Fatsias, to 15 ft., from Japan, are evergreen shrubs with lobed leaves much like those of a castor-bean plant. The foliage of *F. japonica* is a glossy dark green, while that of *F. japonica variegata* displays

Fatsia japonica

an irregular edging of cream-white. Either may be called "rice-paper plant," a name more properly applied to Tetrapanax, which see.

Fatsias are best used as specimen plants indoors to provide an exotic, tropical accent that is highly decorative. Pot them in fairly large containers, and shift, as they require it, to larger pots until the ultimate size you can handle is reached. Do not keep them too warm, or where the air is stagnant, as either of these conditions may lead to an infestation of red spider mites.

CULTURE: Light, semi-sunny. Temperature, on the cool side, preferably not above 70°F. in winter. Humidity, 30% or more. Soil, equal parts loam, sand, peat moss, and leaf mold; keep evenly moist. If your plant is large enough, propagate by cuttings from the branches in spring.

Hedera

DESCRIPTION: *H. canariensis,* trailer, from the Azores, Canaries, and Morocco, is called Algerian ivy. Its large, leathery leaves to 8 in. across may be plain, glossy green, or colorfully variegated. *H. helix,* trailer, from Asia, Europe, and North Africa, is available in approximately seventy varieties. These include kinds with large leaves, small leaves, some five-lobed, others three-lobed, several with ruffled or marginally curled edges, and numerous kinds with white or yellow variegation. They comprise one of the largest groups of foliage plants from which the indoor gardener may choose. *H. helix* is commonly called "English ivy."

CULTURE: Light, sunny to shady. Temperature, on the cool side, preferably not over 70° in winter. Humidity, average house will do if other conditions are good, but 30% or more is desirable. Provide frequent over-

VARIETIES OF HEDERA (English Ivy)

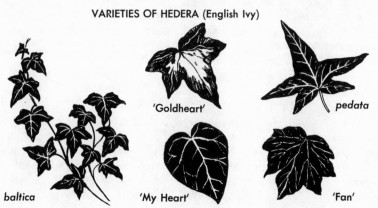

baltica   'Goldheart'   pedata   'My Heart'   'Fan'

ead showering. Soil, equal parts
oam, sand, and peat moss. Propagate by cuttings at any time.

Oreopanax

DESCRIPTION: This genus is composed
of several woody plants of dissimilar
leaf form. *O. nymphaeifolius,* from
Central America, Mexico, and the
West Indies, has broad, entire leaves.
O. salvinii, from Oaxaca, has deeply
lobed leaves. *O. xalapensis,* from Central America and Mexico, has fully
palmate leaves.
CULTURE: Same as Dizygotheca.

Polyscias

DESCRIPTION: *P. balfouriana,* from New
Caledonia, has a variety, *marginata,*
with creamy white edges on its round,
dark-green, leathery leaves. *P. filici-
olia,* from the South Sea Islands,

Polyscias fruticosa elegans

has ferny leaves of bright green on a
small, shrublike plant. *P. fruticosa
elegans,* from Polynesia, has parsley-
like leaves on a shrubby plant usually
under 4 ft. high in cultivation.
CULTURE: Same as for Hedera, except
that average house warmth is needed
in winter, and at least 50% humidity
is required.

Schefflera

DESCRIPTION: This genus of small
trees or shrubs offers three species of
value to the indoor gardener. *S.
actinophylla,* from Australia and Java,
is a rapid-growing plant with large,
palmately compound leaves; often
called "umbrella tree." *S. digitata,*
from New Zealand, has yellowish
veins and hairy margins in the palmately compound leaves, which
have seven to ten leaflets. *S. venulosa,*
from India, commonly mislabeled as
S. digitata, has only five or six leaflets
at maturity.

The compound leaves of all these
plants are umbrella-like. The main
stems develop a bark with age, and
the plants tend to grow as a single
trunk. Branching is sometimes induced by cutting back to the height
at which more bushy growth is
desired.
CULTURE: Light, sunny to shady.
Temperature, average house. Humidity, average house. Soil, equal parts
loam, sand, and peat moss; water
thoroughly, then not again until the
surface is dry. Propagate by cuttings
of half-ripened stems.

Schefflera actinophylla

Tetrapanax

DESCRIPTION: *T. papyriferum,* from Formosa, is the popular rice-paper plant. Its great, umbrella-like, lobe leaves are like felt when they ar young. For culture and suggeste uses, see Fatsia.

MILKWEED FAMILY   Asclepiadace

Mostly tropical herbs, shrubs, vines, and cactuslike succulents with regul flowers and milky juice.

Ceropegia

DESCRIPTION: *C. barkleyi,* from Cape Province, is very similar to *C. woodii* (see below), except that its leaves are more pointed. *C. caffrorum,* from eastern South Africa, has plain green, arrowhead leaves set on long wiry stems. *C. debilis,* from Nyasaland, has plain green, very slender leaves, scarcely ⅛ in. wide. *C. sandersonii,* from Natal, has succulent stems, set at distant intervals with plain green leaves. *C. stapeliaeformis,* from Cape Province, has stout succulent stems, ½ to 1 in. in diameter, with stapelialike flowers about 3 in. long in sum-

mertime. *C. woodii,* from Natal, ha small, silver-mottled, heart-shape leaves on long wiry stems, henc "string of hearts." Small bulbs de velop along these, giving rise t "rosary vine." The purplish flower are about 1½ in. long, and bottlelik —round at the bottom, slender i the middle, and capped by sever hairy spokes, hence "umbrella vine.

The ceropegias compose a strang genus. Only *C. barkleyi* and *C. wood* are truly attractive. The others ar interesting because they are bizarr or grotesque.

CULTURE: Light, sunny to semi-shad Temperature, average house. Humid ity, average house. Soil, equal par loam, sand, and peat moss; wate thoroughly, then not again unt surface is dry. Propagate by cutting or plant the bulblets which forr along the stems.

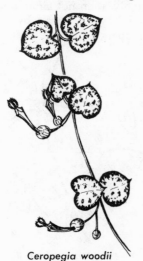

Ceropegia woodii

Hoya

DESCRIPTION: *H. bella,* from India, i a dwarf, nearly upright plant wit pink- or purple-centered flowers. *H carnosa,* the popular wax plant, fron Queensland and southern China has very fragrant, pinkish whit flowers, each set in the center with

Hoya carnosa

ters rapidly, and odd, five-petaled blossoms having an appearance which gives rise to the popular name "starfish flower." In most species, the flowers have an unpleasant odor. *S. gigantea,* from Zululand to Rhodesia,

Stapelia variegata

ed, star-shaped crown. *H. carnosa variegata* has leaves broadly bordered ι white, and pink-tinged. 'Silver ,eaf' has silver and pink markings n long green leaves; maroon flowers.

Although hoyas are well known as ouse plants, the major points in heir care seem to be little under-tood. As a consequence, too few mateur growers have the satisfac-ion of seeing the plants bloom. The nost important rule is this: Do not emove the stem or "spur" from vhich flowers have been borne; next eason's flowers will come from the ame place.

ULTURE: Light, sunny or semi-sunny. Temperature, average house. Humid-ty, average house. Soil, equal parts oam, sand, peat moss, and leaf nold; water heavily, then not again ιntil top inch or more has dried out. This partial drying-out is necessary or the development of healthy roots n these plants. Propagate by cut-ings of the top growth in spring, nd by layering at any time.

tapelia

ESCRIPTION: A well-known genus of ucculent plants having short, erect, ιur-angled stems which form clus-

has blooms to 18 in. across, pale yel-low with irregular crimson lines crossbanding the petals. *S. hirsuta,* from Cape Province, has hairy, brownish purple flowers marked transversely with creamy yellow or purple. *S. variegata,* from South Africa, grows 4 to 6 in. tall, and bears char-treuse and maroon-brown flowers about 3 in. across. These are not as evil-smelling as those of the larger-flowered species.

CULTURE: Light, sunny to semi-sunny. Temperature, average house. Humid-ity, average house. Soil, equal parts loam, sand, and leaf mold; keep evenly moist in summer. In winter, apply only enough water to keep the stems plump. Propagate by division of the clumps, or by cuttings in late spring or summer.

Stephanotis

DESCRIPTION: *S. floribunda*, the Madagascar jasmine, is better known as
the "bride's flower." It is a wiry
twiner with opposite, oblong, leathery
leaves of glossy deep green. The
clusters of tubular flowers, most
abundant in June, are waxy white
and deliciously fragrant.
CULTURE: Light, sunny to semi-sunny.
Temperature, average house. Humid-
tiy, 30% or more. Soil, equal parts
loam, sand, peat moss, and leaf
mold; keep evenly moist at all times.
Feed biweekly in spring, summer,
and fall; withhold food, reduce
amount of watering slightly, and
lower temperature in winter. Propa-

Stephanotis floribunda

gate by cuttings of half-matured
stems in spring; keep warm and in
high humidity until roots form.

BALSAM FAMILY   Balsaminacea

Watery-stemmed, warm-climate herbs with simple leaves and showy, spurre
flowers. Only one genus is of interest to the indoor gardener.

Impatiens

DESCRIPTION: *I. holstii*, to 3 ft., from
tropical East Africa, has small, reddish leaves and burgundy-colored
stems veined with red. Countless
hybrids exist, many nearly indistin-
guishable from those of *I. sultanii*.
The basic flower color is fiery scarlet,
but varieties exist in salmon, rose,
and white. *I. platypetala aurantiaca*,
from the Celebes, has green leaves
and 2-in. flowers of subdued salmon-
orange. Each has a scarlet eye, the
center of which is set with an emerald-green ovary. *I. sultanii*, to 1 ft.,
from Zanzibar, and its varieties usually have fresh green foliage set with
an endless array of carmine, pink,
salmon, scarlet, or white flowers. Any

of these may be called "patient Lucy."
Outdoors in the summer, in a spo
where there is partial to full shade
plants of impatiens are without pee
for giving season-long color. Man
strains are cultivated from seed
sown in midwinter, and thus brough
to blooming size by warm weather
It is not unusual for some seedling
to bloom more profusely than others
and these can be carried over by
rooting cuttings in late summer o
early fall. The only real problem wit
impatiens is that red spider mite
cannot resist them. The best contro
is high humidity and evenly mois
soil at all times. I once revived a
young plant of impatiens 'Orange

Impatiens sultanii

Baby' which carried a near-fatal mite infestation by placing it alone

in a covered terrarium. Within a few days new growth was evident, and in a matter of weeks there were numerous blooms. I left the plant in its private greenhouse until warm weather permitted placing it in the open garden.

CULTURE: Light, sunny to semi-shady. Temperature, average house, but preferably not over 72°F. in winter. Humidity, 50% or more. Soil, equal parts loam, sand, and peat moss; keep evenly moist. Propagate by cuttings inserted in moist sand, Perlite, or in a glass of plain water, at any time.

BEGONIA FAMILY

Begoniaceae

Mostly succulent herbs from tropical parts of the world; each flower is of one sex only. Typically the leaves are lopsided, and male flowers have two petals, the females two to five, with a three-angled ovary (seed capsule).

Begonia

DESCRIPTION: The various kinds of begonias are as different as any members of the same genus could be. There are miniature, terrarium-size begonias, and giants which can top 5 ft.; begonias with innumerable small round leaves, and those with star-shaped or lobed leaves a foot across; varieties which grow like dwarf bushes completely covered with clusters of colorful blooms, those which dangle heavy bouquets from the tips of their stems, kinds which end up tall stems with airy showers of flowers on top, and types which hide their flowers under some of the most brilliant foliage in the whole world of plants.

Because of the many variations, begonias do not fall neatly into clear-cut classifications. Generally they are grouped according to types of roots —fibrous, rhizomatous, and tuberous—and each type is then subdivided into several smaller groups.

WAX BEGONIAS: Among the fibrous-rooted begonias, the best known are the *semperflorens* (everblooming) or wax begonias, with many compact branches covered with nearly round, waxy green or reddish leaves and flowers all over, at intervals throughout the year. The old-fashioned single-flowering varieties are still popular for window boxes and semi-sunny garden borders. Today's indoor favorites are the semi-double (thimble or crested) and double (rosebud or camellia) hybrids with foliage rich green, bronzy, or mahogany-red. Because these begonias are succu-

SEMPERFLORENS OR EVERBLOOMING BEGONIAS

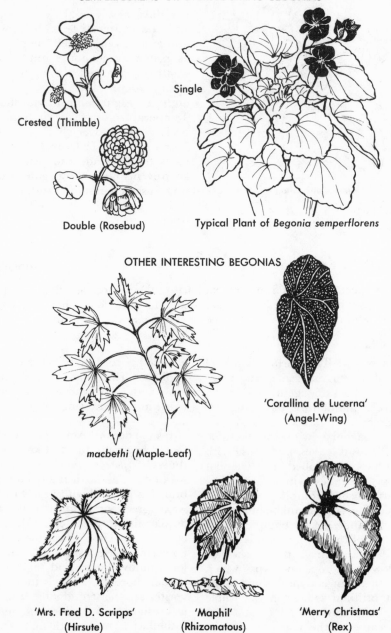

Crested (Thimble)

Single

Double (Rosebud)

Typical Plant of *Begonia semperflorens*

OTHER INTERESTING BEGONIAS

macbethi (Maple-Leaf)

'Corallina de Lucerna'
(Angel-Wing)

'Mrs. Fred D. Scripps'
(Hirsute)

'Maphil'
(Rhizomatous)

'Merry Christmas'
(Rex)

lent, their soil needs to become nearly dry before it is moistened. For fullest flowering, provide several hours of sun daily in winter, and all but the hottest in summer.

CANE-STEMS, also fibrous-rooted, are popularly called *angel-wing begonias* because the lopsided leaves are shaped like, and hang like, wings. They have sturdy stems with swollen, widely spaced joints. While quite small they may begin to drip heavy clusters of large flowers. These, too, resent constant moisture in the soil and will quickly drop their lower leaves. Pinching out the growing tips occasionally will keep them more compact and attractive.

HAIRY-LEAVED BEGONIAS, which are mostly fibrous-rooted, wear a coat of bristly or velvety hair on their leaves and outside the flower petals.

To complete the fibrous-rooted types, there are those which trail beautifully from hanging baskets (Chapter 8) and a great number of unclassifiable odd and rare types.

RHIZOMATOUS BEGONIAS have a rhizome that is thick, scarred, a ground-level stem which creeps over the soil (not through it) and sends down shallow roots. From the top of the rhizome, leaf- and flower-stems grow up out of the "eyes." The blooms generally appear high above the foliage in late winter and spring.

REX BEGONIAS are also mostly rhizomatous, but they are known and grown as a separate class because their main attraction is foliage of gorgeous colors and patterns. As a rule, they require more warmth and humidity than most other begonias, but much less sunlight—often none at all, but only bright daylight.

TUBEROUS BEGONIAS—the best known ones, at any rate—are the summer-flowering aristocrats for semi-sunny garden beds. For indoor growing, there are also the semituberous "maple-leaf" species and their hybrids; and the winter-flowering tuberous types called "Christmas begonias," usually sold as florists' gift plants. These require cooler temperatures (60-65°F.).

The new Rieger hybrids are related to the tuberous species *B. socotrana,* but culture indoors is more like *B. semperflorens.* They grow best in a soilless medium; keep evenly moist. Feed lightly, regularly.

CULTURE: Light, sunny to semi-shady. Temperature, average house. Humidity, average house satisfies most common begonias, excepting the rexes and tuberous types which need 50% or more; all grow more luxuriantly in a relative humidity of 30% or more. Soil, equal parts loam, sand, peat moss, and leaf mold; keep evenly moist, unless noted otherwise in descriptions above. Propagate by cuttings or seeds.

PINEAPPLE FAMILY   Bromeliaceae

Mostly epiphytic plants from the American tropics with rosettes of stiff leaves. The foliage is almost always interesting, the flowers showy. Besides the genera listed, try *Dyckia, Guzmania, Nidularium, Quesnelia* and *Tillandsia.*

Aechmea

DESCRIPTION: *A. fasciata,* 1½ ft., from Brazil, has a variety, *purpurea,* that has purple to maroon bands with silver markings on the leaves. In late summer a flower spike bearing pink bracts and blue flowers appears. They age to purple and rose, and may last five months. 'Foster's Favorite' is one of the most colorful aechmeas. It has glossy, wine-red leaves and pendent spikes of deep-blue flowers in winter, followed by blue berries. Other aechmeas bloom at various seasons, with long-lasting flowers, making it possible to have a continuous display from these bromeliads.

Aechmea fasciata 'Silver King'

The leaf rosettes of aechmeas are vaselike in their ability to hold water, hence, the "living vase plant." In the tropics it is not uncommon to see orchid or hibiscus flowers placed within these "vases" to give additional color to plants not in bloom. Since these flowers do not require water in order to stay fresh for short periods of time, and since neither has a long stem which can penetrate to the base of the rosette, this does no harm. However, many amateur growers have taken up this practice, often using cut flowers which use up water and, even worse, have long, stiff stems which can easily damage the heart of the plant, where its own flower spike develops. If you have an aechmea, don't risk injury to the plant by trying to "gild the lily," in this case an aechmea. Have patience and your plant will send up its own magnificent spike of long-lasting, highly colored blossoms.

CULTURE: Light, sunny to semi-sunny. Temperature, average house. Humidity, average house, but preferably 30% or more. Soil, osmunda fiber, shredded bark, or coarse leaf mold; water the roots sparingly, but keep the vases filled with water. Propagate by removing offsets from the parent plant when they are large enough to handle.

Ananas

DESCRIPTION: *A. comosus,* from Baía (Bahía) and Mato Grosso, is the pineapple of commerce. Indoor gardeners frequently slice off a rosette of leaves from the top of a fruit, and root it by planting the base about 1 in. deep in moist potting soil. It is not unusual for the pineapple top to form roots and grow into a strikingly handsome foliage plant. After eighteen months to two years, sometimes more, a new pineapple may develop out of the center of the leaf rosette.

CULTURE: Same as Aechmea, except that high humidity is more important, and a soil mixture of equal parts of loam, sand, peat moss, and leaf mold may be used.

Billbergia zebrina

Ananas comosus

Billbergia

DESCRIPTION: Primarily, billbergias are grown for their extraordinary flowers. They are borne in clusters on tall, sometimes drooping, spikes well above the foliage. The bracts surrounding the true flowers are colorful, and frequently contrast with the color of the blossoms. *B. amoena,* from southern Brazil, has rose bracts and blue-edged, green flowers. *B. iridifolia concolor,* from Espírito Santo, Brazil, has pale-pink bracts and yellow flowers. *B. venezueleana* has rose bracts, white sepals, and chartreuse petals.

CULTURE: Light, sunny to semi-sunny. Temperature, average house. Humidity, average house. Soil, osmunda fiber, sphagnum moss, or pieces of charcoal; billbergias need a potting medium which will hold moisture, yet allow good aeration of the root system. Give them ample water during the hot months but withhold almost entirely from the roots in winter, keeping the centers of the leaves filled, however. During flowering, usually in the spring, do not give overhead showering as this will shorten the flower life. After flowering is over, the plant will normally send up suckers from its base, then die. Propagate by detaching the suckers and potting them individually when they are large enough to handle.

Cryptanthus

DESCRIPTION: The name cryptanthus means hidden flower, and refers to the fact that these bromeliads have their flowers almost wholly concealed beneath the leaves instead of in erect, showy spikes as others in the family do. The plants are generally low-growing, ground-hugging rosettes of colorfully marked leaves. One of the loveliest is *C. bromelioides tricolor,* whose bright-green leaves are vivid rose at the base and on the margins, edged and striped ivory-white. Another colorful favorite is *C. zonatus zebrinus,* from Brazil, with bronzy purple leaves crossbanded brown. These and other cryptanthus may be referred to as "earth stars."

CULTURE: Semi-sunny to semi-shady. Temperature, average house. Humidity, average house. Soil, equal parts loam, sand, peat moss, and leaf mold; keep growing medium barely moist, but syringe the foliage as often as possible. Propagate by removing offsets when they are large enough to handle.

Neoregelia

DESCRIPTION: Neoregelias are mostly erect bromeliads, many with colorful foliage, often spiny-edged, and bearing their blossoms low within the leaf rosettes. One of the hybrids, called "painted fingernail," has green leaves tipped with bright rosy red. Another has straw-colored leaves, and one (*N. carolinae marechalii*) has foliage salmon-crimson. *Neoregelia carolinae tricolor,* from Brazil, is one of the showiest of all. Its rosettes of bright green leaves, precisely striped with lengthwise bands of ivory, become suffused with phosphorescent rose-pink in the spring. This coloration stays bright well into autumn.

CULTURE: Light, semi-sunny to semi-shady. Temperature, average house. Humidity, average house, preferably 30% or more. Soil, osmunda fiber or fir bark mixed with chipped char-

Cryptanthus zonatus zebrinus

Neoregelia carolinae tricolor

coal. Keep soil barely moist, and replace water in rosette at least once a week. Propagate by removing the suckers when they are large enough to handle.

Vriesia

DESCRIPTION: Vriesias are compact, mostly colorful bromeliads which have spectacular flower spikes. Because the cups formed by the rosettes of leaves will catch and hold water, they are often called "living vase plants." The name "flaming sword" has been given to hybrids which send up fiery red, swordlike flower spikes.
CULTURE: Light, semi-sunny to semi-shady. Temperature, average house. Humidity, 30% or more. Soil, equal parts loam, sand, peat moss, and leaf mold; keep barely moist, but be lavish in syringing the foliage, using tepid

Vriesia carinata 'Marie'

water. Propagate by removing the suckers when they are large enough to handle, or, as with "flaming sword" varieties, remove the new plant which develops in the center of the old one.

CACTUS FAMILY

Cactaceae

Succulents from the American tropics with fleshy, thickened stems, usually spiny, and colorful, decorative flowers.

Aporocactus

DESCRIPTION: *A. flagelliformis,* from Mexico, the rattail cactus, has slender stems with ten to twelve ribs, and showy, bright-red flowers. It is ideal in a hanging basket or as a shelf plant.
CULTURE: Light, sunny to semi-sunny. Temperature, average house. Humidity, average house, with some fresh air. Soil, 2 parts sand, 1 part each of loam and leaf mold; allow to become dry between waterings. Propagate by removing offsets, or by rooting cuttings in damp sand.

Aporocactus flagelliformis

Astrophytum

DESCRIPTION: *A. asterias,* from northern Mexico, forms a low, spineless dome divided into eight segments, marked in such a way as to give the popular names "sand dollar" and

Astrophytum myriostigma

"sea-urchin cactus." It has large, red-throated, yellow flowers. *A. myriostigma,* 2 in., from central Mexico, is called "bishop's cap." It is spineless, star-shaped, divided into five segments, and covered with soft white scales. Golden-yellow flowers with many petals arise from the center in summer.
CULTURE: Same as Aporocactus.

Cephalocereus

DESCRIPTION: *C. senilis,* from Mexico, is called "old-man cactus" because of its covering of long, snowy white, hairlike spines.
CULTURE: Same as Aporocactus.

Chamaecereus

DESCRIPTION: *C. silvestri,* from Argentina, is commonly called "peanut cactus" because it has clusters of short,

Chamaecereus silvestri

cylindrical branches. The entire plant is covered with soft white spines.
CULTURE: Same as Aporocactus.

Cleistocactus

DESCRIPTION: *C. baumannii,* from Argentina and Paraguay, is an old-time favorite with bright-red, tubular blossoms, hence "scarlet bugler." *C. strausii,* from Bolivia, also red-flowered, is distinguished by long silvery hairs which give the popular name "silver torch cactus."

Cleistocactus baumannii

CULTURE: Light, semi-sunny. Temperature, average house, preferably not over 75°F. in winter. Humidity, average house. Soil, 2 parts sand, 1 part each of loam and leaf mold; water only when dry. Propagate by removing offsets.

Echinocactus

DESCRIPTION: Echinocacti form a large group of very spiny plants, popular as specimens in their juvenile stages, and especially attractive when they form clumps. They are easily raised from seeds, making balls of spines when young, aging to broadly cylindrical shape, and maturing to huge size. These may be called "barrel cacti," but related genera (Notocactus, Rebutia, and Lobivia) are known by the same popular name.
CULTURE: Same as Aporocactus.

Echinocereus rigidissimus

"rainbow cactus."
CULTURE: Same as Aporocactus.

Echinopsis

DESCRIPTION: Small globular or cylindrical plants noted for a wealth of large, outstandingly beautiful, trumpet-shaped blossoms. Normally, the pink or white flowers unfurl toward dusk, remaining open through most of the following day. They are among the easiest of all cacti to grow, and very free-flowering. *E. multiplex,* from southern Brazil, is the popular "Easter-lily cactus."
CULTURE: Same as Aporocactus.

Echinocactus horizonthalonius

Echinocereus

DESCRIPTION: Echinocereus blossoms are large and brightly colored, in red, purple, pink, yellow, and white, and appear during the summer months. These plants are of easy culture, small-sized, and begin bearing large blossoms at an early age. They are among the easiest of all cacti to bring into flower. Their popular names include "hedgehog cactus" and

Echinopsis multiplex

Epiphyllum

DESCRIPTION: *E. oxypetalum,* from Mexico to Brazil, is one of the cacti known as "night-blooming cereus." In addition, there are countless day-blooming hybrids called "orchid cacti." All are large, strong-growing, spineless plants, but some of the latest hybrids are smaller in growth and more free-flowering. Among the thousands of named epiphyllum hybrids available, nearly any size, shape, or color of flower can be found. CULTURE: Light, semi-sunny to semi-shady. Temperature, average house, preferably not over 75°F. in winter.

Gymnocalycium mihanovichii

Epiphyllum 'Professor Ebert'

Humidity, 30% or more. Mist the stems with tepid water as often as possible, preferably daily. Soil, equal parts of loam, sand, and leaf mold; keep evenly moist, in winter keeping only damp enough to prevent leaf shrinkage. Feed biweekly through spring and summer. Propagate by rooting cuttings in spring and summer.

Gymnocalycium

DESCRIPTION: Species of gymno-calycium, known as "chin cacti," are especially recommended for beginning window gardeners because they are easily grown, small globular plants which have large and beautiful, long-lasting flowers. They received their common name from the protuberant growth beneath each areole which looks like a double chin. CULTURE: Same as Aporocactus.

Hylocereus

DESCRIPTION: *H. undatus,* from Brazil, is semi-trailing, and probably the largest-flowered of the cacti known as "night-blooming cereus." CULTURE: Same as Epiphyllum.

Lobivia binghamiana

Lobivia

DESCRIPTION: *L. aurea,* to 4 in., from Argentina, with large yellow flowers, and *L. binghamiana,* to 3 in., from southeastern Peru, with purple-red flowers, are merely a sampling of these small cacti with large flowers. They are outstanding for window gardens.

CULTURE: Same as Aporocactus.

Mammillaria

DESCRIPTION: An extremely large genus, comprising hundreds of species. Mammillarias blossom from a hairy or woolly areole between the older nodular growths at the top of the plant. Among favorites in this group are species called "old lady cactus," "golden stars," "feather cactus," "powder puff," "lady finger," "thimble," and "rose pincushion." Most of these are clustering types, soon filling a small pot with clumps of unusual beauty.

CULTURE: Same as Aporocactus.

Mammillaria elongata

Notocactus

DESCRIPTION: Notocacti are prized for their easy culture and free-blooming habits. They are small plants with brightly colored spines and large, showy flowers, predominantly yellow. Lemon ball (*N. submammulosus*) is a good one. It is a very free-blooming

species which will mature in three years. Golden ball (*N. leninghausii*) has golden spines.

CULTURE: Same as Aporocactus.

Notocactus leninghausii

Opuntia

DESCRIPTION: The opuntias are probably the best known of all cacti. Some of them, the platyopuntias, are known as "prickly-pears," or "pad cacti," the first name from their fruit, and the second from the shape of their disk-like branches. Others, the cylindropuntias, known as "cholla" (pronounced "choya"), have branches which are almost perfectly cylindrical, joined together in link fashion. Of

Opuntia microdasys

the two groups, the pad cacti are preferred for indoor use, as the chollas
have vicious spines which are unusu-
ally tenacious.

"Bunny-ears," a pad type (*O.
microdasys*), has spineless pads covered
with bright golden tufts of soft
glochids. "Beaver-tail" (*O. basilaris*) is
another spineless one. The pads of
others may be variegated with white
and pink, or thickly hairy, or of odd
shapes. They do not flower freely in
cultivation.

CULTURE: Same as Aporocactus.

Rebutia kupperiana

Rebutia

DESCRIPTION: Rebutia species make
valuable house plants. They bear a
circle of large blooms near the lower
part of the tiny barrel-shaped stems,
hence "crown cactus." Rebutias form
clumps, with the small plants also
encircling the parents crown-fashion.

CULTURE: Same as Aporocactus.

Schlumbergera

DESCRIPTION: *S. bridgesii,* often called
Zygocactus truncatus, is the much-loved
"Christmas cactus." It has wide,

Pereskia aculeata

Pereskia

DESCRIPTION: Pereskia is unusual for
a cactus in that it bears normal leaves.
P. aculeata, from tropical America, is
a leafy small shrub or vine in pot
cultivation. Its woody stems are set
with thorns. In late summer or fall the
branches are laden with greenish
white flowers which yield a delightful
fragrance like that of citrus blossoms,
hence "lemon vine."

CULTURE: Same as Aporocactus.
Prune back as necessary after flowering each year.

Schlumbergera bridgesii

green, spineless stems that are jointed and winged. *S. gaertneri* is the "Easter cactus." It has bright-red flowers in the spring. (See also Zygocactus.) CULTURE: Light, semi-sunny to semi-shady. Christmas cactus may not set buds if it receives any artificial light in autumn or if water is not withheld when vegetative growth begins to cease in September or October. Temperature, average house, except slightly cooler in autumn. Humidity, average house, preferably 30% or more. Plant benefits from frequent misting with tepid water. Soil, equal parts loam, sand, peat moss, and leaf mold, or unmilled sphagnum moss. Propagate by rooting cuttings at any time.

Zygocactus truncatus

Selenicereus

DESCRIPTION: A genus of vinelike, climbing cacti, often called "night-blooming cereus." *S. macdonaldiae* is an extraordinarily beautiful one with gold and white blossoms often a foot across and equally long. "Princess of the night," *S. pteranthus,* is another with very large, white, fragrant blossoms. "Queen of the night," *S. grandiflorus,* has blossoms which are white inside with salmon-colored outer parts, with a very pleasing vanilla odor. CULTURE: Same as Epiphyllum.

Zygocactus

DESCRIPTION: *Z. truncatus,* from South America, is the popular "Thanksgiving cactus." It differs only slightly from species of *Schlumbergera* (described above), and has the typical flat, narrow stems which are joined like the links of a chain. The hose-in-hose flowers vary in color from rose-red, purple, and pale pink, to orange and salmon. Flowering occurs in fall and winter. CULTURE: Same as Schlumbergera.

BELLFLOWER FAMILY   Campanulaceae

Herbs from temperate as well as tropical parts of the world, with alternate leaves and regular flowers, often bell-shaped, and usually lavender, blue, or white. Only one genus is of interest to the indoor gardener.

Campanula

DESCRIPTION: *C. elatines,* from south-eastern Europe and the Adriatic region, is a variable species, the cultivated forms of which are known as

Campanula isophylla alba

"Adria bellflowers." The variety *alba plena* has double white flowers; *flore plena,* double blue. *C. fragilis,* from Italy, is a delicate trailer with

small, intense-blue flowers. *C. isophylla alba* (white) and *C. isophylla mayii* (blue), from Italy, are much loved for their starry masses of flowers. All of these campanulas make excellent hanging basket plants. They have bright green leaves set on tender stems. While several kinds are sometimes known as "star of Bethlehem," this name more properly belongs to Ornithogalum.

CULTURE: Light, sunny to semi-sunny. Temperature, cool, preferably not over 70°F. in winter. Humidity, 30% or more. Soil, equal parts loam, sand, peat moss, and leaf mold; keep evenly moist, except on the dry side in winter. Trim back and keep cool, even in the range of 40-50°F. in fall and winter. Propagate by cuttings taken in the spring.

BITTERSWEET FAMILY   Celastraceae

Evergreen and deciduous vines, trees, and shrubs widely cultivated in American gardens. Only one genus is of interest to indoor gardeners.

Euonymus

DESCRIPTION: Many varieties of *E. japonicus,* from Japan, are available for indoor use, and all of them are

Euonymus japonicus medio-pictus

easily grown. Variegations in these small-leaved plants include green with gold centers, white borders or marginal coloration, and even the kinds with all-green leaves are decorative. Euonymus may be pruned into any desired shape, and is useful for bonsai (Chapter 9).

CULTURE: Light, semi-sunny to semi-shady. Temperature, cool, preferably not over 70°F. in winter. Humidity, 30% or more, otherwise red spider mites will be troublesome. Soil, equal parts loam, sand, and peat moss; keep evenly moist at all times. Propagate by cuttings of half-ripened wood in fall or winter.

SPIDERWORT FAMILY

Commelinaceae

This family contains the several familiar plants known as "wandering Jew." These and others in the group are cultivated mostly for showy leaves which alternate along succulent, watery stems. The flowers usually have three sepals and three petals, and may be regular or irregular.

Cyanotis

DESCRIPTION: *C. kewensis,* from Malabar, has velvety brown hair on both leaves and stems, hence "teddy-bear plant." *C. somaliensis,* from Somaliland, has triangular green leaves covered with white hair, thus, "pussy ears." *C. veldthoutiana,* from South Africa, is the most colorful, having deep-green leaves with purplish reverses, purple stems, all covered with a thick coat of fluffy white wool; popularly known as "white gossamer." These plants are all small creepers.

CULTURE: Light, sunny to semi-sunny. Temperature, cool, preferably not over 72°F. in winter. Humidity, average house. Soil, equal parts loam, sand, and peat moss; keep on the dry side. Propagate by cuttings at any time.

Cyanotis veldthoutiana

Geogenanthus

DESCRIPTION: *G. undatus,* from Peru, is a low-growing foliage plant whose puckered leaves give rise to the name "seersucker plant." They are broad,

Geogenanthus undatus

oval, dark green with the metallic sheen characteristic of the family, and are banded with silvery gray. The reverses are deep purple-red, as are the stems. This is one of the most rewarding of all members of the family because it develops suckers freely, and will soon fill a pot with its colorful and unusual foliage.

CULTURE: Light, semi-shady. Temperature, average house. Humidity, 30% or more. Soil, equal parts loam, sand, and peat moss; keep evenly moist. Propagate by detaching the suckers described above.

Rhoeo

DESCRIPTION: *R. spathacea* (or *R. discolor*), to 1 ft. or more, from Mexico, has an upright rosette of lance-shaped leaves, dark green above, iridescent purple beneath. Above each leaf base two large bracts hold a number of small white flowers. This habit gives rise to a picturesque name, "Moses in the cradle." *R. spathacea vittata* has creamy yellow vertical stripes along the leaves.

CULTURE: Light, sunny to semi-shady.

Setcreasea purpurea

Rhoeo spathacea

Temperature, average house. Humidity, average house. Soil, equal parts loam, sand, and peat moss; keep evenly moist. Propagate by removing offsets, or by transplanting seedlings which often spring up around the parent plant.

Setcreasea

DESCRIPTION: *S. purpurea*, from Mexico, is an erect, fleshy-stemmed, white-hairy plant, that has a strong purple leaf color, hence "purple heart."

CULTURE: Same as Tradescantia.

Siderasis

DESCRIPTION: *S. fuscata*, from Brazil, would not be taken for a member of the spiderwort family at first glance, as it has long, densely hairy leaves in clustering rosettes. Closer inspection, however, reveals the kinship through the contrasting band of silver discernible in the leaves, the barely visible taffeta-like sheen, and the deep-purple leaf reverses. The flowers of lavender-blue are produced close to the base of the plant, sometimes hidden beneath the arching leaves.

CULTURE: Same as Geogenanthus, except allow soil to go partially dry before applying water.

Tradescantia

DESCRIPTION: *T. albiflora albo-vittata*, from Central America, has large blue-green leaves striped generously with white. *T. albiflora laekenensis*, or 'Rainbow,' has iridescent lavender and white stripes on green. *T. blossfeldiana*, from South America, has the coloration of *Rhoeo spathacea*, but trails rampantly and bears loose clusters of lavender flowers. *T. multiflora,* from Jamaica, is a small trailer with narrow dark-green leaves and white flowers. *T. navicularis,* from Peru, is a small plant with boat-shaped, brownish green leaves. It seems to have an affinity for desert conditions, and is often listed along with cacti and other succulents. Any of these tradescantias may be called "inch plant" or "wandering Jew." (See also Zebrina.)

Tradescantia albiflora laekenensis 'Rainbow'

CULTURE: Light, sunny to semi-shady. Temperature, cool, preferably not over 75°F. in winter. Humidity, average house, but dry drafts will disfigure leaf edges. Soil, equal parts loam, sand, and peat moss; allow to become slightly dry between waterings. Propagate by cuttings at any time.

Zebrina

DESCRIPTION: *Z. pendula,* from Mexico, and its many varieties, are the "wandering Jews" which have long been favorite indoor plants. They are characterized by trailing, fleshy, almost watery stems, which will root at each node if in contact with damp soil. Strong light intensifies the foliage coloration, which includes green, red, purple, yellow, pink, and silver, the bands of contrasting colors running the length of the leaves, and with reverses often highly colored. CULTURE: Light, sunny to semi-sunny. Temperature, average house. Humidity, 30% or more. Soil, equal parts loam, sand, and peat moss; keep evenly moist. Propagate by cuttings at any time.

COMPOSITE FAMILY   Compositae

This, the world's largest plant family, includes trees, shrubs, vines, and herbs. The foliage varies widely, but the flower heads are similar. They may consist of petal-like ray flowers as in a daisy, of tubular, tiny disk flowers, as in the center of a daisy, or of both, hence "composite." Only three genera are of interest to the indoor gardener. A fourth, Ligularia, makes an interesting pot plant in a cool, moist place.

Chrysanthemum

DESCRIPTION: The chrysanthemums received as potted gift plants need as cool a place as possible (60-70°F.), evenly moist soil at all times, and protection from direct sun except in early morning and late afternoon.

After the blooms wither, cut back stems to an inch or two, place in cool basement, frost-free garage, or cold frame, and keep soil barely moist until spring. Then set out in the garden. Four-in. cuttings rooted from the resultant growth may be placed five to an 8-in. pot to give a showy display the following autumn.

Chrysanthemums bloom when the days are short. Florists force them out of season by covering the plants with black material a few hours each day until buds show color. This is an exacting process, best left to the professional grower.

Felicia

DESCRIPTION: *F. amelloides* is the kingfisher or blue daisy. Not for a warm, dry apartment, but if you can give it a sunny, moist, airy, cool atmosphere, it will bloom all winter. CULTURE: Light, sunny. Temperature, cool. Humidity, 30% or more. Soil, equal parts loam, sand, and peat moss; keep evenly moist. Feed biweekly. Propagate by seeds or cuttings in the spring every year.

Gynura

DESCRIPTION: *G. aurantiaca*, 2 ft., from Java, is a stout, branchy plant with leaves and stems completely overlaid with short, close-set, vivid purple hairs. This feature has been both its salvation and its downfall—salvation because it provides the beauty which keeps people trying to grow it, and downfall because the hairs give a fragile look which results in too much pampering. Remember that Gynura, or "purple velvet plant," is a composite (in season you may see typical yellow daisies on it) whose relatives

include such sun-worshipers as true sunflowers, daisies, and marigolds. While this family does have a few members which prefer partial shade (Ligularia, for example), Gynura is not one of them.

CULTURE: Light, sunny. Temperature, average house. Humidity, average house. Soil, equal parts loam, sand, and peat moss; keep evenly moist. Propagate by cuttings any time. Begin pruning when the plant is small to eliminate the spindly, single-stalked development which is normal with unattended gynuras.

Gynura aurantiaca

Senecio

"Cineraria"

DESCRIPTION: Hybrids of *S. cruentus,* 1 to 2 ft., from the Canaries, are the popular florist plants known as cinerarias. They are showy plants with large heads of big, daisylike flowers in many colors from purple through blue and red and pink to white. Often the rays of the flower are white at the base, vividly colored on the outer edges.

CULTURE: Light, sunny to semi-sunny. Temperature, cool (50-65°F.). Hu-

Senecio mikanioides

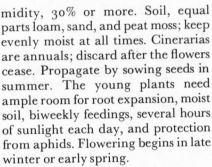

Senecio cruentus

midity, 30% or more. Soil, equal parts loam, sand, and peat moss; keep evenly moist at all times. Cinerarias are annuals; discard after the flowers cease. Propagate by sowing seeds in summer. The young plants need ample room for root expansion, moist soil, biweekly feedings, several hours of sunlight each day, and protection from aphids. Flowering begins in late winter or early spring.

Vining Senecios

DESCRIPTION: *S. confusus,* from Mexico, is a vine with neat, toothed, pointed-oval leaves and clusters of orange-red flowers during winter. It is often called "flame vine." *S. mikanioides,* from South Africa, is the much-loved parlor- or German-ivy, with thin, bright green, ivylike leaves and thin stems.
CULTURE: Light, semi-sunny to semi-shady. Temperature, moderately cool

to average house. Humidity, preferably 30% or more. Soil, equal parts loam, sand, and peat moss; keep evenly moist. Propagate by cuttings.

Succulent Senecios

DESCRIPTION: *S. scaposus,* from South Africa, is a succulent composite which forms rosettes of long, slender leaves covered with white felt. *S. gregorii* is called "peppermint stick" because its leafless, jointed stems are sometimes striped lengthwise with green, cream, and pink. *S. stapeliaeformis* has thick, many-angled stems, and may be called "candy stick."
CULTURE: Light, sunny to semi-sunny. Temperature, average house. Humidity, average house. Soil, 2 parts sand, 1 part each of loam and peat moss; water thoroughly, then not again until dry. Propagate by cuttings in the spring or summer.

MORNING-GLORY FAMILY   Convolvulaceae

Vines, shrubs, and trees, mostly from the tropics, with alternate leaves, and trumpet- or funnel-shaped flowers twisted in the bud stage. Only one genus is of interest to the indoor gardener.

Ipomoea

DESCRIPTION: *I. batatas,* from the East Indies, is the sweet potato of commerce, and the vine often cultivated in window gardens as a beautiful and easily grown hanging basket plant. Since many of the potatoes in commerce have been treated to prevent sprouting, it is necessary to start with a tuber which shows sprouts. Plant upright or horizontally, depending on container. Any planting medium which will hold moisture may be used. Vermiculite, Perlite, or a mixture of equal parts of sand, soil, and peat moss are examples of good mediums. Or, clear water with the lower half of the tuber submerged is a time-honored way to grow sweet potato vines. Change water weekly. Chips of charcoal in container help to keep the water fresh.

Growth becomes active in from one to three weeks after planting, if the container has been set in a warm, well-lighted place. At the outset, water the growing medium thoroughly; not again until it becomes dry. Once plant is in active growth, water enough to keep moist at all times.

The common morning-glory, *Ipomoea tricolor,* is sometimes cultivated indoors as a vine for a sunny window. Plant seeds of hybrid variety such as 'Heavenly Blue' in 6- to 10-in. pot containing equal parts of loam, sand, and peat moss. Keep evenly moist, and thin to allow three or four seedlings to mature. Provide a trellis of some kind; a simple framework with crisscrosses of string is ample.

DOGWOOD FAMILY   Cornaceae

Hardy shrubs or trees, noteworthy for showy flowers, fruit, and, in some species, colorful bark. *Aucuba* is the genus most useful indoors.

Aucuba

DESCRIPTION: *A. japonica,* the Japanese laurel, has large, leathery leaves, usually yellow-splotched. Hardy outdoors and air pollution tolerant to U.S.D.A. Zone 7. Also called gold dust tree. A durable foliage plant except in a hot, dry atmosphere. Bold texture.
CULTURE: Light, semi-sunny to semi-shady. Temperature, on the cool side in winter. Humidity, 30% or more. Soil, equal parts garden loam, sand, and peat moss. Keep evenly moist. Propagate by cuttings in the spring or summer; these will root in water.

Aucuba japonica

STONECROP FAMILY Crassulaceae

Succulent plants with fleshy, pliable stems and leaves, and small, perfect flowers in showy clusters.

Crassula

DESCRIPTION: *C. argentea*, from South Africa, is typical of one distinct type of crassula. It has visible, branching stems which form shrub- or treelike

Crassula argentea

plants. The other, typified by *C. hemisphaerica*, from Southwest Africa, consists of small, low plants with the stems all but hidden under closely packed rosettes of leaves. There are hundreds of crassulas, most of them splendid house plants, and many well known by popular names such

as "propeller plant" (*C. cultrata*), "silver beads" (*C. deltoidea*), "scarlet paintbrush" (*C. falcata*), "string o' buttons" (*C. perfossa*), "rattlesnake" (*C. teres*), and "miniature pine tree" (*C. tetragona*).

CULTURE: Light, sunny to semi-sunny. Temperature, average house. Humidity, average house. Soil, 2 parts sand, I part each of loam and peat moss; keep evenly moist most of the time, but allow to approach dryness between waterings. Propagate by sowing seeds in the spring, or by stem or leaf cuttings at any time.

Crassula perfossa

Echeveria affinis

Echeveria

DESCRIPTION: Tender rosette-forming plants noted for beautifully colored and textured leaves. They display a variety in form, some being tiny ground covers, while others form rosettes at the ends of heavy stems.

Most are free-flowering, producing bright, long-lasting spikes of tubular blossoms. There are nearly countless different echeverias. Here are three good ones: *E. affinis,* from Mexico, has leaves which are almost black if given enough sun. *E. elegans,* from Hidalgo, has leaves of waxy pale blue with white, translucent margins and coral-pink flowers on pink stems. *E. pulv-oliver,* a hybrid, has red-tipped, plushlike leaves.

CULTURE: Light, sunny to semi-sunny. Temperature, average house with some fresh air. Humidity, average house. Soil, 2 parts sand, 1 part each of loam and peat moss; keep on the dry side. Propagate by removing offsets, or by stem cuttings of upright species.

Kalanchoe

DESCRIPTION: There are many kinds of kalanchoe, mostly from Malagasy (Madagascar), and they vary greatly in manner of growth. *K. beharensis* has large lobed leaves completely

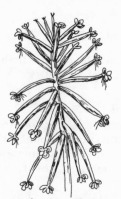

Kalanchoe tubiflora

Kalanchoe blossfeldiana 'Tom Thumb'

covered with a heavy felting of brown hair. *K. blossfeldiana* and its hybrids are shrubby plants with fleshy leaves and clusters of showy, though individually small, blossoms. These are predominantly red, sometimes orange or yellow, and they bloom when the days are short, often at Christmas and on through winter. *K. pinnata,* from India, is called "air plant" or "magic-leaf" because baby plants form along its scalloped leaf edge if it is pinned to a window curtain or laid on moist soil. *K. tomentosa* has small leaves covered with white felt, with the tips toothed and marked with brown; it is called "panda plant." *K. tubiflora* is called "palm plant" from the fancied resemblance of its curved stems to a palm tree. Like *K. pinnata,* this kalanchoe also forms plantlets along the leaf edges.

CULTURE: Light, sunny to semi-sunny. Temperature, on the cool side, but they do reasonably well in the average house. Humidity, average house. Soil, equal parts loam, sand, and peat moss; water only when dry on the surface. Propagate by potting up the naturally formed plantlets, by sowing seeds in the spring, or by tip cuttings. Leaves of named *K. bloss-feldiana* varieties will root exactly like those of the African violet (see Saintpaulia), and send up clusters of new plants which may be divided and potted separately or left in clumps.

Pachyveria

DESCRIPTION: Crosses between two members of the Crassulaceae, Echeveria, and Pachyphytum, have resulted in an intergeneric hybrid known as Pachyveria. Numerous pachyverias exist today, and they are so attractive and useful as house plants that mention is made here of them. Pachyverias are succulents with plump, richly colored leaves in thick rosettes.

CULTURE: Same as Echeveria.

Sedum

DESCRIPTION: There are more than three hundred species of sedum, with an unbelievably wide range of form, color, and habit. *S. morganianum,* from Mexico, is an outstanding plant for hanging baskets. It is often called "burro's-tail" for its chains of waxy, pale, blue-green leaves up to 3 ft.

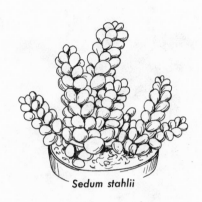

Sedum stahlii

long. *S. multiceps,* from Algeria, looks like a miniature Joshua tree. *S. stahlii,* from Mexico, is called "coral beads" because of its small, fat, egg-shaped leaves of reddish color (poor soil enhances this coloration). Other sedums may be shrubby, to a foot or more in height, or they may be mat-forming.

CULTURE: Light, sunny to semi-sunny. Temperature, cool to average house. Humidity, average house, with plenty of fresh air. Soil, 2 parts sand, and 1 part each of loam and peat moss; keep on the dry side. Propagate by sowing seeds in the spring, or by cuttings or division at any time.

CYCAS FAMILY   Cycadaceae

Primitive, palmlike, evergreen shrubs or trees. The frondlike leaves, in rosettes, are so stiff to the touch, they are sometimes mistaken for plastic. The genus here, and the similar *Zamia,* are of interest for pots.

Cycas

DESCRIPTION: *C. revoluta,* the sage palm, grows to 10 feet tall, the individual fronds to 5 feet. Extremely slow growing; a bushel-size specimen is a costly investment, but it will stay house-size indefinitely.

Cycas revoluta

CULTURE: Light, sunny to shady; best kept outdoors in strong light during warm weather. Temperature, moderate to average house. Humidity, 30% or more. Soil, equal parts loam, sand, peat moss, and leaf mold. Keep evenly moist. Propagate by removing and rooting basal growth buds in spring.

SEDGE FAMILY   Cyperaceae

Superficially similar to, but not the same as true grasses. Sedges have triangular, solid stems and small, inconspicuous, green flowers.

Carex

DESCRIPTION: *C. elegantissima,* from Japan, is, as its name indicates, an elegant, water-loving plant which resembles tufts of tall-growing grass, white-striped along the margins. It is of limited use in the indoor garden except in terrariums with other plants which like wet soil and semi-sunny to semi-shady lighting.

Cyperus

DESCRIPTION: *C. alternifolius,* to 4 ft., from Madagascar, is the well-known "umbrella plant." For indoor use, its dwarf form, *gracilis,* to 2 ft., is generally preferred. *C. diffusus,* from Mauritius, suckers freely, has fairly broad leaves, is a rapid grower, and will fill a pot nicely within a short time. *C. elegans,* from tropical Africa, is very similar, but has narrow leaves. *C. papyrus,* from Egypt, is the Egyptian paper plant. If you find yourself the owner of this cyperus, pot it in a large tub and give it room to grow

Cyperus alternifolius gracilis

—the stems often exceed 8 ft. in height! CULTURE: Light, semi-sunny to semi-shady. Temperature, on the cool side in winter. Humidity, 30% or more, with enough fresh air to discourage red spider mites. Soil, equal parts loam, sand, and peat moss; keep wet at all times. Propagate by division at any time.

OLEASTER FAMILY
Elaeagnaceae

Generally hardy trees and shrubs with smooth-edged leaves, golden or silver underneath, and inconspicuous flowers. Only one genus is of interest to indoor gardeners.

Elaeagnus

DESCRIPTION: *E. pungens,* from China and Japan, is known in its form called *aureo-variegata* as an evergreen shrub with oval, wavy-edged leaves bordered with yellow, the undersides silvery. The fragrant white flowers flare above a cylindrical tube, and are borne in clusters arising from the leaf axils.

CULTURE: Light, semi-sunny to semi-shady. Temperature, cool to average house. Humidity, 30% or more. Soil, equal parts loam, sand, and peat moss; keep evenly moist. Propagate by cuttings taken in the spring and kept warm, moist, and in high humidity.

HEATH FAMILY
Ericaceae

Mostly evergreen shrubs from the north temperate zone, widely cultivated outdoors in American gardens. Only the rhododendrons known in commerce as azaleas are of interest to the indoor gardener.

Azalea

DESCRIPTION: Growers force these cool-growing perennials for bloom at Christmas, on through the winter to spring and Easter. Coolness (50-60°F.) will help the flowers stay on longer, and the foliage to stay greener. Syringe the plants daily with room-temperature water. In mild climates, greenhouse-forced plants may be planted outdoors in spring in a semi-shaded place where there is humusy soil enriched by quantities of sand and peat moss. There they will resume their natural perennial habit. In cold climates, transplant to a pot one size larger, using moist German peat moss, and place outdoors in the summer in a cool, partially shaded place. Keep moist throughout the summer, apply biweekly feedings of liquid house plant fertilizer, and supplement occasionally with an iron chelate such as Sequestrene. Bring indoors in autumn, place in a cool place (about 50°F.) and keep the soil barely moist until December or January. Then move to a sunny, moist, cool place, and begin to apply more water and occasional feedings.

SPURGE FAMILY   Euphorbiaceae

Trees, shrubs, herbs, and cactuslike succulents with alternate leaves, milky juice (generally somewhat poisonous) and inconspicuous flowers surrounded by colorful bracts.

Acalypha

DESCRIPTION: *A. hispida,* from western Pacific regions, is prized for its showy flower spikes which dangle gracefully from the leaf axils. They are long,

Acalypha hispida

fluffy, bright red (pinkish white in the variety *alba*). Often called "chenille plant." *Macafeana* is one of several varieties of *A. wilkesiana.* Its red, ovate leaves are colorfully marbled in crimson and bronze. This and others in the genus are called "copper leaf."
CULTURE: Light, sunny to semi-sunny. Temperature, average house. Humidity, average house. Soil, equal parts loam, sand, and peat moss; keep evenly moist at all times. Propagate by cuttings taken in the fall.

Codiaeum

DESCRIPTION: Species and varieties of codiaeum, known everywhere as crotons, are a source of equal parts pleasure and anguish to the indoor gardener. If kept warm and humid, given enough sunlight to color well, and enough fresh air circulation to reduce red spider mite attacks, crotons are nearly unequaled as colorful foliage plants. However, if any phase of culture is not agreeable, they will drop their leaves within a matter of hours.

C. interruptum, from Polynesia, is red and yellow, with the midrib appearing to extend beyond the leaf blade. Another, possibly a sport of this, has two distinct leaf blades connected by the main rib. *C. spirale,* from Malaysia, has green leaves brightly splashed with yellow and red, and twisted like a corkscrew. *C. variegatum pictum,* from Ceylon,

Codiaeum variegatum pictum hybrid

Malaya, southern India, and the Sunda Islands, has given rise to almost countless hybrids. There are oak-leaf shapes, and broad elliptical ones. Colors range from palest yellow through pinks, reds, oranges, and browns, to every possible shade of green. There are spots, blotches, marginal colorings, and veins often showing contrasting colors. Many crotons have young growth of one color that matures to quite another. Very seldom will two leaves on any plant be exactly alike.

CULTURE: Light, sunny to semi-sunny. Temperature, average house. Humidity, 30% or more, and ample circulation of fresh air. Soil, equal parts loam, sand, peat moss, and leaf mold; keep evenly moist. Propagate from cuttings whenever warmth (70-80°F.) and high humidity can be provided.

Euphorbia

DESCRIPTION: *E. pulcherrima,* from southern Mexico, is the beloved poinsettia of our Christmas holidays. It has succulent, tender new growth

which matures to a woody, shrublike structure, and large, colorful bracts when the days are short in fall and early winter. *E. splendens,* the only other species widely cultivated by indoor gardeners, is the popular "crown of thorns." Its stems are covered by stout, thickly set gray spines; the small leaves are sparse and short-lived; the ½ to 1-in. floral bracts range in color from yellow to salmon-pink, rosy red, and scarlet.

To prolong the life of a flowering poinsettia, protect it from chilling or

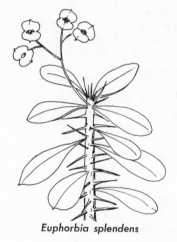

Euphorbia splendens

drying drafts. Provide enough water to keep the soil evenly moist at all times. Give at least two or three hours of sunlight each day, and a temperature range of 65-72°F. A moist atmosphere (30% humidity or more) helps to prolong the life of the colorful bracts. When these (red, pink, or white parts which resemble large flower petals) finally begin to fall, set the plant in a light place where the temperature will not fall below 55°F., and keep the soil barely moist. Repot in new soil in the spring, and, when the weather is warm out-

Euphorbia pulcherrima

doors, sink the pot to its rim where it will have morning sun and protection from strong winds.

During June, July, or August, take cuttings of the new growth and root them in moist sand and peat moss, or in vermiculite. When roots have formed, pot the young plants in a mixture of equal parts of loam, sand, and peat moss. When fall approaches, and nights begin to be cool, bring the pots to an enclosed porch or indoors. Sudden high or low temperatures, dryness in the air and soil, and lack of sunlight may cause the lower leaves of poinsettias to yellow and fall, leaving unsightly bare stems.

The plant from which cuttings were taken can be kept year after year. When propagation is complete, cut back the stems to about 12 inches from the soil. Pinch out the growing tips of new growth until the middle of July to encourage more flowering terminals. A large and showy poinsettia will result, even though it has served as a parent plant for others.

When poinsettias are brought indoors in autumn, if any artificial light strikes them during the normal dark period of each twenty-four hours, they may fail to bloom for the Christmas holidays.

CULTURE for poinsettias is outlined above. This outline is for the crown of thorns, *E. splendens,* and its many varieties: Light, sunny to semi-sunny. Temperature, average house. Humidity, average house. Soil, equal parts sand, loam, and peat moss; allow to be quite dry between waterings. Propagate by cuttings, first allowing the cut portions to dry in the open air, then inserting them in moist sand.

Jatropha

DESCRIPTION: *J. multifida,* from Texas to Brazil, is a fairly recent introduction as a house plant. It is an attractive shrub with almost-round, palmate leaves which are finely cut and lobed. "Coral plant," the common name, came from its showy clusters of coral-red flowers which are nearly everblooming.

CULTURE: Light, sunny to semi-sunny. Temperature, average house. Humidity, 30% or more. Soil, equal

Jatropha multifida

parts loam, sand, and peat moss; keep evenly moist. Propagate by sowing the seeds (very large and rapid germinators), or by cuttings of hard young branches; let these dry slightly before inserting them in the rooting medium.

Pedilanthus

DESCRIPTION: *P. tithymaloides,* from Central America, may be called "devil's-backbone" because of its strange, zigzag stems, or "redbird cactus" because of the small, birdlike,

scarlet blossoms which appear in the spring after the plant has been chilled in winter. The lance-shaped leaves of this succulent are light green with suffusions and splashes of rosy red, white, and dark green.
CULTURE: Light, sunny to semi-shady. Temperature, average house. Humidity, average house. Soil, equal parts loam, sand, and peat moss; keep evenly moist. Propagate by cuttings taken in the spring.

Synadenium

DESCRIPTION: *S. grantii,* the African milk-bush, is a succulent plant with the milky sap typical of its family. The variety *rubra* has fleshy, wine-red leaves to 3 in. in length, set on thick, fleshy stems which become shrubby with age. This makes a showy, unusual foliage plant in the sunny window garden.
CULTURE: Light, sunny to semi-sunny. Temperature, average house. Humidity, 30% or more. Soil, equal parts loam, sand, and peat moss; allow soil to go slightly dry between waterings. Propagate by cuttings; these lose their milky juice so rapidly, it is necessary to seal them with a flame.

GENTIAN FAMILY   Gentianaceae

Herbs, all except exacum, from cool parts of the world. They have opposite leaves and much admired flowers, frequently of true blue. Exacum is the only genus of interest to indoor gardeners.

Exacum

DESCRIPTION: *E. affine,* from Socotra in the Indian Ocean, is a free-flowering, fragrant plant which deserves a place in almost every window garden. Unlike most plants recommended for indoor growing, exacum is a biennial, completing its life cycle within two growing seasons. Thus it requires the raising of a new generation from seed each year to assure having a constant supply of flowering-age plants. Its blossoms are blue with prominent golden stamens. In the variety *atrocoeruleum* the color is more nearly purple. The plants are bushy, a foot high or more, with neat, waxy, oval leaves.
CULTURE: Light, semi-sunny to semi-shady. Temperature, average house. Humidity, average house, preferably 30% or more. Soil, equal parts loam, sand, and peat moss; keep evenly moist. Propagate by sowing seeds in February for plants to flower through the following fall and winter.

Exacum affine

GERANIUM FAMILY   Geraniaceae

Herbs, sometimes woody-stemmed, sometimes succulent, with simple leaves and umbels of showy flowers. Only one genus is of interest to the indoor gardener, the one which furnishes the many forms of potted "geraniums."

Pelargonium

DESCRIPTION: The most popular geraniums are varieties of *Pelargonium hortorum*. These are the upright, thick-stemmed, branching plants with scalloped, roundish leaves marked with a horseshoe-shaped zone of brownish green (hence the name "zonal geranium") and heavy clusters of large single to double flowers in shades of red, salmon, pink, lavender, and white. Hundreds of named varieties are available.

FANCY-LEAF GERANIUMS: The fancy-leaf geraniums are zonal types with green leaves variegated with white; or leaves in shades of brick, brown, bronze, and gold; or extra-fancy tricolor combinations. The most brilliant is probably 'Mrs. Velma Cox' with blending tones of gold, bright red, rosy pink, and brown—crowned by heads of single salmon flowers.

Zonal geraniums are available also as 3-in. miniatures, and only slightly taller semi-dwarfs. The leaves may be as small as a thumbnail, but shaped and marked—often variegated—like their larger counterparts. Yet the flowers are disproportionately large. Sometimes a cluster will cover the whole plant. Among these miniatures, 'Imp' is one of the smallest with single, peach-pink flowers. 'Kleiner Liebling' ('Little Darling') is a wee one with fine white trimming on the edge of the leaf, and single, pale-pink flowers.

MARTHA WASHINGTON GERANIUMS are varieties of *Pelargonium domesticum,* different from the zonals in many ways. The all-green leaves are crisply crinkled by the veins; and the late spring flowers are extraordinarily large and plentiful, in flamboyant colors and combinations, often distinctively blotched on the upper petals. Several dozen named varieties are available. The small-flowered pansy types, like purple-and-white 'Madame Layal,' are most likely to succeed indoors. After flowering, the plant should be cut back severely and the pot set outdoors in partial to full sun for the summer. Bring it back indoors in fall and cut down on watering during the winter months. Start weak but regular weekly feedings of balanced fertilizer when flower buds first appear.

SCENTED-LEAVED GERANIUMS: Some hobbyists concentrate on the geranium species and varieties with scented leaves. They are slightly less demanding and need less sun. Several different "scent categories" are listed in "A Selection of Herbs To Grow Indoors," Chapter 6.

SUCCULENT GERANIUMS: One odd, and relatively rare, succulent geranium is often mistaken for a cactus, and rightly so, for the stems of *Pelargonium echinatum* are nearly as thorny as an opuntia. In the winter and

FAVORITE GERANIUMS

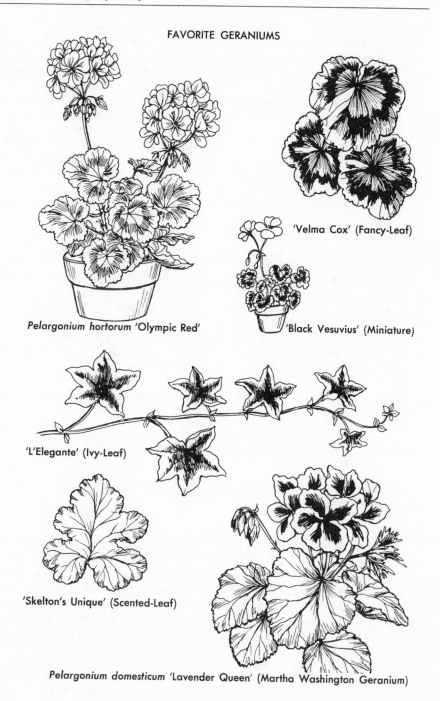

Pelargonium hortorum 'Olympic Red'

'Velma Cox' (Fancy-Leaf)

'Black Vesuvius' (Miniature)

'L'Elegante' (Ivy-Leaf)

'Skelton's Unique' (Scented-Leaf)

Pelargonium domesticum 'Lavender Queen' (Martha Washington Geranium)

spring it grows rampantly, and when provided with sunlight for several hours daily, the stems will be laden with white and crimson flowers. During summer and fall the plant goes dormant, loses all foliage, and needs to be kept nearly dry throughout this period.

IVY-LEAVED GERANIUMS: Another fascinating group of geraniums—the ivy-leaved varieties of *Pelargonium peltatum*—have long, trailing stems angled at the joints, and glossy ivy-like leaves. They give a bountiful display of bloom in the summer. In California these are often planted to cover sunny banks; and anywhere they are exquisite in hanging baskets and window boxes. 'Galilee' is an excellent, free-flowering double pink variety; 'Charles Monsolet' is double cerise; 'Mrs. W. H. Martin' is double orchid. For delicately variegated leaves, choose 'Sunset' ('L'Elegante'), a variety whose ivy-shaped leaves are tinged with pink when the soil is kept dry and there is plenty of warm sunlight; it bears light-lavender flowers.

CULTURE: Light, sunny to semi-sunny. Temperature, on the cool side (anywhere from 50-70°F. in winter, except Martha Washingtons, which require 60°F. or less in order to set buds). Humidity, average house, preferably 30% or more, with plenty of fresh air. Soil, 3 parts loam, 1 part each of sand and peat moss; add a teaspoonful of steamed bone meal to each 5-in. pot. Pack firmly around the geranium roots. Water thoroughly, then not again until surface is dry. Geraniums flower best when slightly pot-bound; over-potting is particularly unwise for the miniatures. Fertilize geraniums biweekly when they are in active growth and flower; not when they are resting, as the Martha Washington and ivy-leaf varieties do in winter. Propagate by rooting cuttings, in spring for following winter bloom, in autumn for following spring and summer.

GESNERIAD FAMILY   Gesneriaceae

Handsome, often velvety-leaved plants from the tropics with wheel-shaped, tubular, or bell-shaped flowers.

Achimenes

DESCRIPTION: Several species from tropical America, and many hybrids, make achimenes one of the most valuable of all summer-flowering plants, both in window gardens and outdoors, in partially shaded places. The tubular, five-lobed blossoms have been likened to a small petunia, a cattleya (hence, "nut orchid") and a slipper-flowered gloxinia (species of Sinningia, which see). The latest hybrids have extra rows of petals, thus giving a double, hose-in-hose kind of flower. Colors include white, pink, rose, red, violet, purple, and blue; some are solid, others may be veined or dotted with contrasting colors. There is also variation in leaf shape, color, and in the manner of growth. Generally the plants are low and hairy with toothed, elmlike leaves. Flowers arise from the leaf

Achimenes 'Vivid'

axils and are borne singly, paired, or even several on a single peduncle.

Plants of achimenes grow from scaly underground rhizomes or small tubers. Small catkinlike bodies of similar appearance sometimes occur in the leaf axils or among the flowers. These may appear insignificant, but if six are planted in a 6-in. pot, the growing tips pinched out when plants are 2 or 3 in. tall, you will be amazed at the floral display from July until fall.

CULTURE: Light, semi-sunny to semi-shady. Temperature, average house. Humidity, 30% or more. Soil, equal parts loam, sand, peat moss, and leaf mold; keep this evenly moist whenever plants are in active growth, nearly dry in fall and winter during dormancy, when they may be stored at 50-55°F. Order achimenes rhizomes from January to April; cover with ½ to 1 in. soil and start with gentle bottom heat (70-80°F.). Fertilize biweekly while plants are making active growth. When the plants begin to go dormant, either because of short days or lack of sufficient moisture, the scaly rhizomes may be left in the pot until replanting time in spring; or sift them out in autumn and store through the winter

in a cool place in a bag of dry vermiculite. Propagate by breaking large rhizomes in two, by leaf or stem cuttings in summer, or by sowing seeds in midwinter.

Aeschynanthus

DESCRIPTION: *A. lobbianus,* from Java, formerly known as a trichosporum, is a trailing epiphytic plant of plain green leaves set opposite on stems which may reach a length of 2 ft. or more. At the ends of these, clusters of downy, maroon-brown calyxes form. Inside each is a scarlet flower bud; this arrangement suggests a common name, "lipstick plant," which may also be applied to the similar *A. pulcher.* At maturity the flowers extend to twice the length of the calyxes, flaring wide enough to reveal creamy yellow throats. *A marmoratus,* from Siam, is cultivated more for its waxy dark-green leaves netted yellow-green and flushed with ma-

Aeschynanthus pulcher

roon, than for its infrequent brown-spotted, green flowers.

CULTURE: Light, semi-sunny to semi-shady. Temperature, average house. Humidity, 50% or more. Soil, un-milled sphagnum moss, osmunda fiber, or a mixture of equal parts loam, sand, peat moss, and leaf mold; keep evenly moist at all times. Fertilize biweekly except when weather conditions are not conducive to rapid growth (for example, several weeks of cloudy, wet days in fall or winter). Propagate by stem or tip cuttings at any time that warmth (70-80°F.) and high humidity can be provided.

Chirita sinensis

Alloplectus

DESCRIPTION: Species vary from shrubby to kinds like *Columnea* and *Episcia*. For baskets, grow *A. ambiguous* (yellow flowers) or *A. nummularia* (red pouch flowers; formerly called *Hypocyrta nummularia*); for general culture in window garden or under lights, grow *A. calochlamys* (yellow flowers, showy salmon-pink calyces).

CULTURE: Same as Columnea.

Boea

DESCRIPTION: *B. hygroscopica* has quilted, velvety, light green leaves. Yellow-centered bright blue flowers. Likes warmth, high humidity. A fine subject for terrarium gardening.

CULTURE: Same as Columnea.

Chirita

DESCRIPTION: *C. asperifolia* has soft green leaves. Flowers waxy, the tube dark blue, the face white. *C. sinensis* has silver-veined oval leaves. Flowers tubular, pale lilac on red stems.

C.s. 'Silver Leaf' has fancier foliage. All excellent for fluorescent-light gardening.

CULTURE: Same as Columnea.

Chrysothemis

DESCRIPTION: These gesneriads have tuberous roots and need an early winter rest. Species C. *friedrichsthaliana, pulchella* 'Cooper Leaf' and 'Green Leaf' and *villosa* are noteworthy for glossy foliage and yellow flowers borne from orange calyces (excepting the first which are green).

CULTURE: Same as Sinningia.

Codonanthe

DESCRIPTION: These trailing gesneriads are excellent for hanging baskets, especially in a greenhouse. Species C. *carnosa, crassifolia,* and *uleana* have white flowers followed by attractive berrylike fruit.

CULTURE: Same as Columnea.

Columnea

DESCRIPTION: Columneas are mostly pendent or trailing plants of tropical America, with small, opposite leaves and large, showy flowers in their axils.

Many come from Costa Rica. *C. arguta,* from Panama, has waxy,

Columnea gloriosa

pointed, bronze leaves and large, red, tubular blossoms. *C. gloriosa* has brown-tinted, velvet-covered, green leaves and showy, orange-red flowers to 3 in. long. *C. hirta* is similar to *C. gloriosa,* but has smaller, more linear leaves. Large orange-red flowers are produced in abundance. *C. linearis* has narrow, shiny leaves on semi-upright stems and pink flowers. *C. microphylla* has tiny, buttonlike leaves covered with coppery hairs; orange-scarlet flowers 3 in. long extend out horizontally from the vertically drooping stems.

Hybrid columneas derived from these species tend to be everblooming. They are also more easily cultivated and are among the best new house plants.

CULTURE: Light, semi-sunny to semi-shady. Temperature, average house. Humidity, 50% or more. Soil, equal parts loam, sand, peat moss, and leaf mold; or, preferably, a soilless medium prepared according to the recipe of Michael Kartuz, page 39.

Keep evenly moist. Propagate by rooting tip cuttings or by sowing seeds in warmth and high humidity.

Episcia

DESCRIPTION: Episcias are luxuriant foliage plants, handsome with or without flowers. The first species to attract the attention of commerce was *E. reptans,* known formerly as *E. coccinea* or *E. fulgida,* and promoted as the "flame violet." Its pebble-surface, bronzy leaves with distinctive green or silver veining have become a familiar sight wherever tropical plants are grown. Today there are dozens of other episcia species and cultivars available. You may choose hairy or smooth-leaved kinds; leaves with contrasting veins or zones; flowers of white, yellow, pink, red, blue, or lavender; plain, spotted, marked, or lined. Episcia flowers are five-lobed, long-tubed, and all are fringed, some more noticeably than others.

Episcias are best displayed when allowed to trail and grow unimpeded, as from a shelf or hanging basket. They grow strawberrylike stolons one after the other, and these soon produce a magnificent cascade of foliage unequaled by any other plant. The effect is highlighted by the blossoms which arise in the leaf axils, in some varieties only seasonally, in others almost constantly. If room does not permit fullest spreading for episcias, they may be kept cut back into a rounded, bushy form. Root the plantlets along the cut-off stolons by pinning them to moist soil.

CULTURE: Light, semi-sunny to semi-shady. Temperature, warm. Humidity, 30% or more. Soil, equal parts loam, sand, peat moss, and leaf mold;

keep evenly moist and give biweekly feedings except in late fall and early winter. Propagate by rooting the stolons.

Kohleria amabilis

Gesneria cuneifolia

Gesneria

DESCRIPTION: Rapidly rising new stars in the Gesneriad Family. Dwarf, compact plants are everblooming, ideal for fluorescent-light culture and terrariums. *G. cuneifolia* has glossy, dark green leaves; tubular red flowers. Hybrid 'Lemon Drop' bears a nonstop crop of yellow flowers.

CULTURE: Same as Columnea.

Kohleria

DESCRIPTION: *K. amabilis,* from Colombia, is a small, bushy plant with silver-green, hairy leaves, veined with chocolate-brown. Its red-spotted pink flowers come for months on end, borne on airy, fuzzy stems. *K. eriantha,* from Colombia, a plant sold for many years as *Isoloma hirsutum,* has downy, erect stems to 4 ft., with many dark-green leaves, conspicuously marked on the edges with red plush; it bears

a great display of scarlet-orange flowers. *K. lindeniana,* from Ecuador, is a bushy plant of olive-green leaves boldly veined with silver. In warmth, good light, and high humidity it produces an almost never-ending array of fragrant, white, blue-throated flowers.

Kohlerias grow from scaly rhizomes, considerably larger than those of achimenes. They may be planted whenever available, brought to maturity, then dried off and stored in coolness (50-60°F.), barely moist, for a resting period of two to four months.

CULTURE: Light, semi-sunny to semi-shady. Temperature, average house. Humidity, 30% or more. Soil, equal parts loam, sand, peat moss, and leaf mold; keep evenly moist. Fertilize biweekly when growth is active. Propagate by dividing the scaly rhizomes at repotting time.

Nautilocalyx

DESCRIPTION: Though relatively unknown, plants of this genus are valuable for cultivation indoors. *N. bullatus,* from Amazonian Peru, is an upright plant cultivated for pebbly-

Nautilocalyx forgetii

Nematanthus wettsteinii

surfaced, bronze-green leaves. The tiny yellow flowers borne in the leaf axils are interesting but not showy. *N. forgetii*, from Peru, has olive-green leaves boldly patterned with a maroon-red midrib; underneath, the stems are fuzzy; flowers small, creamy yellow. *N. lynchii*, from Colombia, has bronze- or maroon-red leaves, sometimes nearly black, and small, cream-colored flowers.
CULTURE: Light, semi-sunny to semi-shady. Temperature, average house. Humidity, 30% or more. Soil, equal parts loam, sand, peat moss, and leaf mold; keep evenly moist and give biweekly feedings. Propagate by rooting tip cuttings in warmth and high humidity.

Nematanthus

DESCRIPTION: These trailing or semi-upright spreaders resemble the related columneas. They have showy, pouch-shaped flowers. *N. wettsteinii,* the gold-fish plant, was known until recently as *Hypocyrta.* A perfect miniature basket plant; tiny, glossy leaves, red-and-yellow pouch flowers.
CULTURE: Same as Columnea.

Rechsteineria

DESCRIPTION: This genus name has now been changed to Sinningia. However, the species names remain the same, and in this edition, we have retained the old name *Rechsteineria*. *R. cardinalis,* from Central America, is widely cultivated for its scarlet, tubular flowers. The downy, bright green, heart-shaped leaves grow on upright stems, with the flowers borne in the leaf axils toward the top of the plant. *R. leucotricha,* from western Paraná, is known as

Rechsteineria macropoda

"Brazilian edelweiss." Like other rechsteinerias, it grows from a large, fleshy tuber, similar to a yam or sweet potato, but more or less round with a concave top. The dull-green leaves are covered heavily with white hair, and when the rosy coral flowers come, this rechsteineria makes a breath-taking sight. *R. macropoda*, from southern Brazil, has large heart-shaped leaves of bright green, and loose umbels of nodding, tubular flowers of fiery scarlet. *R. purpurea*, from Brazil, often bears only two whorls of dark-green leaves, topped by old-rose, tubular flowers, dotted with red; thus it came to be called the "double- or triple-decker plant." CULTURE: Same as Sinningia.

Saintpaulia

DESCRIPTION: Among the many plants which botanical explorers have endured hardship to collect and introduce into cultivation, none could give the discoverer more pride and satisfaction than the saintpaulia. If Baron Walter von Saint Paul could see today's thousands of glamorous African violet varieties—descendants of the species he collected in Africa around 1890—he should feel that his work was worth while. Few house plants give so many people such pleasure.

The popularity of African violets in this country began in 1936 with the introduction of the first-named varieties. It spread fast, like a harmless but infectious disease. And today, a plant lover has only to see a well-grown specimen, with a lush rosette of velvety leaves nearly hidden under a blanket of colorful flowers, to catch the contagion. Only one with a very strong character (or a completely disinterested person) can bring one plant into bloom without wanting more.

Nobody can count accurately the number of named varieties of African violets available today. Hundreds of new hybrids are introduced every year, some of them very similar to others—only the names are different. If you want a few plants to bloom on a window sill, you might stay with well-known kinds which have been proved sturdiest and most free-flowering. If you're building a collection, you'll shop through catalogues and swap with other collectors until you have plants in several sizes—miniature, standard, and extra large—with all types of foliage and flowers. Leaves may be nearly smooth or soft-velvety; corrugated with indented veins, fringed or waved on edge, round or pointed, flat or cupped, solid green or variegated with creamy white.

African violet flowers may be single, semi-double, or double; fringed or ruffled on the edge; in varying shades of blue, pink, lavender, wine, purple, and white. The bicolors have two shades of the same color; multicolors have more than two colors per flower. And there are novelties like star-shaped flowers, or petals bordered with another color, or contrastingly streaked and splashed.

It's easy to understand why African violets are popular, for these plants will flower not just during one annual season but off and on all year long. They take up little space, and they keep healthy and contented without a great deal of fuss and trouble. But don't let the popular name mislead you. They are not violets, and they do not grow like the "Russian" or

THE SAINTPAULIA (African Violet)

Hybrid of *S. ionantha* with plain or "boy" leaves and single flowers

FLOWER TYPES

LEAF TYPES

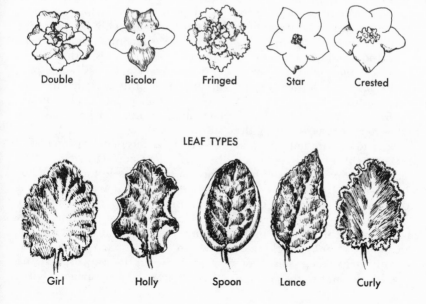

| Double | Bicolor | Fringed | Star | Crested |

| Girl | Holly | Spoon | Lance | Curly |

"English" violets as we know them. Rather, take "African" as a clue to their culture, and try to give them growing conditions similar to their tropical homelands.

CULTURE: Light, semi-sunny to sunny in winter months; shade from hottest sun in summer. Insufficient light is the most frequent cause of failure to flower. African violets thrive under fluorescent-light culture, described in Chapter 11. Temperature, average house, specifically, 70-80°F. Humidity, 30% or more in winter. Average indoor air, particularly in winter, is likely to be too dry. This condition will cause leaves to crisp on the edge; buds will fail to open; flowers may be few or none. Set pots on (not in) a layer of sand or gravel kept constantly moist, in a tray or similar shallow container. Soil, equal parts loam, sand, and peat moss; or buy the handy, packaged mediums recommended specifically on the labels for African violets. It is advisable to pasteurize the soil as described in Chapter 2. Feed biweekly except the first two months after repotting. Keep soil evenly moist by applying water of room temperature (cold water makes spots on the leaves). Water alternately from the top and from the bottom, so nutrient salts cannot form a crust on the soil. Bottom watering means setting the pot in water to the rim until pot and soil are thoroughly moist. Repot when roots completely cover the soil ball, usually not more than once a year. To insure perfect drainage, put a ½-in. or inch-deep layer of pebbles or small pieces of broken pot in the bottom; small chunks of charcoal added will help keep soil fresh-smelling. Place plant so the crown is slightly elevated, with the soil sloping down around it, to prevent crown rot. Overpotting also invites rot; keep pot sizes as small as possible.

African violets are usually healthiest and flower best when they have only one crown (the "collar" near the soil where the stems come together and join the roots). On show plants, remove such new growth as soon as it appears. Or let the new crowns grow for a while, then cut them off and root them for new plants. Keep the leaves clean and free from dust with a camel's-hair brush, or, and this is even better, turn the pot upside down (hold the soil in place with your fingers or a piece of foil) and gently swish the leaves through lukewarm water containing a little mild household detergent. Set the plant aside to drain before returning to its growing quarters.

The most common problem with African violets—failure to flower—is usually caused by insufficient fluorescent light or sunlight, temperature too high, humidity too low, too many crowns on a plant, chilling plant with icy water, or a combination of these factors. It's true also that some varieties flower more easily and profusely than others. African violet growers' catalogues offer clues to the current varieties which have the most stamina.

African violets may be propagated by seeds, leaf cuttings, or division. For leaf cuttings, select a mature but not old leaf, cut it with an inch of stem, using a sharp knife, and insert in a moist rooting medium (even plain water) up to the leaf blade. For division, use a sharp knife to cut down between the crowns, severing them below the soil surface. There are many specific suggestions for African violet propagation techniques in Chapter 3.

Sinningia

DESCRIPTION: What a triumph it is to plant a thick, dry, brown, and barren-looking tuber—and watch it produce a luxuriant plant with layers of large, oval, velvety leaves topped with a crowning glory of immense, flaring, tubular flowers in rich patterns and glowing colors. That's what happens when you grow gloxinias, known correctly as sinningias.

At home in tropical Brazilian forests, sinningia species flower naturally in spring and summer, drop their leaves and go dormant during winter's less favorable months. But because we can control indoor weather, and because today's hybrids are bred for strength and fullest

flowering, our new gloxinias often flower at intervals during most of the year. Some almost never go dormant, others may rest for a few days or several months. And the tubers can be started into growth whenever they are available—from mail-order suppliers in all but the coldest winter or hottest summer months.

A fresh gloxinia tuber feels firm and lively; it is neither dry and shriveled nor soft with rot. If it is a large tuber, it should go in a 5- or 6-in. pot (preferably a shallow bulb pan). Put a 1-in. layer of gravel or broken pieces of crockery in the bottom. Add enough soil (equal parts loam, sand, and peat moss) to fill the pot halfway; set in the tuber, cupped side up, and cover it completely with soil. The finished soil level will be about ½ in. below the pot rim, and will cover the top of the tuber with about ½ in. of soil.

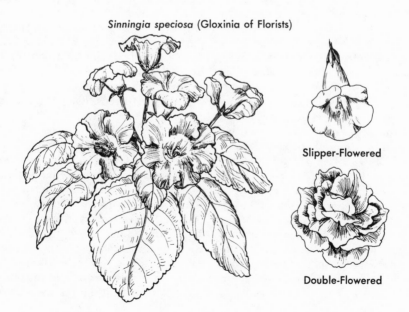

Sinningia speciosa (Gloxinia of Florists)

Slipper-Flowered

Double-Flowered

Moisten the soil and pot thoroughly by setting it in water nearly to the rim. When the top of the soil is shiny and moist, remove the pot and let it drain. Then, put it in some warm (60°F. minimum) spot where it is shaded and protected from drafts. Bottom heat (70-80°F.) will speed up rooting. Water only enough to keep the soil slightly moist until leaves begin to show at the top.

Now, move the plant to its permanent growing quarters—a warm window where some sun will reach it but where it's shaded against very hot sun; or, perhaps, under an installation of fluorescent lights as described in Chapter 11. In either case, if indoor air is dry (and in winter it usually is), increase humidity by setting the pots on, not in, a layer of sand or gravel in a tray at least as large as the plant's mature leaf-spread.

Step up the watering schedule so that whenever you touch the soil, it always feels nicely moist—but never so much that the roots are constantly soggy-wet. Water of room temperature is safest, and won't make white marks on the leaves. Every two weeks, water with a solution of house plant fertilizer. If stems begin to grow long, if the plant gets spindly, if the leaves curl under on the edges, you'll know that the light is too dim, the air too dry, and your gloxinia probably won't flower freely; the buds, if formed, may drop. You may need to enclose the plant in a tent of polyethylene, at least until flowering gets a good start.

When the last bud has opened and the last flower has faded, cut off the old stems and leaves and look for signs of new growth from the tuber. If you see the new leaves, continue watering

and fertilizing; and repeat the complete process as long as new sprouts are produced after flowering. If there is no new growth, water the plant a little less each time, until the soil is nearly dry. Store the tuber in the pot, in warmth (50-60°F.) and dim light. Check resting tubers frequently, and water often enough to keep them plump. When small new leaves appear, repot in fresh soil and start over.

The slipper-type gloxinias comprise a separate group of modern hybrids, and many of the original species in this category are still cultivated. These include *Sinningia eumorpha* (white slipper flowers, yellow- and lavender-throated), *S. pusilla* (a miniature with leaf span of 1½ in., and ⅜-in. lavender flowers on 1-in. stems), and *S. regina* (maroon-green leaves, beautifully veined with silver, suffused beneath with rosy purple, and reddish purple flowers).

Gloxinias are easily propagated from seeds sown at any season in warmth and high humidity; by leaf cuttings with an inch of petiole (leaf stalk) attached; by stem cuttings; and occasionally by tuber division. Specific techniques for gloxinia propagation are discussed in Chapter 3.

Smithiantha

DESCRIPTION: *S. cinnabarina,* from Mexico and Guatemala, was known until recently as a naegelia, and the arrangement of its beautiful flowers gave rise to the name "temple bells." The red-plush-covered, dark-green, heart-shaped leaves are magnificent, and when the nodding bells of scarlet and yellow rise above the foliage, the sight is nearly breath-taking. Numerous other smithiantha species and hybrids are in cultivation today. All have the plush-covered leaves, among the most richly textured of all plants, and they send up racemes of nodding bells in pastel colors, sometimes fiery orange-scarlet also.

Sow smithiantha seeds in April, May, or June; or plant the scaly rhizomes in summer. Blossoms come from November to April. Afterward, dry off and leave in dormancy and near dryness for several weeks until replanting time in summer.

CULTURE: Light, semi-sunny to semi-shady. Temperature, 60-75°F. in winter. Humidity, 50% or more. Soil, equal parts loam, sand, peat moss, and leaf mold; keep evenly moist, and fertilize biweekly, except during the season of dormancy described above. Propagate by dividing the rhizomes at potting time.

Streptocarpus

DESCRIPTION: *S. grandis,* from Zululand, Natal, is a strange plant which has only one leaf in its lifetime. From a dust-size seed, only twelve to eighteen months are required to attain a leaf up to 3 ft. long and 2 ft. wide. Near its base, along the midrib, small blue flowers appear on clustered stalks. *S. hybridus* 'Weismoor,' from Germany, and others, represent the wedding of most streptocarpus species into a modern-day plant with superb foliage, and bounteous clusters of colorful, tubular flowers which may reach a diameter of 5 in. *S. rexii,* from South Africa, is the original "Cape primrose," only common name for the genus, and it is still grown by collectors and used in breeding programs. *S. saxorum,* from Tanganyika, is entirely different from the other species. It has small, oval, fuzzy leaves in whorls on succulent stems. From the base of these grow the wiry stems which bear the white-throated, lavender-blue flowers. *S. saxorum* requires culture like episcia, but can get along nicely with other kinds of streptocarpus. It propagates easily from stem cuttings taken at any time, kept warm and in high humidity.

CULTURE: Light, semi-sunny to semi-shady. Temperature, 60-75°F. in winter. Humidity, 50% or more. Soil, equal parts loam, sand, peat moss, and leaf mold; keep evenly moist and provide biweekly feedings whenever plants are making active growth. Propagate by sowing seeds in January or February (for blooms about one year later); or, with species which grow like *S. rexii,* or hybrids like 'Weismoor,' by dividing old clumps.

Streptocarpus saxorum

GRASS FAMILY   Gramineae

Mostly slender plants with round, hollow stems and slender, pointed, parallel-veined leaves arising from swollen joints. They are cultivated as cereals and fodder, sugar and molasses, for starches, beverages, and many industrial uses, for pastures and lawns, and for garden ornament. It is the genera in this category which are of interest to the indoor gardener.

Arundinaria

DESCRIPTION: *A. falcata,* to 15 ft., from the Himalayas, is often called "sickle bamboo." Its hollow canes, to ½-in. thick, mature a warm, yellow-green. They are set with blue-green leaves 1 to 6 in. long.

CULTURE: Same as Bambusa.

Bambusa

DESCRIPTION: *B. nana,* 3 to 10 ft., from China and Japan, is the smallest bamboo commonly cultivated as a pot plant. Its small, light-green leaves with bluish reverses are sparsely set on dense-growing, thin, hollow canes.

CULTURE: Light, sunny to semi-sunny. Temperature, average house. Humidity, average house, with ample fresh air. Soil, equal parts loam, sand, peat moss, and leaf mold; keep evenly moist. Propagate by dividing large clumps in the spring.

Oplismenus

DESCRIPTION: *O. hirtellus variegatus,* from the West Indies, has thin, papery leaves striped with white and pink. It is often called "basket grass," and may be used also as a regular pot plant.

CULTURE: Same as Bambusa.

Stenotaphrum

DESCRIPTION: *S. secundatum variegatum,* from the tropical parts of America, creeps rapidly by stolons, and sends up straight, slim, round-tipped leaves of creamy white on green. In its plain-leaved form, this is the popular St. Augustine grass of the South.

CULTURE: Same as Bambusa.

IRIS FAMILY   Iridaceae

Herbs with flattened fans of sword-shaped or grassy leaves, and showy flowers. Only two genera are of real interest to the indoor gardener, although lapeyrousia (grown like freesia) is increasing in popularity.

Freesia

DESCRIPTION: An extensively hybridized group of South African plants, growing about 20 in. high from corms. The fragrant, flaring, tubular flowers occur in a one-sided cluster at right angles to the stem and to the tall, erect leaves. Mostly yellow or white in the species, the flowers of hybrids appear in pastel colors. Corms are planted from August to November, 1 in. deep and 2 in. apart; blooms come January to April.

CULTURE: Light, sunny to semi-sunny. Temperature, cool, not above 70°F.

in winter. Humidity, 50% or more. Soil, equal parts loam, sand, and peat moss; keep evenly moist and give biweekly feedings while growth is active; keep dry balance of year. Propagate by sowing seeds in spring, and by removing offsets at repotting time.

Neomarica

DESCRIPTION: *N. gracilis,* from Brazil to Mexico (white with blue flowers), and *N. northiana,* from Brazil (white with violet, brown, and yellow flowers) are known as apostle plants because legend says that twelve sword-shaped leaves, grouped in a fan, will form before one turns brown. Unfortunately, this is not always true. The flowers, small and irislike, are short-lived, and appear on a leaflike scape.

When flowering has finished on *N. northiana,* baby plants develop from the same place which produced blossoms. When these are large enough, the scape bends over so that the new plants may take root in soil. This habit gives this neomarica another common name, "walking-iris." *Marica* was the former name of this genus. CULTURE: Light, sunny to semi-sunny. Temperature, on the cool side, preferably not over 72°F. in winter. Humidity, 30% or more. Soil, equal parts loam, sand, and peat moss; keep evenly moist at all times. Propagate from the small plants which may be pinned down to small pots of soil, and severed from the scape when sufficiently rooted, or by division of the rhizomes.

MINT FAMILY   Labiatae

Tender and hardy herbs, some tropical shrubs, mostly with square stems, opposite, aromatic leaves, and irregular flowers. Nine of these—lavandula, majorana, marrubium, mentha, nepeta, ocimum, origanum, rosmarinus, and thymus—are discussed in Chapter 6. Two other genera are of interest to the indoor gardener.

Coleus

DESCRIPTION: *C. blumei,* 1 to 3 ft., from Java, and its countless hybrids are erect plants with highly colored leaves, most of them displaying two or more colors in more or less regular patterns. *C. rehneltianus,* from Ceylon, is the parent of most of the prostrate or creeping forms. All are primarily foliage plants which will grow more luxuriantly if the flower buds are picked off as soon as they are noticed. CULTURE: Light, sunny to semi-sunny. Temperature, average house. Hu-

midity, average house, with some fresh air. Soil, equal parts loam, sand, and peat moss; keep evenly moist. Propagate by seeds sown in late winter or spring, or by stem cuttings taken at any time. They root readily in water or soil.

Plectranthus

DESCRIPTION: *P. australis,* from Australia and other Pacific islands, has waxy green, scalloped leaves on trailing stems; spikes of white flowers. *P. oertendahli,* from Natal, has silver-

Plectranthus oertendahli

veined leaves, purple-margined and purple beneath; spikes of pale-pink

flowers. *P. purpuratus,* from Natal, is smaller than the other species. It has velvet-textured, fleshy leaves with purple beneath, and lavender flowers.

Recent interest in this genus has made known, and sometimes available, other species which are equally valuable as basket or shelf plants. *P. coleoides,* for example, is a small, upright plant, with white-margined, green leaves.

CULTURE: Same as Coleus, except that plectranthus is more tolerant of dim lighting.

PEA FAMILY   Leguminosae

The legumes are characterized by butterflylike flowers, as in the sweet pea. Of approximately 500 genera in the family, several are of interest to the indoor gardener. *Poinciana* and *Tamarindus* seedlings, for example, grow easily in a fluorescent-light garden. Also adapt to bonsai training. Two favorite genera are included here.

Acacia

DESCRIPTION: These shrubs or trees are famed—and loved—for sprays of puffy yellow, fragrant flowers from February to April. They will grow only in a winter atmosphere that is sunny, airy, moist, and cool—preferably 35 to 40°F. If you can provide these conditions, grow *A. armata, A. baileyana,* or *A. farnesiana.*

CULTURE: Light, sunny to semi-sunny. Temperature, cool from fall to spring. Humidity, 30% or more, and fresh air. Soil, equal parts loam, sand, and peat moss; keep evenly moist. Prune after flowering. Propagate from seeds or cuttings in the spring.

Calliandra

DESCRIPTION: Tub-sized trees with locustlike leaves and red, powder-puff flowers. Recommended for pot culture: *C. haematocephala, C. surinamensis,* and *C. tweedii;* winter-flowering, except *tweedii* tends to be everblooming. Foliage attractive all year.

CULTURE: Light, sunny. Temperature, moderate in winter. Humidity, 30% or more, with some fresh air. Soil, equal parts loam, sand, and peat moss; keep evenly moist. Prune back after flowering. Propagate by air-layering or cutting in the spring.

LILY FAMILY

Liliaceae

Herbs, vines, and treelike plants, often bulbous, with leaf veins mostly running parallel. The regular flowers are six-parted and have a superior ovary (that is, it occurs inside the flower).

Agapanthus

DESCRIPTION: *A. africanus,* 1½ to 2 ft., from the Cape of Good Hope, is known as blue African lily. The white-flowered *A. orientalis albus,* 2 to 3 ft., from South Africa, is called lily-of-the-Nile; it is available also in a blue-flowered form. These are large, tuberous-rooted, summer-flowering plants which are best handled in roomy tubs instead of the more conventional pots (the roots are so strong, they may burst clay pots).

Agapanthus is generally kept dormant during the winter, with only enough water and light given to keep the strap-shaped leaves from falling. Beginning in the spring, give the plants full light with some sun, and keep the soil constantly moist. Feeding at this time with any complete, balanced plant food will aid in producing flowers with the finest color and texture; supplemental feedings during and after bloom will result in stronger roots for the following season.

Other worthy varieties of agapanthus include *A. orientalis* 'Dwarf White,' with flower stems only about 18 in. tall; 'Peter Pan,' a graceful miniature with foliage to 8 in. and blue flowers on 2-ft. stalks; and *A. globosus flore plena,* a small plant with fully double, deep-blue blossoms. For limited areas, as in window gardens, these smaller plants are more satisfactory than the usual, larger ones.

CULTURE: Light, sunny to semi-shady. Temperature, cool to average house, preferably not over 72°F. in winter. Humidity, average house. Soil, equal parts loam, sand, and peat moss; follow moisture directions given above. Propagate by division in early spring.

Aloe

DESCRIPTION: This genus contains succulent members of the lily family, native principally to South Africa. Although many amateur gardeners mistake aloes for agaves, and vice versa, the two are easily distinguished by even a superficial examination of the leaves. Those of agaves are tough and fibrous, while those of aloes are

Agapanthus africanus

Aloe variegata

juicy and tender. Nearly 200 species of aloe are known, ranging in size from plants less than an inch in height to ones which are treelike both in size and in shape.

Aloes form rosettes of leaves, and suckers sent up from the base of the parent plant (which can be used for propagating) soon fill a pot with showy foliage. Some varieties have spotted leaves, some are plain, some are smooth-margined, while others are equipped not only with teeth but also with a sharp terminal spine. Some aloes (partridge-breast, A. variegata, for example), have three-sided leaves.

South African plants normally bloom during our winter; thus, aloes are treasured for the bloom they provide in our bleak months. The spirelike racemes held well above the foliage bear tubular flowers, predominantly red.

CULTURE: Light, sunny to semi-sunny. Temperature, average house, but preferably not over 75°F. in winter. Humidity, average house. Soil, equal parts loam, sand, and peat moss; keep evenly moist, allowing to become dry occasionally. Overwatering

will kill aloes. Propagate by removing offsets or by sowing seeds.

Asparagus

DESCRIPTION: A. asparagoides myrtifolius, small climber from the Cape of Good Hope, is the "baby smilax" used by florists in wedding and other decorations. A. plumosus, from South Africa, grows naturally as a climber, but can be kept in cultivation as a small clump of exceedingly fine, fernlike growth. It is this foliage which so often comes with roses from the florist. A. sprengeri, from western Africa and Natal, bears inch-long needles of bright green on thorny stems. Its small, fragrant, white flowers are followed by showy red berries.

CULTURE: Light, semi-sunny to shady. Temperature, average house, preferably not over 72°F. in winter. Humidity, average house, with ample fresh air. Soil, equal parts loam, sand, and peat moss; keep evenly moist. Propagate by sowing seeds, or by dividing the clumps in spring or fall.

Aspidistra

DESCRIPTION: A. elatior, from China, has been a favorite for generations. Sometimes called "cast-iron plant" because of its ability to withstand all sorts of vicissitudes. Commercial florists and amateur flower arrangers find the leaves effective and long-lasting.

In addition to the species with plain, shiny, blackish green leaves, which often measure over 2 ft. in length, there is available a variegated type, A. elatior variegata, with leaves alternating green and white stripes in varying widths.

CULTURE: Light, semi-sunny to shady.

Temperature, cool, preferably not over 75°F. in winter. Humidity, average house, but 30% or more will result in more luxuriant growth. Soil, equal parts loam, sand, and peat moss; keep evenly moist. Propagate by dividing the roots in late winter or spring.

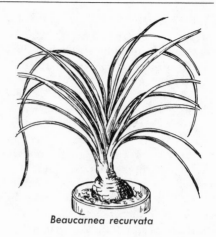

Beaucarnea recurvata

Aspidistra elatior variegata

Beaucarnea

DESCRIPTION: *B. recurvata,* the elephant foot plant, or "pony-tail," is an unusual, desert-dwelling member of the lily family, notable primarily for a large, swollen base in which it can store a year's supply of water. With great age, beaucarnea may attain a height of 30 ft., but small plants are ideal as indoor specimens, and slow-growing enough to remain a convenient size for many years. Topping the bulbous base, the bottle plant has a rosette of thin, exceedingly long, tough leaves. In lily fashion, it produces panicles of whitish flowers, small and lightly fragrant.
CULTURE: Light, sunny to semi-sunny. Temperature, average house, preferably not over 75°F. in winter. Humidity, average house. Soil, equal parts loam, sand, and peat moss;

keep evenly moist. Propagate by removing offsets.

Bowiea

DESCRIPTION: *B. volubilis,* from South Africa, is a novelty sometimes grown in the indoor garden. Above ground it has a fat, light-green bulb which sends up almost leafless, branched stems which twine if support is furnished. The flowers are insignificant, small and greenish white. Often called "climbing onion."
CULTURE: Light, semi-sunny to semi-shady. Temperature, cool, not over 72°F. in winter. Humidity, average house. Soil, equal parts loam, sand, and peat moss; keep evenly moist, except dry during dormancy in fall and early winter. Propagate by removing offsets.

Chlorophytum

DESCRIPTION: *C. bichetii,* from Siam, is a miniature, tuft-forming, grassy plant of white-margined and striped leaves. *C. comosum mandaianum,* with white-striped leaves; *C. comosum picturatum,* with yellow-striped leaves;

and *C. elatum vittatum*, with white-striped leaves, are all South African plants with informal rosettes of daylilylike foliage. All send up tall, slender racemes of small white flowers which are followed later by new plants, thus giving rise to the popular names "airplane-plant" and "spider plant." As soon as the weight of the new plants is great enough, the stem will bend over, and, if it comes in contact with soil, prompt rooting occurs; after a few weeks the stolon may then be cut away.
CULTURE: Light, semi-sunny to shady. Temperature, average house. Humidity, average house. Soil, equal parts loam, sand, and peat moss; keep evenly moist. Propagate by removing aerial plantlets (see above), or by division.

Convallaria

DESCRIPTION: *C. majalis,* from temperate Asia and Europe, is known everywhere as "lily-of-the-valley." It is hardy outdoors, but can be forced inside. Buy specially prepared roots which are available in the fall. Space them 1 or 2 in. apart with the buds just above the surface in equal parts loam, sand, and peat moss. Keep evenly moist and on the cool side, preferably not over 70°F. Keep in a dark place for about ten days, then gradually expose to light, finally moving to a place which receives about two hours of sun each day. They will bloom in about three weeks. Afterward, either plant outdoors in a shady place, or discard. Be sure to order forcing roots; otherwise, your nurseryman may wait until late March or early April to ship.

Cordyline

DESCRIPTION: *C. terminalis,* from India, and its many varieties, including the popular "Hawaiian ti" are outstanding and durable foliage plants. They mature with a crown of palmlike leaves atop a trunk or cane which may grow to a height of 10 ft. or more outdoors in warm climates, but considerably less when roots are restricted by a pot. Cordylines differ only slightly from Dracaenas, and may sometimes be listed as such.
CULTURE: Same as Dracaena.

Dracaena

DESCRIPTION: Dracaenas are decorative foliage plants with sword-shaped leaves, hence "corn plant," usually crowded at the top of canelike stems. Most common of the genus is *D. marginata,* with dark green leaves banded marginally in red set in rosette fashion along slender, twisting canes. *D. sanderiana* and its variety 'Margaret Berkery' have white-striped green leaves, wider than *marginata.*

Dracaena sanderiana
'Margaret Berkery'

Dracaena marginata

D. fragrans, from Ethiopia, Guinea, and Sierra Leone, was the species best known to Victorian homes, a large-growing plant with soft-leathery leaves of shining green. Its varieties show extremely colorful variegation, being banded, striped, or margined in yellow or cream. The species sends up terminal racemes of small, creamy white, fragrant flowers occasionally.

Dracaena fragrans 'Victoriae'

D. godseffiana, from Guinea and the Congo, and its numerous varieties display an entirely different growth habit from the dracaenas described above. These are mostly small plants, inclined to be shrubby, with wiry stems bearing leaves in pairs or tiers of three, irregularly

Dracaena goldieana

marked with yellow or white. *D. goldieana,* from Upper Guinea, is halfway between these two types. It is broad-leaved but grows in rosette form. The foliage is spectacularly crossbanded with pale green or white. It is considered the most beautiful of all dracaenas. (See also Cordyline.) CULTURE: Light, semi-sunny to shady. Temperature, average house. Humidity, average house. Soil, equal parts loam, sand, and peat moss; keep evenly moist. Propagate by stem cuttings, or by root division.

Gasteria

DESCRIPTION: All species of gasteria have stiff, tongue-shaped leaves, often smooth but sometimes warted, from which they receive the common name of "ox-tongue plant." They are perfectly suited to pot culture for, while they stand some neglect, they will re-

Gasteria lingua

Gloriosa rothschildiana

parts peat moss, sand, and leaf mold; an azalea or bulb pan makes a good container. Provide strings or wires for the plants to climb on, as their heavy, branching stems require firm support. G. rothschildiana blooms in

ward the thoughtful grower with numerous offsets and freely-borne spikes of green-tipped pink or red tubular flowers. All come from South Africa.

CULTURE: Light, semi-sunny to semi-shady. Temperature, average house. Humidity, average house. Soil, equal parts loam, sand, and peat moss; keep evenly moist, except slightly less so in winter. Propagate by sowing seeds or by removing offsets.

Gloriosa

DESCRIPTION: G. rothschildiana, from Uganda, the climbing- or glory-lily, climbs by means of tendrils which are long extensions of the leaf tips. The flowers, of true lily form, with sharply reflexed petals, arise from the leaf axils as the plant grows. Most species have blossoms crimson at the outer parts, golden toward the base, but some are pure yellow. A few have crisped petals, a trait which adds to the beauty of the flowers.

Plant the cigarlike tubers of gloriosa 4 in. deep in a mixture of equal

spring and summer, but by resting the tubers after flowering, it may be brought into bloom any time. Other species flower in late summer and fall.

CULTURE: Light, sunny to semi-sunny. Temperature, average house. Humidity, 50% or more. Soil, see paragraph above. Keep evenly moist in growing season, nearly dry at other times. Propagate by tuber division at repotting time in spring, or by sowing seeds in winter or spring.

Haworthia

DESCRIPTION: There are nearly a hundred species of haworthia, succulents native to South Africa, and their rosettes of thick leaves exhibit a wide variety of forms. One of the best known is H. fasciata, called "zebra haworthia" because its dark-green leaves are banded crosswise

Haworthia fasciata

with rows of white warts. *H. attenuata* has these raised white dots set so thickly on its leaves that it is called the "wart plant."

The windowed haworthias are completely different from those with firm-fleshed leaves. Their rosettes are of soft leaves which have transparent or translucent edges or tips, thus permitting light to penetrate to the main part of the plant even when it is mostly underground during the extreme droughts of its native habitat.

H. viscosa represents a third type, which forms a stiff, triangular column nearly 8 in. tall.

CULTURE: Light, sunny to semi-sunny. Temperature, average house. Humid-

Haworthia cuspidata

ity, average house. Soil, equal parts loam, sand, and peat moss; water only when the surface has become dry. Propagate by sowing seeds or removing offsets.

Lachenalia

DESCRIPTION: Members of this South African genus are called "Cape cowslips." They are small, bulbous, spring-flowering plants, with spikes of bloom similar in form to those of hyacinths but brightly and variously colored.

CULTURE: Light, sunny in fall, winter, and spring; darkness during summer dormancy. Temperature, cool, not over 70°F. in fall and winter. Humidity, 30% or more. Soil, equal parts loam, sand, and peat moss; keep evenly moist, except dry in summer. Propagate by removing offsets at potting time in early fall.

Lilium

DESCRIPTION: The only lilium which indoor gardeners have much to do with is *Lilium longiflorum eximium,* the Easter lily, and it is a transient in the window garden. When a gift plant is received, punch your thumb through the foil covering the pot base to be sure the drainage hole is unobstructed. Then set the pot in a bowl of water to soak for a few hours. Remove, drain, and water again only when the topsoil begins to feel dry. Keep in a fully bright place, but without too much direct sunlight. A cool location will prolong the life of the blossoms. After flowering has finished, and the stalk begins to look yellow, reduce the amount of water given until the plant goes completely dry and the top can be removed with a slight, twisting pull. Set the pot in a cool, dark place until the weather permits setting the bulb (unpotted) in the outdoor perennial bed, covering with 6-8 in. of sandy, humusy soil. Here it may flower again, either the same season or another year. Once forced for pot-flowering, lily bulbs are of no further use in the indoor garden.

Ophiopogon

DESCRIPTION: Interesting plants grown for grassy foliage, and also for the bright-blue berries which sometimes form. The foliage is evergreen, and may be plain or variegated. Flowers are usually white, nodding, on foot-long stems. Often called "lily-turf." Most ophiopogons grow from short, thick rhizomes, with underground fibrous roots which may act as stolons, or thicken into tubers. *O. arabicum* is distinguished by having almost black leaves and berries, with lavender flowers.

CULTURE: Light, semi-sunny to semi-shady. Temperature, on the cool side, not over 72°F. in winter. Humidity, 30% or more, with ample fresh air. Soil, equal parts loam, sand, and peat moss; keep evenly moist. Propagate by division at any time.

Phormium

DESCRIPTION: *P. tenax*, the New Zealand flax, has leathery, sword-shaped leaves 18 in. to several feet long; they are deep, brownish green with orange-red at the margin. The variety *atropurpureum* has leaves in shimmering red-purple and deep bronze. Both are good for accent in a collection of house plants.

CULTURE: Light, sunny to semi-sunny. Temperature, on the cool side, prefer-

ably not over 75°F. in winter. Humidity, average house, with ample fresh air. Soil, equal parts loam, sand, and peat moss; keep evenly moist. Propagate by removing offsets.

Pleomele reflexa variegata

Pleomele

DESCRIPTION: *P. reflexa* surrounds tall (to 12 ft.), graceful cane stems with short, narrow, dark green leaves. Its variegated form, called Song of India, has yellow stripes. *P. thalioides* looks more like a compact form of *Spathiphyllum*. In profile its reflexed leaves may remind you of a Balinese dancer.

CULTURE: Same as Dracaena.

Sansevieria

DESCRIPTION: *S. cylindrica*, to 5 ft., from South Africa, has round, tapered, dark-green leaves; pink flowers. *S. trifasciata* ("snake plant" or "mother-in-law's tongue"), from India and tropical Africa, and its

Sansevieria 'Golden Hahnii'

of small, blue-tinted, white flowers with reflexed petals on delicate stems. CULTURE: Light, semi-sunny to semi-shady. Temperature, average house, but preferably not over 75°F. in winter. Humidity, 50% or more, with

Scilla violacea

many varieties are grown for their stiff, usually spearlike, often variegated leaves. They may be divided into two classes—the bird's-nest types which form low (to 8 in.), neat, compact rosettes of foliage, and the tall kinds (to 5 ft.), whose leaves stand erect from the soil surface. The leaves may be plain green or crossbanded with lighter or darker shades, or banded or margined with near-white or bright yellow. Occasionally sansevierias send up tall, showy, arching sprays crowded with small, greenish white, fragrant flowers. CULTURE: Light, sunny to shady. Temperature, average house. Humidity, average house. Soil, equal parts loam, sand, and peat moss; water heavily, then not again until soil begins to feel dry. Propagate by division of the creeping rootstock, or by inserting 3-in. sections of the leaves to half their length in sandy soil.

Scilla

DESCRIPTION: *S. violacea,* to 8 in., from South Africa, has fleshy, slender, olive-green leaves attractively spotted with pewter, and lined maroon beneath. In winter it sends up spikes

ample fresh air. Soil, equal parts loam, sand, and peat moss; keep evenly moist, except slightly less so in summer and early fall. Propagate by removing offsets at repotting time in autumn.

Tulbaghia

DESCRIPTION: *T. fragrans,* from Transvaal, sends up slender stems crowned by an umbel of lavender-pink, fragrant flowers, above an attractive fan of strap leaves about 15 in. tall. Sometimes called "pink agapanthus." *T. violacea,* from South Africa, has narrow, garlic-scented leaves, and umbels of showy, lilac, star-shaped flowers atop 18- to 24-in. stems. CULTURE: Light, sunny to semi-sunny. Temperature, average house, preferably not over 72°F. for long periods in winter. Humidity, average house, with some fresh air. Soil, equal parts loam, sand, and peat moss; keep evenly moist. Propagate by removing offsets in spring or fall.

Veltheimia

DESCRIPTION: Handsome bulbous plants from South Africa, having shiny green leaves 1 ft. long and tubular flowers borne in dense racemes atop tall stalks above the basal foliage. *T. viridifolia*, the species customarily grown as a house plant, has green-tipped, pink flowers.
CULTURE: Same as Lachenalia.

LOGANIA FAMILY   Loganiaceae

This large family includes two popular ornamental shrubs, *Buddleia* and *Gelsemium*, neither of particular interest as house plants. However, the genus *Nicodemia* provides one excellent indoor shrub.

Nicodemia

DESCRIPTION: *N. diversifolia*, the indoor oak, has bluish-green leaves shaped like those of the English oak (to which it is not related). It makes an interesting color contrast in a collection of green plants.
CULTURE: Light, semi-sunny to semi-shady. Temperature, moderate to cool in winter. Humidity, 30% or more. Soil, equal parts loam, sand, and peat moss; keep evenly moist at all times. Propagate by cuttings.

Nicodemia diversifolia

LOOSESTRIFE FAMILY   Lythraceae

Shrubs, trees, and herbaceous plants, characterized by whorled or alternate leaves and showy flowers. Two genera are of interest here.

Cuphea

DESCRIPTION: *C. hyssopifolia*, or elfin-herb, has wiry branches densely set with small leaves and starlike, purplish-rose flowers. It is easily kept under 12 in. as a pot plant; excellent for bonsai work, also for fluorescent-light culture.
CULTURE: Light, sunny to semi-sunny. Temperature, moderate to average house. Humidity, 30% or

more, with some fresh air. Soil, equal parts garden loam, sand, and peat moss; keep evenly moist. Propagate from cuttings in spring.

Lagerstroemia

DESCRIPTION: *L. indica* is the ever-popular crape-myrtle of Southern gardens. A new miniature form from the George W. Park Seed Company, called crape-myrtlette, is excellent for pot culture in a window or in a fluorescent-light garden. It can also be trained as a bonsai.

CULTURE: Light, sunny to semi-sunny. Temperature, moderate to average house. Humidity, 30% or more, with some fresh air. Soil, equal parts loam, sand, and peat moss; keep evenly moist. Propagate by sowing seeds or taking cuttings in spring.

MALPIGHIA FAMILY   Malpighiaceae

Trees, shrubs, and vines from tropical America with evergreen, opposite leaves, and insignificant, five-petaled flowers. Only one genus is of interest to the indoor gardener.

Malpighia

DESCRIPTION: *M. coccigera,* from the West Indies, is called "miniature holly" because of its spiny-margined, small, glossy leaves; delicate, crepe-textured ½-in. pink flowers come in summer. *M. glabra,* the Barbados cherry, from tropical America, is a slender-branched shrub with neat, pointed-oval leaves, and umbels of fringed, rose-red blossoms followed by scarlet, cherry-sized fruit.

CULTURE: Light, sunny to semi-sunny. Temperature, cool, preferably not over 75°F. in winter. Humidity, 30% or more. Soil, equal parts loam, sand, and peat moss; keep constantly moist. Propagate by sowing seeds or taking cuttings in spring.

MALLOW FAMILY   Malvaceae

Herbs, shrubs, and trees from all over the world. The alternate leaves are usually lobed, or deeply cut, and the flowers of most genera are showy.

Abutilon

DESCRIPTION: This evergreen shrub, known in the past as "parlor-maple," and today as "flowering-maple," has soft-haired, long-stalked, attractively lobed leaves. Except for *A. megapotamicum variegatum,* from Brazil, which is cultivated both for colorful foliage and blossoms, abutilons are most prized for their showy, bell-shaped, hollyhocklike, pendent blossoms of white, yellow, salmon, orange, pink, or red. Most are everblooming.

The abutilon grows rapidly and needs shifting to larger pots as it develops. When the plant is in the largest-sized pot which can be

Abutilon megapotamicum variegatum

handled conveniently allow it to become pot-bound, and make up for the restricted root room by giving supplemental feedings at biweekly intervals. Prune the plant as it grows, to encourage more symmetrical, compact growth and greater branching. Since the plant flowers on new, terminal growth, an increase in the number of branches results in more bloom.

CULTURE: Light, sunny to semi-sunny. Temperature, average house. Humidity, average house. Soil, equal parts loam, sand, and peat moss; keep evenly moist at all times. Propagate by sowing seeds in winter or spring, or by taking cuttings at any time.

Hibiscus

DESCRIPTION: *H. rosa-sinensis,* the rose-of-China, or "flower-of-a-day," and

its varieties are ideally suited to pot culture. Do not confuse these tender tropical evergreen shrubs with their hardy relatives known as rose-of-Sharon (*H. syriacus* varieties, sometimes called altheas), or with the herbaceous, non-woody, rose-mallows (*H. moscheutos* varieties).

The Chinese hibiscus are noted for their hollyhocklike blossoms, which may be single or double, and in shades of yellow through salmon and pink to red. Sunlight is necessary for flower production, with the long-stalked blossoms forming in the leaf axils of new growth. Ample moisture, at the roots and in the air, will prevent premature bud drop. Normally the flowers remain open only for a day, and, if removed from the shrub, will not require water in order to stay fresh for their usual length of time. Conversely, no amount of water, or other treatment, will keep them open past closing hour. Only a few varieties remain fresh longer than a day.

Hibiscus begin to bloom when only a few inches high, and are almost everblooming when grown properly.

Hibiscus rosa-sinensis

In time they will develop into shrubs which can easily be maintained at any desired size by pruning.

While most of these hibiscus have large, toothed, glossy-green leaves, a few show attractive variegation. *H. rosa-sinensis cooperi* is grown primarily for leaves which are highly variegated with metallic green, white, pink, and crimson.

CULTURE: Light, sunny. Temperature, average house. Humidity, 30% or more. Soil, equal parts loam, sand, and peat moss; keep evenly moist at all times. Propagate by rooting 4-in. stem cuttings.

ARROWROOT FAMILY   Marantaceae

Herbs from tropical America, with handsome foliage, many with tuberous roots. Basal leaves narrow toward the stem to sheath it, and the flowers, usually not showy, are sheathed by bracts.

Calathea

DESCRIPTION: Calatheas, often identified as marantas, comprise an extremely large group of highly decorative foliage plants which have proved themselves worth while for indoor cultivation. More than a dozen are readily available, with another three dozen or so identified, named, and well on their way into commerce. Calatheas have rhizomatous roots, and the leaves arise from the crown in tufts. They sucker readily, and in no time will fill a pot with foliage.

Leaves of calatheas are long, broad, and pointed at the tip. The veins run diagonally from the main rib to the outer edge of the leaf, and most coloration follows this general direction. In some varieties, the leaf reverses are also highly colored.

CULTURE: Light, semi-shady. Temperature, average house. Humidity, 50% or more. Soil, equal parts loam, sand, peat moss, and leaf mold; keep evenly moist. Feed established plants biweekly except in late fall and early winter. Propagate by division of the roots at repotting time, preferably in the spring.

Maranta

DESCRIPTION: *M. leuconeura kerchoveana*, from Brazil, has broad, bright-green leaves with rows of brownish to dark-green blotches on either side of the midrib, hence "rabbit-track plant." At night the leaves fold upward like hands in supplication, thus giving rise to the name "prayer plant." *M. leuconeura massangeana* is strikingly colored, with parallel stripes of silver

Calathea zebrina

Maranta leuconeura kerchoveana

and pink from the midrib to the leaf margins, the leaf surface feathered in silver along the main rib, shading into bright brown to blue-green at the edges.
CULTURE: Light, semi-shady. Temperature, average house. Humidity, 30% or more. Soil, equal parts loam, sand, peat moss, and leaf mold; keep evenly moist, but slightly drier during December, January, and February. This partial rest will result in more vigorous growth, after repotting in March. Propagate by division at transplanting time.

MEADOW-BEAUTY FAMILY   Melastomataceae

Tropical herbs, shrubs, and trees, frequently from the Amazon valley, with opposite or whorled, showy leaves. The decorative flowers sometimes have colorful bracts.

Bertolonia

DESCRIPTION: Bertolonias are among the most beautiful of all the small tropical foliage plants. *B. maculata,* from Brazil, with brown oval leaves margined in red, sprinkled with silver along the midvein, with red reverses and completely covered with long hairs, is a choice plant which has been offered in the trade, but not frequently. *B. pubescens,* from Ecuador, another gem, has puckered oval leaves of green, banded through the center with purple-brown, and shorter hairs than *B. maculata.* Other bertolonias, species, and cultivars may display clear carmine, bright white or brilliant purple in the leaves, and distinctively colored veins and reverses. Small blossoms often are produced atop erect stems just above the leaves. These are not easy plants to grow.
CULTURE: Light, semi-shady to shady. Temperature, evenly warm (65-75°F.). Humidity, 50% or more. Soil, equal parts loam, sand, peat moss, and leaf mold; keep evenly moist. If

Bertolonia maculata

he leaves begin to turn brown at the ips, increase the humidity and check o be sure the plant is not receiving oo much direct sunlight. Propagate y sowing seeds, or by rooting cuttings n warmth and high humidity.

Schizocentron

DESCRIPTION: *S. elegans,* from Mexico, s a succulent, creeping plant which vill root at each node if the reddish tems are in contact with damp soil. t has small, deep-green, slightly hairy eaves, and bears large, magenta-colored blossoms during summer. When these cascade from a basket, or drape a table edge, it is obvious vhy the plant is called "Spanish hawl."

CULTURE: Light, semi-sunny to semi-hady. Temperature, cool, preferably not over 72° F. in winter. Humidity, 0% or more. Soil, equal parts loam, and, and peat moss; keep evenly moist. Propagate by cuttings rooted n warmth and high humidity.

Tibouchina

DESCRIPTION: *T. semidecandra,* from outhern Brazil, is a medium-sized

evergreen shrub popularly called "princess-flower" or "glory-bush." It has bronze-green, hairy leaves and large royal-purple, velvety flowers. It is a winter-flowering plant which begins to bloom when scarcely more

Tibouchina semidecandra

than a foot high, and does best grown fresh each year from cuttings made in spring or summer. Often trained in tree form (see Chapter 9).

CULTURE: Same as Schizocentron, except provide more sun.

FIG FAMILY   Moraceae

Vines, shrubs, and trees of temperate as well as tropical origin, grown for edible fruit or handsome foliage; rubber is derived from some. Only one genus is of interest to the indoor gardener.

Ficus

DESCRIPTION: *F. carica,* common fig, rom the Mediterranean region, makes a striking foliage plant in a arge tub (14-in. diameter, or more). *F. diversifolia,* from India, Java, and Malaya, is a twiggy, small plant with dark-green leaves to 2 in., shaped

like a fig fruit, and ½-in. yellow "figs," which are not edible. *F. elastica,* from India and Malaya, and its varieties are the durable "rubber plants," widely cultivated for large, bold-textured, sometimes colorfully variegated foliage. *F. lyrata* (often

Ficus elastica decora

Ficus benjamina

called *F. pandurata*), from tropical
West Africa, has very large, shiny,
leatherlike, wavy-edged leaves whose
shape suggests the popular name
"fiddleleaf rubber plant."

Weeping fig, *F. benjamina,* is one
of the best, and consequently most
popular, of all indoor trees. The
leaves, about 2 in. long, are shiny,
bright to dark green, on gracefully
drooping branches. Indian laurel,
F. retusa nitida, is similar, except
erect in habit. In fact, it can be
pruned to stylish, formal shapes.
The more light these receive, the
more foliage they can retain. Both
tolerate maintenance under Cool
Beam or Cool-Lux spotlight illumination.

The creeping figs, *F. pumila* from
Australia, China, and Japan, and
F. radicans, from the East Indies, are

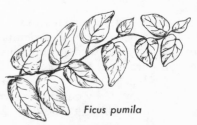

Ficus pumila

remarkably different from the upright kinds. They have heart-shaped
leaves from ½ to 2 in. long, plain
green or variegated, on prostrate
stems. Occasionally these climb by
clinging to a damp surface.

CULTURE: Light, semi-sunny to shady.
Temperature, average house. Humidity, average house, but preferably
30% or more. Soil, equal parts loam,
sand, and peat moss; keep evenly
moist. Propagate by air-layering or
from cuttings, especially in spring

BANANA FAMILY   Musaceae

The largest of all herbs, some tree-sized, of tropical origin, cultivated for edible fruit, showy flowers, or distinctive foliage.

Heliconia

DESCRIPTION: *H. rostrata,* to 6 ft., from Brazil, has banana-like leaves, and exceedingly showy red bracts with yellow ends, which surround the flowers. Other species of interest to the indoor gardener include *H. aurantiaca, H. brasiliensis,* and *H. velutina.*
CULTURE: Light, semi-sunny. Temperature, average house. Humidity, 50% or more, with ample fresh air. Soil, equal parts loam, sand, peat moss, and leaf mold; keep evenly moist. Propagate by dividing the roots in late winter or spring.

Musa

DESCRIPTION: *M. coccinea,* the red banana, to 5 ft., from Vietnam, has golden flowers and yellow-tipped scarlet bracts followed by ornamental orange fruit. *M. nana* (or *M. cavendishii*), the dwarf, ladyfinger banana

Musa rosacea

from southern China, bears edible fruit over 3 in. long. *M. rosacea,* from India, is grown for its bright-green leaves, which have an iridescent purple-red midrib, and yellow flowers; 3-in. fruit not edible. *M. velutina,* 3 to 6 ft., from Assam, is probably the most dwarf species discussed here. It bears erect clusters of pale yellow or pinkish flowers in red bracts, and soft, pink fruit.
CULTURE: Light, sunny to semi-shady. Temperature, average house. Humidity, 30% or more, with ample fresh air. Soil, equal parts loam, sand, peat moss, and leaf mold; keep evenly moist. Feed biweekly in spring and summer. Plant in large pots, at least 12 in. across. Propagate in March by removing suckers which form at base of parent plant; also by sowing seeds in warmth and moisture in winter or spring.

Orchidantha

DESCRIPTION: Sometimes listed as lowea, orchidanthas are fairly low-growing plants, resembling in leaf and habit an aspidistra. The flowers are orchidlike, pale yellow and purple in *O. borneensis,* while in *O. maxillarioides,* from Malaya, a slightly taller plant, the blossoms are green-lipped, with purple variegation and calyx. Although seldom offered in the trade, the plants are not difficult to grow.

CULTURE: Light, semi-shady. Temperature, average house. Humidity, 50% or more. Soil, equal parts loam, sand, peat moss, and leaf mold; keep evenly moist. Propagate by division in spring.

Strelitzia

DESCRIPTION: *S. reginae,* the bird-of-paradise flower, from South Africa, has become a favorite house plant in recent years. It has large banana-like foliage, and flowers of unusual form. They are orange-petaled, with a blue tongue, and appear from red-edged, green, boat-shaped bracts at the top of the plant or in the upper axils. A dwarf form of this species grows only about 18 in. tall.

CULTURE: Light, sunny to semi-sunny. Temperature, cool, not over 75°F. for long periods in winter. Humidity, 30% or more. Soil, equal parts loam, sand, and peat moss; keep evenly

Strelitzia reginae

moist, allowing to become slightl dry occasionally. Propagate by divi sion of the rhizomes, or by removin suckers in the spring. Plant in larg pot or tub (10- to 15-in. size) an avoid disturbing until container nearly bursting. Feed biweekly excep during the shortest days of the yea

MYRSINE FAMILY   **Myrsinacea**

Tropical trees and shrubs with opposite, evergreen, leathery leaves an insignificant flowers which are often followed by colorful berries. Only on genus is of interest to the indoor gardener.

Ardisia

DESCRIPTION: *A. crispa* (or *A. crenulata*), from China and Malaya, is often used for Christmas decoration because of its red, hollylike berries and leaves. The plant makes a graceful small tree, and attains considerable maturity before it will produce the fragrant white or pinkish blossoms which precede the berries. Often called "coral-berry."

CULTURE: Light, semi-sunny to semi-shady. Temperature, slightly cool, preferably not over 75°F. for long

Ardisia crispa

periods in winter. Humidity, 30% or more; frequent misting of the foliage with tepid water is beneficial. Soil, equal parts loam, sand, and peat moss; keep evenly moist. Propagate by sowing seeds or rooting cuttings.

MYRTLE FAMILY — Myrtaceae

Tropical shrubs and trees with aromatic foliage. Some bear showy flowers, others are cultivated for foliage or edible fruit. Only two genera are of interest to the indoor gardener.

Callistemon

DESCRIPTION: *C. lanceolatus,* from New South Wales, is an open shrub with sparsely set leaves. The numerous small blossoms feature showy crimson stamens with golden anthers; they are arranged in such a way as to suggest the popular name "bottle-brush."
CULTURE: Light, sunny. Temperature, average house. Humidity, average house. Soil, equal parts loam, sand, and peat moss; allow to become nearly dry between waterings. Propagate by sowing seeds in spring.

Eugenia

DESCRIPTION: *E. uniflora,* the Surinam cherry, has shiny, dark green leaves on a shrub or small tree, easily kept to house-size. Fragrant white flowers in season are followed by the edible red fruit.
CULTURE: Light, sunny to semi-sunny. Temperature, average house.

Humidity, 30% or more. Soil, equal parts loam, sand, and peat moss; keep evenly moist. Propagate by cuttings.

Myrtus

DESCRIPTION: *M. communis,* the Greek myrtle, resembles boxwood. It is cultivated for its fragrant foliage. *M. communis microphylla* has smaller leaves on a more compact plant. *M. communis variegata* has leaves marked attractively with white. All are excellent indoor plants, well adapted to pot culture, and easily grown.
CULTURE: Light, sunny to semi-sunny. Temperature, cool, not over 72°F. for long periods in winter. Humidity, average house. Soil, equal parts loam, sand, and peat moss; allow to become nearly dry between waterings, but keep evenly moist in summer. Propagate by rooting cuttings of firm or partially ripened wood.

FOUR-O'CLOCK FAMILY — Nyctaginaceae

Herbs, trees, and shrubs, mostly from tropical America, with simple, smooth-edged leaves and showy flowers. Only one genus is of interest to the indoor gardener.

Bougainvillea

DESCRIPTION: Bougainvilleas are in a class by themselves both structurally and decoratively. They are the only representative of the family cultivated

Bougainvillea 'Temple Fire'

indoors. The minute flowers appear in dense clusters, and while they themselves are insignificant, the three-parted, papery bracts which surround them are colorful and so long-lasting that the plants appear to be in almost continuous bloom.

These Brazilian plants may be divided into two groups—those which climb vigorously, and those which can be trained easily into pot-plant form. All have spines sparsely set along the stems. In the vining types there is 'Fire Chief' with vivid red bracts; *B. glabra* has purplish pink bracts, and those of *B. spectabili. praetoriensis* are multicolored—golden bronze overlaid with pink and yellow. Other vining bougainvilleas are equally colorful.

Shrubby types include 'Temple Fire,' which has brick-red bracts turning cerise with age. 'Barbara Karst' is amenable to trimming and pruning, which will force it into bushy growth. Others, not vigorous vining types, may also be trained as shrubby plants.

CULTURE: Light, sunny. Temperature average house. Humidity, 30% or more. Soil, equal parts loam, sand and peat moss; keep evenly moist. Propagate by sowing seeds in spring or by rooting 6-in. lengths of half ripened or old wood taken from April to June.

OLIVE FAMILY   Oleacea

Evergreen and deciduous shrubs and trees from many parts of the world cultivated for ornament (lilac, for example), as well as food (olive). Two genera are of interest to the indoor gardener.

Jasminum

DESCRIPTION: Jasmines are erect or climbing shrubs prized for their fragrant blossoms. Usually they have small, shining, dark-green leaves which may be simple or pinnate. The white or yellow flowers are tubular with spreading lobes, and they appear in clusters, either at the branch tips or in the leaf axils. *J. officinale grandiflorum* and *J. polyanthum* require coolness; *J. sambac* and its varieties like average house warmth.

CULTURE: Light, sunny to semi-sunny. Temperature, see paragraph above. Humidity, 50% or more. Soil, equal parts loam, sand, and peat moss; keep evenly moist. Propagate by rooting cuttings of nearly mature wood, or by layering.

Osmanthus

DESCRIPTION: The most valuable os manthus available as a pot plant i *O. fragrans*, the sweet-olive. It is an evergreen shrub from the Orient, with finely toothed, glossy leaves and clusters of tiny white flowers in the leaf axils. The blossoms are so heavily fragrant that their perfume will fill a whole room, and the plants are nearly everblooming.

Another osmanthus often seen indoors is *O. ilicifolius variegatus,* or false holly, a variety with leaf margins of white. It has smaller leaves than true holly, but there is a resemblance, and the osmanthus is a much better keeper indoors than the real thing. CULTURE: Light, sunny to semi-sunny. Temperature, on the cool side, not over 75°F. for long periods in winter. Humidity, 30% or more, with ample fresh air. Soil, equal parts loam, sand, and peat moss; keep evenly moist. Propagate by rooting cuttings of half-ripened wood in late summer.

EVENING-PRIMROSE FAMILY   Onagraceae

Herbs from temperate as well as tropical parts of the world. Leaves may be alternate or opposite; the flowers are showy. Only one genus is of interest to the indoor gardener.

Fuchsia

DESCRIPTION: Fuchsias are handsome small shrubs or trees with simple, usually opposite leaves, and spectacular blossoms arising from the leaf axils on new growth. Fuchsia flowers are unusual in having brilliantly colored sepals instead of the inconspicuous green ones of many other flowers. The fuchsia sepals are elongated tubes with four widely flaring petal-like parts which open to expose the pendent petals and extruding stamens. Petals may be four or five in number, often twice that in the double forms, and may match or contrast with the sepals in coloring. The tones range from pure white through pale pink to rose, red, lavender, violet, purple, and blue in the hybrids, with hundreds of named varieties from which to choose. Some are hanging basket or shelf plants, others grow as graceful upright shrubs.

CULTURE: Light, semi-sunny to semi-shady. Temperature, cool, not over 75°F. in winter. Humidity, 50% or more, with ample fresh air. Soil, equal parts loam, sand, and peat moss; keep evenly moist, and feed biweekly except in fall and early winter. Propagate by rooting cuttings in the spring.

Fuchsia 'Black Prince'

ORCHID FAMILY   Orchidaceae

Epiphytic as well as terrestrial herbs, from both tropical and temperate parts of the world; some 30,000 species are known.

Brassavola

DESCRIPTION: *B. nodosa,* from South America, is called "lady of the night" in Mexico. Its greenish white flowers appear from September through January, and they are incredibly fragrant at night.

CULTURE: Light, semi-sunny to semi-shady. Temperature, average house, preferably not over 75°F. in winter. Humidity, 50% or more. Soil, osmunda fiber or shredded bark; keep on the dry side. Propagate by division in late winter or spring.

Cattleya

DESCRIPTION: There are numerous cattleya species in cultivation, and countless hybrids. Of all orchids, these are probably the ones to which most indoor gardeners aspire. *C. skinneri,* from Guatemala, is good for the beginner. It has clusters of white

Cattleya skinneri

flowers in spring, borne on a small plant (about 12 in. tall).

CULTURE: Same as Brassavola.

Cycnoches

DESCRIPTION: *C. chlorochilon,* from South America, has chartreuse, creamy white, and dark-green flow-

Cycnoches chlorochilon

ers whose shape suggests the popular name "swan orchid."

CULTURE: Light, semi-sunny to semi-shady. Temperature, average house. Humidity, 50% or more. Soil, osmunda fiber, shredded bark, or equal parts loam, sand, peat moss, and leaf mold; provide even moisture and feed biweekly, except to keep dry and withhold fertilizer during dormancy, which occurs after flowering, in spring. Propagate by division in spring or summer.

Epidendrum

DESCRIPTION: A genus of epiphytic orchids, native to Mexico, Central and South America, noted for being almost weedlike in growth. One of the best species for the beginner is *E. o'brienianum,* with long spikes of bright scarlet blossoms. There are similar varieties in commerce today sold merely by color, including white, orange, pink, lavender, red, and yellow. The stems of these and other epidendrums are canelike, with two large leaves at the top, from which the flower stalks emerge. Do not be hasty in severing the old canes from the roots when new growth begins; often the old canes will bloom again. CULTURE: Light, semi-sunny to semi-shady. Temperature, average house. Humidity, 50% or more. Soil, unshredded sphagnum moss; soak, then allow to become nearly dry before watering again. Feed biweekly except in fall and early winter. Stake and tie long canes. Propagate by air-layering or division in spring or summer.

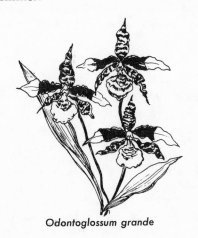

Odontoglossum grande

Odontoglossum

DESCRIPTION: *O. grande,* and the similar but smaller-flowered *O. schlieperianum,* both from South America, have yellow petals crossbanded with reddish brown, hence the name "tiger orchid." CULTURE: Light, semi-shady. Temperature, cool, not over 72°F. in winter. Humidity, 50% or more. Soil, osmunda fiber or shredded bark. Propagate by division in spring or summer.

Oncidium

DESCRIPTION: *O. kramerianum,* from Colombia and Ecuador, is a spectacular "butterfly orchid," with spring and fall flowers of golden yellow spotted brown. All oncidiums offered

Oncidium kramerianum

in commerce are showy. Two miniatures, *O. triquetrum* and *O. variegatum,* are especially appropriate for window collections. CULTURE: Light, semi-sunny to semi-shady. Temperature, average house, preferably with no prolonged periods over 72°F. in winter. Humidity, 50%

or more. Soil, osmunda fiber or shredded bark; keep evenly moist, but occasionally allow to be nearly dry. Propagate by division in spring.

Paphiopedilum

DESCRIPTION: *P. maudiae* and other lady-slipper orchids cultivated in-

Paphiopedilum maudiae

doors are sometimes confused with the related and similar cypripediums which grow as wild flowers in our woodlands. *P. maudiae* blooms twice a year, with long-lasting flowers of green and white above attractively mottled leaves.

CULTURE: Light, semi-shady. Temperature, average house. Humidity, 50% or more. Soil, osmunda fiber, shredded bark, or equal parts loam, sand, peat moss, and leaf mold; keep evenly moist. Propagate by division in spring.

Phalaenopsis

DESCRIPTION: Hybrids of these "dogwood" or "moth" orchids make excellent house plants. They are breathtaking when in flower.

CULTURE: Light, semi-sunny to semi-shady. Temperature, average house. Humidity, 50% or more. Soil, osmunda fiber or shredded bark; keep evenly moist. Propagate by division in spring.

WOOD-SORREL FAMILY   Oxalidaceae

Bulbous or tuberous herbs, usually with palmately divided leaves, and small, showy, funnel-shaped flowers. Only one genus is of interest to the indoor gardener.

Oxalis

DESCRIPTION: Species of oxalis are mostly rather small, rounded, delicate-appearing plants with attractive flowers and foliage, the leaves generally with three leaflets. *O. bowieana*, from South Africa, has large rosy red flowers in summer and fall. *O. carnosa*, from Chile and Peru, has yellow flowers in spring. *O. cernua*, from South Africa, called "Bermuda buttercup," has fragrant yellow flowers

in spring. Its double-flowered form, *flore pleno*, is also called 'Capri.' *O. deppei*, from southern Mexico, has yellow-throated, rosy red flowers above attractive foliage. *O. hedysaroides rubra*, the "fire-fern" from South America, has wiry stems set with small, delicate, wine-red leaves; under good culture it will bear a profusion of small yellow flowers. *O. hirta*, from South Africa, grows semi-

Oxalis deppei

upright and bears yellow-tubed, rose-colored flowers in winter. *O. melanosticta,* from South Africa, forms a very compact rosette of leaves covered by glistening, silvery hair; the yellow flowers come in autumn. *O. ortgiesii,* from the Andes of Peru, grows strongly upright to 1½ ft. or more and is called "tree oxalis." It has brown-red foliage, and a never-ending display of small yellow flowers. *O. regnelli,* from South America, is nearly everblooming, with white flowers set among or slightly above square-cut leaflets of deep bronze-green, flushed maroon beneath. *O. rubra,* from Brazil, is known often as *O. crassipes.* It has generous clusters of rosy pink or white flowers borne above graceful mounds of bright-green foliage; nearly everblooming.

O. variabilis, from the Cape of Good Hope, is known in commerce as "Grand Duchess." The yellow-throated, vivid rose flowers, to 3 in. across, appear in winter.

CULTURE: Light, sunny to semi-sunny. Temperature, average house. Humidity, 30% or more. Soil, equal parts loam, sand, and peat moss; keep evenly moist during the growing season, dry otherwise. As a rule, winter-flowering species are dormant in summer, and vice versa. Ever-blooming kinds need to be repotted annually, in summer or fall, and trimmed back to promote new growth. Propagate by removing offsets at potting time, or by division of kinds with fleshy rhizomes.

Oxalis regnelli

PALM FAMILY

Palmaceae

Tropical trees, sometimes bushlike, with tough, leathery leaves and inconspicuous flowers. The family includes coconut, date, and oil palms, as well as countless genera grown chiefly for ornament.

Caryota

DESCRIPTION: *C. mitis, C. plumosa,* and *C. urens* are known as "fishtail palms." While young, they are outstanding for growing in containers.

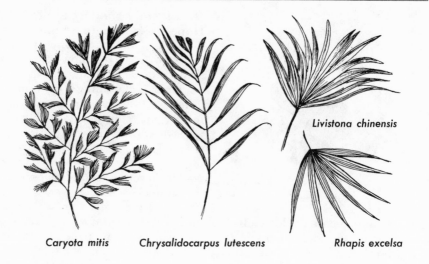

Livistona chinensis

Caryota mitis   Chrysalidocarpus lutescens   Rhapis excelsa

CULTURE: Light, semi-sunny to semi-shady. Temperature, average house. Humidity, average house, preferably 30% or more. Soil, equal parts loam, sand, and peat moss; keep evenly moist. Propagate by sowing seeds in moist soil and warmth (80-85°F.) in March.

Chamaedorea

DESCRIPTION: *C. cataractarum,* from Mexico, is dwarf, and showy indoors; female plants bear scarlet fruits. *C. costaricana,* from Costa Rica, forms clusters of bamboo-like canes with elegant, graceful fronds. *C. elegans,* from Mexico, is known as "parlor palm," and *C. elegans bella,* from eastern Guatemala, is the ever-present "miniature palm." *C. seifritzii,* from Mexico, bears clusters of small, slender canes. It has an overall lacy appearance.

CULTURE: Light, semi-shady to shady. Temperature, average house. Humidity, average house. Soil, equal parts loam, sand, and peat moss;

keep evenly moist. Propagate by removing suckers, or by sowing seeds.

Chamaerops

DESCRIPTION: *C. humilis,* from southern Europe and North Africa, is the fan palm. It is dwarf enough to be cultivated indoors.

CULTURE: Light, sunny to semi-sunny. Temperature, cool, preferably in a range of 50° to 70°F. Humidity, average house, with ample fresh air. Soil, equal parts loam, sand, and peat moss; keep evenly moist to wet. Propagate by sowing seeds in moist soil and warmth in spring, or by removing suckers in spring or summer.

Chrysalidocarpus

DESCRIPTION: *C. lutescens,* from Madagascar, the butterfly or areca palm, has willowy, furrowed, yellow canes in a clump. It may form more than a dozen of these in one small pot, and thus it serves as a showy container-grown plant.

CULTURE: Light, semi-sunny to semi-shady. Temperature, average house. Humidity, average house. Soil, equal parts loam, sand, and peat moss; keep evenly moist. Propagate by sowing seeds, or by division of the clumps, in spring.

Howea

DESCRIPTION: *H. belmoreana* and *H. fosteriana,* both from Lord Howe Island, are sometimes called kentia palms. They are slow-growing, showy in containers, probably the best of all large-size palms for indoors.
CULTURE: Same as Chamaedorea.

Licuala

DESCRIPTION: *L. spinosa,* from Malaya to Java, has fan-shaped leaves, with the segments plaited and terminated as if they had been cut squarely with pinking shears.
CULTURE: Same as Chamaedorea, except that licuala needs more humidity, at least 30%.

Livistona

DESCRIPTION: *L. chinensis,* from China,

is another fan palm (see also Chamaerops). Its individual leaves are sometimes more than 5 ft. wide. This palm grows to a single stem, and makes a striking container plant while young.
CULTURE: Same as Chamaedorea, except that ample humidity and fresh air are more important.

Phoenix

DESCRIPTION: *P. roebelenii,* from Assam to Vietnam, is the dwarf date palm. It is one of the showiest, most graceful palms to grow indoors.
CULTURE: Same as Chamaedorea.

Rhapis

DESCRIPTION: *R. excelsa* and *R. humilis,* both from southern China, have bamboo-like canes and fan-shaped leaves. They are outstanding as house plants.
CULTURE: Same as Chamaedorea, except on the cool side, preferably not over 75°F. in winter.

SCREW-PINE FAMILY   Pandanaceae

Tropical trees and shrubs cultivated as foliage plants. The flowers are insignificant, and seldom appear in cultivation. Only one genus is of interest to the indoor gardener.

Pandanus

DESCRIPTION: *P. veitchi,* from Polynesia, and other screw-pines are remarkable for the perfect spiral arrangement of the long, prickly-margined, sword-shaped leaves, and for the aerial roots which hang down to the soil, seeming to be props to hold the plants upright.
CULTURE: Light, sunny to semi-sunny.

Temperature, average house. Humidity, 50% or more, especially from January until summer. Soil, equal parts loam, sand, peat moss, and leaf mold; evenly moist, except slightly less so in fall. The most active growth occurs from midwinter to summer; repot at this time, if necessary. Propagate by removing suckers at repotting time.

PASSION-FLOWER FAMILY   **Passifloraceae**

The only genus cultivated is Passiflora, discussed below.

Passiflora

DESCRIPTION: Passifloras are exciting
flowering vines. Some people attach
religious significance to the formation of the flowers. The ten petals
are said to represent the apostles at
the Crucifixion; the rays of the
fringed corona, the crown of thorns;
the anthers, the wounds; and the
stigmas, the nails; the five-lobed
leaves, the hands of the persecutors;
and the tendrils resembling the
whips and cords used. Further apoc-
ryphal resemblance is noted by some
in the veil, or fine hairs, of violet
surrounding the crown, five spots
the hue of blood in the center of the
plant, seventy-two filaments equal-
ing the number of thorns which
tradition says set the Lord's crown,
the leaves shaped like the head of a
lance which pierced His side, and
the round spots on the leaf reverses
signifying the thirty pieces of silver.

Passiflora alato-caerulea

P. *caerulea,* from Brazil, has blue
flowers. The hybrid P. *alato-caerulea*
(or P. *pfordtii*) is larger and more
showy, with white, pink, and blue
flowers. P. *coccinea,* from the tropics
of South America, is the scarlet passion flower. P. *coriacea,* from southern
Mexico to Peru, is cultivated first for
its odd "batwing" leaves, but also for
green, yellow, and purple flowers.

CULTURE: Light, sunny to semi-sunny.
Temperature, average house. Humidity, 30% or more. Soil equal
parts loam, sand, peat moss, and leaf
mold; keep evenly moist. Give ample root room, and pinch the plants
as they develop, to produce well-
branched vines. Propagate by seeds
or cuttings at any time.

POKEWEED FAMILY   **Phytolaccaceae**

Herbs, shrubs, and trees, tending to be weedy. Only one genus is of interest
to the indoor gardener.

Rivina

DESCRIPTION: R. *humilis,* from tropical
America, is an erect plant with
spreading branches and slender-
stalked, pointed-oval leaves. It is

grown for clusters of berrylike fruits which follow the small pink and white flowers. Rivina, sometimes called "bloodberry" or "rouge plant," is related to the garden pokeweed, and the berries are just about as short-lived.

CULTURE: Light, sunny to semi-sunny. Temperature, average house. Humidity, average house. Soil, equal parts loam, sand, and peat moss; keep evenly moist. Propagate by seeds or cuttings at any time.

Rivina humilis

PINE FAMILY   Pinaceae

Cone-bearing evergreens from tropical as well as temperate parts of the world. Except for bonsai work (Chapter 9), only the araucaria is of interest to the indoor gardener.

Araucaria

DESCRIPTION: *A. excelsa,* the Norfolk Island pine, resembles a true pine tree. It has stiff needles, resinous sap, and is capable of forming woody cones. On its native island, this pine reaches a height of 200 ft., but in captivity 2 to 5 ft. is more likely. Juvenile specimens have long been favorite indoor plants, especially at Christmas, because of their symmetrical growth, and also because they will stand abuse.

CULTURE: Light, semi-sunny to semi-shady. Temperature, on the cool side, preferably not over 70°F. in winter. Humidity, 30% or more. Soil, equal parts loam, sand, and peat moss; keep evenly moist. Propagate from seeds, or root the top leader of an old plant (side shoots do not make well-shaped specimens).

PEPPER FAMILY   Piperaceae

Tropical herbs and shrubs with fleshy, smooth-edged leaves and insignificant flowers. The genus piper yields common black pepper. Only one other family member is of interest here.

Peperomia

DESCRIPTION: A variable genus of succulent plants, all well-suited to culture indoors. Several dozen peperomias are available in commerce, ranging from plants with a vining habit and small foliage to erect bushes of large, heavy leaves. Foliage color may be almost black, as in *P. griseo-argentea* 'Blackie,' green as in

Peperomia argyreia

P. cubensis, reddish as in *P. rubella,* variegated with creamy white as in *P. obtusifolia variegata,* or the leaves may be silvery, buff, or bronze, quilted or pleated, shiny or hairy, or with blotches, bands, margins, or reverses of contrasting color. *P. argyreia* (sometimes called *P. sandersii*) is the popular "watermelon-begonia." More than sixty peperomia species and varieties are known, and while they may vary widely in appearance, all require the same care.

CULTURE: Light, semi-sunny to shady. Temperature, average house. Humidity, average house. Soil, equal parts loam, sand, and peat moss; water only when the surface becomes dry. Propagate by stem cuttings of the vining types, or by leaf cuttings of the others.

PITTOSPORUM FAMILY   Pittosporaceae

Trees and shrubs, sometimes vinelike, mostly from Australia, with thick, leathery, alternate leaves and showy flowers.

Pittosporum

DESCRIPTION: The finest species of pittosporum is *P. tobira,* with thick, shining, leathery leaves arranged in whorls at the tips of branches. The shrub tends to grow in flat planes, and is especially adapted to bonsai, as it is agreeable to pruning and training. A variegated form is also available, grayish green with creamy-margined leaves. Both have fragrant clusters of small white flowers.

CULTURE: Light, semi-sunny to semi-shady. Temperature, cool, not over 75°F. in winter. Humidity, 30% or more, with ample fresh air. Mist foliage frequently with tepid water.

Pittosporum tobira

Soil, equal parts loam, sand, and peat moss; keep evenly moist, occasionally allowing to approach dryness. Propagate by rooting cuttings of half-ripened wood.

PODOCARPUS FAMILY   Podocarpaceae

Evergreen shrubs and trees cultivated outdoors in the South. Only one genus is of interest to the indoor gardener.

Podocarpus

DESCRIPTION: Japanese, coniferous evergreen trees which remain conveniently small for many years when confined in pots. One of the best is *P. macrophylla maki* which has slender leaves spirally arranged along the stems. Another fine one is *P. nagi,* with elegant spreading branches and shiny green elliptic leaves. Both are good subjects for bonsai (Chapter 9). CULTURE: Light, semi-shady. Temperature, cool, not over 75°F. in winter. Humidity, 30% or more, with ample fresh air. Soil, equal parts loam, sand, and peat moss; keep evenly moist. Propagate by sowing seeds, or rooting cuttings of almost ripened wood.

BUCKWHEAT FAMILY   Polygonaceae

Herbs, shrubs, trees, and vines from all over the world. Some are foodstuffs and others are cultivated for showy flowers or foliage. Two genera are of interest to the indoor gardener.

Antigonon

DESCRIPTION: *A. leptopus,* from Mexico, is a robust vine started from seeds. It will form a tuber, and easiest culture indoors is to keep it dormant in winter. "Coral vine," as it is known, climbs by means of tendrils. Racemes of bright rose-pink flowers, arising from the leaf axils, appear freely from early spring to late fall. CULTURE: Light, sunny. Temperature, average house. Humidity, average house. Soil, equal parts loam, sand, and peat moss; keep evenly moist. Propagate by sowing seeds in early spring.

Coccoloba uvifera

Coccoloba

DESCRIPTION: *C. uvifera,* the "sea-grape" from southern Florida and the

West Indies, is a shrubby evergreen plant of leathery, rounded leaves with prominent red veins which change to white at maturity. A sport, *C. uvifera aurea,* is exceedingly colorful, its almost stemless leaves generously splashed with creamy yellow.

CULTURE: Light, sunny to semi-shady. Temperature, average house. Humidity, average house. Soil, equal parts loam, sand, and peat moss; keep evenly moist. Propagate by seed, by cuttings of ripe wood, or by layering.

FERN FAMILY   Polypodiaceae

Most tender as well as hardy ferns belong in this family. Many genera are of interest to the indoor gardener.

Adiantum

DESCRIPTION: Adiantum, or maidenhair, ferns are distinguished by having thin, wiry black stems and many small, firm leaflets with wedge-shaped bases. *A. cuneatum* is the old greenhouse favorite, but *A. tenerum wrightii*—a medium-sized form with fronds pink when young, maturing to green—and *A. hispidulum,* a handsome dwarf species from Australia and New Zealand, are the two usually seen in cultivation today.

Maidenhair ferns are moisture-loving plants. They need high humidity and wet soil, the latter humusy. Peat moss, leaf mold, or shredded fir bark are all good potting mediums for these plants as their fine roots need a soft, easily penetrated material which will hold ample moisture yet permit air to enter freely. Most authorities state that maidenhair ferns need temperatures ranging from 65°F. (nighttime) to 85°F. (daytime), yet I have seen these ferns growing rampant beside a mountain stream in Mexico which was too cold for the comfort of a

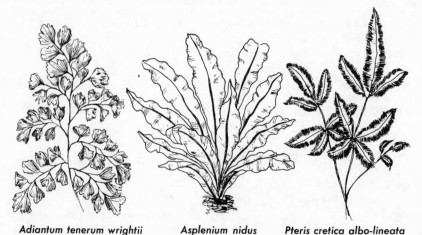

Adiantum tenerum wrightii   *Asplenium nidus*   *Pteris cretica albo-lineata*

heavy-coated human. L. H. Bailey, in *Hortus,* suggests minimum lows of 45-50°F., with highs staying close to 70°F., and I agree with this.

These ferns need to be rested slightly during the winter months by cutting down on watering, and moving to a cool place. If repotting is needed—about every three years, once established in a large container—turn the plant out of its pot in February, remove as much topsoil as convenient, and replace it with fresh rich soil, peat moss, or leaf mold. If more plants are desired, propagate by dividing the clump before repotting it.
CULTURE: See above.

Asplenium

DESCRIPTION: *A. nidus,* from India to Queensland and Japan, the "bird's-nest fern," has fairly wide, entire fronds which rise in rosettes. It is a durable fern for indoor use, although it lacks the lacy charm usually associated with these plants.

The "mother ferns," *A. bulbiferum,* from Australia, Malaya, and New Zealand, and *A. viviparum,* from Mauritius, are notable primarily for bearing baby plantlets upon the fronds. As soon as the small plants are large enough to handle, cut them loose together with a piece of the old frond. Place in small pots, with the piece of old frond just below the soil to hold the young plant in position until roots form.
CULTURE: Light, semi-sunny to semi-shady. Temperature, cool, not over 75°F. in winter. Humidity, 30% or more, although an excess in the dead of winter may cause browning of the fronds. Soil, equal parts loam, sand,

peat moss, and leaf mold; keep evenly moist. Propagate by removing offsets of bird's-nest types, or rooting plantlets of others (see above).

Cyrtomium

DESCRIPTION: *C. falcatum,* from the Orient, India, Celebes, and Hawaii, and its varieties are handsome, robust plants with leathery, shining, dark-green leaflets. In *C. falcatum rochefordianum* the leaflets have sharply toothed, wavy edges, giving them some resemblance to ilex, hence the name "holly fern."
CULTURE: Light, semi-shady to shady. Temperature, cool, not over 75°F. in winter. Humidity, 30% or more. Soil, equal parts loam, sand, peat moss, and leaf mold; keep evenly moist. Propagate by division of the rhizomes in spring.

Davallia

DESCRIPTION: *D. fejeensis,* from the Fiji Islands, the "rabbit's-foot fern," has fur-covered creeping rhizomes with finely cut, wiry fronds and an airy habit of growth which results from the fronds springing up at intervals from the rhizomes (instead of arising from a central crown). This and other davallias are choice ferns, but not the easiest to grow.

Do not pot davallias in the usual way. Instead, fasten the rhizome with strong copper wire staples to the surface of the soil. Use a shallow pot or hanging basket filled with equal parts loam, sand, peat moss, and leaf mold; keep evenly moist at all times.
CULTURE: Light, semi-shady. Temperature, cool, not over 75°F. in winter. Humidity, 50% or more; mist frequently with tepid water. Soil, see

paragraph above. Propagate by division of the rhizomes, cut into sections and placed on sand. Cover them with peat moss or sphagnum and keep moist.

Nephrolepis

DESCRIPTION: *N. exaltata,* from South America, southern Asia, and Australia, and its many varieties including "sword ferns" and "Boston ferns," are a valuable group to the indoor gardener. The rapidly growing fronds, which rise directly from the soil surface, are long and variously cut.

CULTURE: Light, semi-sunny to semi-shady. Temperature, average house, preferably not over 75°F. in winter. Humidity, average house, with ample fresh air. If frond edges turn brown, provide more humidity, less heat. Soil, equal parts loam, sand, peat moss, and leaf mold; keep evenly moist. Propagate by division in the spring.

Platycerium

DESCRIPTION: *P. bifurcatum,* from Australia, New Guinea, New Caledonia, and the Sunda Islands, is the bizarre, much admired staghorn fern.

CULTURE: Light, semi-sunny to semi-shady. Temperature, average house. Humidity, 50% or more, with fresh air. Soil, osmunda fiber, or bark; keep evenly, but not excessively, moist. Syringe the leaves frequently. Platyceriums are usually mounted

on a slab of rough wood or bark, with a pocket of osmunda fiber to contain the roots, but they may also be pot-grown. Propagate by removing offsets at any time; root in moist osmunda, warmth, and high humidity.

Polypodium

DESCRIPTION: *P. aureum,* from Australia—and the West Indies to Brazil—and its varieties, especially *mandaianum,* are durable ferns for large indoor planters. The bold-textured fronds, sometimes suggestive of tropical foliage such as cutleaf philodendron, rise from cinnamon-colored, hairy, creeping rhizomes, which suggest the common names "bear's-paw" and "hare's-paw" ferns.

CULTURE: Same as Nephrolepis.

Polystichum

DESCRIPTION: *P. tsus-simense,* from Korea, is a miniature fern of dark-green leathery fronds, not often more than 8 in. tall. It is useful for bottle gardens and terrariums.

CULTURE: Same as Nephrolepis, except little or no direct sun.

Pteris

DESCRIPTION: This very large genus, called "table fern," is best known for its species which display irregular forking and cresting of the fronds. Varieties of *P. cretica* and *P. serrulata* show these attractive characteristics most prominently. Some of these, as well as some of the other species and varieties, are variegated with white.

CULTURE: Same as Davallia.

PURSLANE FAMILY Portulacaceae

Herbs and shrubs from temperate as well as tropical parts of the world, with fleshy leaves and often showy flowers. Only one genus is of interest to the indoor gardener.

Portulacaria

DESCRIPTION: *P. afra,* from South Africa, a stout shrub, has small, succulent leaves set on thick, fleshy, brownish red stems. The foliage of the variety *variegata* is colorfully splashed with creamy white, pink, and green. The small flowers are delicate pink.

Portulacaria afra variegata

CULTURE: Light, sunny to semi-sunny. Temperature, average house. Humidity, average house. Soil, equal parts loam, sand, and peat moss; water when the surface is dry. Propagate by rooting stem cuttings in moist sand.

PRIMROSE FAMILY Primulaceae

Herbs from many parts of the world with attractive foliage and showy flowers. Only two genera are of interest to the indoor gardener.

Cyclamen

DESCRIPTION: *C. persicum giganteum,* from Greece to Syria, and its many hybrids have handsome rosettes of fleshy, heart-shaped leaves and colorful flowers like those of the woodland shooting-star (*Dodecatheon* species), except much larger and borne on individual stems. These arise from a fleshy tuber, similar to that of tuberous begonia and sinningia (gloxinia of florists).

CULTURE: Light, semi-sunny to semi-shady. Temperature, cool, not over 72°F. in winter. Humidity, 50% or more, with ample fresh air. Soil, equal parts loam, sand, peat moss,

Cyclamen persicum giganteum

and leaf mold; keep evenly moist, except dry in July and August, but not to the point of shriveling the tuber. Repot in September with the tuber kept at the same level at which it grew previously; keep barely moist until new growth shows. Propagate by sowing seeds in August for bloom eighteen months later.

Primula

DESCRIPTION: Three species of primula, all from China, and many varieties of each, can be grown as pot plants although they require temperatures below those found in the average home. However, a glassed-in porch which is unheated, yet well above freezing, may provide a good place for them.

P. malacoides, the "fairy" or "baby" primrose, is considered the most choice by many indoor gardeners. It has slender stalks bearing multitudes of small blossoms in tiers. *P. sinensis,* or Chinese primrose, has lobed leaves and umbels of typical primrose flowers of many colors. *P. obconica,* called "poison primrose" because many people are sensitive to

Primula malacoides

its foliage, has large, broad leaves. Flowers may be white or shades of pink, rose, or red, or lavender.

CULTURE: Light, semi-sunny to semi-shady. Temperature, cool, not over 65°F. Humidity, 50% or more, with ample fresh air. Soil, equal parts loam, sand, peat moss, and leaf mold; keep evenly moist. Propagate by sowing seeds in April or August. Treat as annuals, discarding at the end of the flowering season.

PROTEA FAMILY   Proteaceae

Mostly tropical trees and shrubs, only one genus of interest here.

Grevillea

DESCRIPTION: *G. robusta,* the silk oak, has large seeds that sprout easily and grow quickly (3 ft. in one year is not uncommon). The leaves

Grevillea robusta

are fernlike in texture on upright stems. This is a fine house plant tree.
CULTURE: Light, sunny to semi-sunny. Temperature, moderate to average house. Humidity, 30% or more. Soil, equal parts loam, sand, and peat moss; evenly moist to slightly dry between waterings. Propagate by sowing seeds.

POMEGRANATE FAMILY   Punicaceae

There is only one genus in this family.

Punica

DESCRIPTION: *P. granatum,* the pomegranate of southwestern Asia, is best known to indoor gardeners in its dwarf form, *nana.* It has single red flowers followed by small, but edible fruits. It makes a dense, twiggy bush with narrow, shiny, apple-green leaves. The variety 'Chico' has double flowers of many crepe-textured petals; it does not bear fruit.
CULTURE: Light, sunny to semi-sunny. Temperature, average house, preferably not over 75° F. in winter. Humidity, 30% or more with ample fresh air. Soil, equal parts loam, sand, and peat moss; keep evenly moist. Propagate by sowing seeds or rooting cuttings.

ROSE FAMILY   Rosaceae

Herbs, shrubs, and trees from many parts of the world, cultivated for garden ornament and as foodstuffs. Often divided into three tribes: the rose, apple, and peach. In addition to the dwarf fruit trees which are of interest for bonsai work (Chapter 9), three genera may be cultivated indoors.

Fragaria

DESCRIPTION: *F. vesca,* from Europe, has a variety *albo-marginata,* called the "variegated wild strawberry," because its small leaves are marked attractively with creamy white and red. The white flowers are followed by delectable, slender, inch-long strawberries. Runnerless varieties,

easily grown from seed to fruit in a few months, are also of interest. They include 'Baron Solemacher' and 'Harzland,' with red fruit, and the golden-fruited 'Alpine Yellow.'
CULTURE: Light, sunny. Temperature, near 40°F. from frost-time in autumn until January, then on the cool side, preferably not over 72°F. for long periods. Humidity, 30% or more, with ample fresh air. Soil, equal parts loam, sand, and peat moss; keep evenly moist and feed biweekly except during period of cold described above for fall and early winter. Propagate by rooting stolons or "runners" when they appear, by division, and by sowing seeds in the spring.

Pyracantha

DESCRIPTION: *P. coccinea lalandii,* from southern Europe and Asia Minor, and varieties of *P. crenato-serrata* such as 'Victory,' are the popular "firethorns" of the outdoor garden. They are easily cultivated, thorny shrubs which bear spring or early summer clusters of white flowers followed by showy orange, scarlet, or red berries which persist well into winter: ideal plants for espaliering.
CULTURE: Light, sunny. Temperature,

cool in winter, preferably not over 72°F. Humidity, average house, with ample fresh air. Soil, equal parts loam, sand, and peat moss; keep evenly moist, and feed biweekly except in the dead of winter. Pyracanthas, 2 to 3 ft. tall, will need a 12- to 14-in. tub. Propagate by rooting softwood cuttings in early summer.

Rosa

DESCRIPTION: *R. chinensis minima,* or *R. roulettii,* from China, and other pygmy or miniature roses, make interesting house plants. They are perfect replicas of large hybrid tea roses, though on a small scale.
CULTURE: Light, sunny to semi-sunny. Temperature, average house, preferably not over 72°F. for long periods. Humidity, 30% or more, with ample fresh air. Soil, equal parts loam, sand, and peat moss; keep evenly moist, and feed biweekly except in late fall and early winter. During this period, miniature roses are best cut back to 4 or 5 in., and stored in a cool, but frost-free place (about 40°F.). In January bring to a sunny, warm place to force growth and flowers. Propagate by sowing seeds, or rooting cuttings.

MADDER FAMILY **Rubiaceae**

Herbs, shrubs, trees, and vines from temperate as well as tropical parts of the world, including genera cultivated for medicinal purposes, for fruit, or showy flowers.

Coffea

DESCRIPTION: *C. arabica,* the coffee tree of commerce, has glossy, dark green leaves, nearly identical to its relative, the gardenia. Requires thoughtful pruning to make it a shapely shrub or small tree. Fra-

Coffea arabica

grant white flowers in spring and summer are followed by bright red beans.

CULTURE: Light, semi-sunny to semi-shady. Temperature, average house; not below 60°F. in winter. Humidity, average house. Soil, equal parts loam, sand, and peat moss; keep evenly moist. Yellowing, chlorotic leaves indicate the need of an acid-type fertilizer. Propagate by sowing very fresh seeds or from tip cuttings.

Gardenia

DESCRIPTION: Gardenias are tender evergreen shrubs prized for fragrant, double, velvety, white blossoms, and deep-green, glossy, ovate leaves. *G. jasminoides veitchii*, from China, has smaller leaves and flowers than the gardenia used by florists, but it is more easily cultivated as a house plant. *G. radicans floreplena*, from Japan, is dwarf in habit, easily kept to 18 in. Its leaves seldom exceed 3 in. in length, and the double flowers measure about 2 in. across.

CULTURE: Light, sunny to semi-sunny in winter, less in summer. Temperature, 62-65°F. at night, 70°F. or slightly more in the daytime, during fall, winter, and spring. Humidity, 30% or more, with ample fresh air. Soil, equal parts loam, sand, and peat moss, having an acid reaction, namely a pH range of 5.0 to 5.5; keep evenly moist. Feed biweekly from January to September, alternating between a balanced house plant fertilizer and a solution made by mixing 1 oz. ammonium sulfate in 2 gals. water. Propagate by rooting cuttings of half-ripened wood.

Gardenias are nearly as well known for dropping their buds as for the flowers they manage to produce. Bud drop is frequently the result of a change in environment, as from a controlled-climate greenhouse to a drafty, arid home. This causes leaves and new growth to turn black at the tips, or the plant may completely defoliate. To avoid this situation, provide a balanced supply of moisture—soil kept constantly moist, but never really dry or dripping wet. Give the plant some sunlight, and place it on a tray or dish of pebbles which have been partially covered with water. Be sure base of pot is on pebbles, not in water below. Buds

Gardenia jasminoides veitchii

may fail to form if nighttime temperatures stay constantly above 70°F., or below 60°F. Insufficient light and soil not of the proper acidity are other causes for failure of buds to form.

Hoffmannia

DESCRIPTION: *H. refulgens,* from Chiapas, is known as the "corduroy plant" because its closely set, parallel veins running from the midrib outward to the leaf margins are depressed in such a way that they give a ribbed effect not unlike wales of corduroy,

Hoffmannia refulgens

while the slight hairiness on the leaf surface adds to the similarity. This and other hoffmannia species, such as *H. ghiesbreghtii,* from Mexico, and *H. roezlii,* also from Mexico, are showy foliage plants characterized by unusual texture and vein patterns in the obovate leaves (the broad end away from the stalk). The upper leaf surfaces may be shaded green to copper or rose-purple, while reverses are usually a deep green. Veins may be light green, pinkish, or silvery. CULTURE: Light, semi-shady. Temperature, average house. Humidity, 50% or more. Soil, equal parts loam, sand, peat moss, and leaf mold; keep evenly moist. Propagate by rooting cuttings in warmth, moist soil, and high humidity.

Ixora

DESCRIPTION: *I. coccinea,* a shrub from the East Indies, has clusters of scarlet, tubular flowers in great abundance, hence the name, "flame of the woods." Recent hybrids are available with flowers ranging from palest yellow through orange to dark red, and from pink to deep rose. Ixoras are evergreen and almost everblooming, with leathery leaves of glossy green. The plants are bushy and amenable to pruning at any time. CULTURE: Light, sunny to semi-sunny. Temperature, average house. Humidity, 30% or more. Soil, equal parts loam, sand, and peat moss; keep evenly moist, and feed biweekly except in the dead of winter. Propagate at any time, especially spring, by rooting strong cuttings with four

Ixora coccinea

pairs of leaves. Set them in sand to which some peat moss has been added, and provide warmth (75-80°F.).

Manettia

DESCRIPTION: *M. bicolor,* from Brazil, is a fast-growing, free-blooming plant sometimes called "firecracker vine." The flowers are tubular, yellow-tipped scarlet, arising on short stems from the leaf axils.
CULTURE: Light, semi-sunny to semi-shady. Temperature, cool, not over 75°F. in winter. Humidity, 30% or more, with ample fresh air. Mist foliage frequently with tepid water to discourage infestations of red spider mites. Soil, equal parts loam, sand, and peat moss; keep evenly moist. Propagate by rooting cuttings in the spring or early summer.

Pentas

DESCRIPTION: *P. lanceolata,* from Arabia and tropical Africa, is a small bushy plant easily kept under 2 ft. by

frequent pruning. It yields white, lavender, pink, or red flowers over a long season. They appear in upright clusters, each about ½ in. across, five-petaled and starlike.
CULTURE: Sunny. Temperature, average house. Humidity, 30% or more. Soil, equal parts loam, sand, and peat moss; keep evenly moist. After an

Pentas lanceolata 'Pink Velvet'

extended time of flowering the plants may become scraggly; prune back severely, or start new plants by rooting cuttings of partly ripened wood.

CITRUS FAMILY   Rutaceae

Mostly tropical trees and shrubs cultivated for fruit or ornament. The foliage of most genera is glossy and attractive, often aromatic; frequently the flowers are deliciously fragrant.

Citrus

DESCRIPTION: *C. aurantifolia* is a spiny, small tree, which bears small limes. *C. limonia meyeri,* from China, is known as "Meyer lemon." It is dwarf-growing, with relatively small leaves and branches and edible lemons of average size. *C. limonia ponderosa* is an excellent tub plant which bears

unbelievably large lemons, to more than 2 lbs. *C. mitis,* the calamondin from the Philippines, is often sold as "miniature orange." It is easily kept under 2 ft. in height by pruning in the spring or early summer. The fragrant white flowers are followed by edible fruits which mature to a diameter of 2 in. and bright orange color. *C. nobilis deliciosa,* the tangerine, is a nearly thornless tree with willowy leaves; its fruit is also known as "Mandarin orange." *C. taitensis,* the Otaheite orange, begins to bear fruit, plum-size and lemon-shaped (but inedible), even when less than 12 in. tall.

CULTURE: Light, sunny to semi-sunny. Temperature, average house, prefer-

ably not over 75°F. in winter. Humidity, 30% or more, with ample fresh air. Soil, equal parts loam, sand, and peat moss; keep evenly moist, occasionally allowing to approach dryness. Feed biweekly except in late fall and early winter. Propagate by rooting cuttings of half-ripened wood in spring or early summer.

SAXIFRAGE FAMILY

Saxifragaceae

Herbs, shrubs, trees, and woody vines from many parts of the world cultivated for garden ornament. Three genera are of interest to the indoor gardener, and they are capable of withstanding temperatures of 20°F. or less.

Hydrangea

DESCRIPTION: *H. macrophylla,* from Japan, and its many varieties are deciduous shrubs, large-leaved, with showy clusters of white, pink, or blue flowers. They are widely sold as Easter pot plants. The coloring of the pink and blue varieties is determined by the degree of soil acidity. That is, a plant which is pink one year (in soil with a pH of 6.0 to not above 6.2) can be made blue another year by changing the soil pH to a more acid 5.0 to 5.5. White-flowered hydrangeas have no coloring pigment and cannot therefore be made to change to pink or blue. 'Sister Therese' and 'Regula' are white; 'Merveille' and 'Strafford,' deep pink; 'Red Star' is a dark pink which blues well; 'Rose Supreme,' 'Enziondom' and 'Kuhnert' are all pinks which may be changed to blue.

If you obtain a potted hydrangea in full bloom, be sure to keep the soil from evenly moist to wet at all times. Provide coolness (not over

72°F. for long periods), humidity (30% or more), fresh air, and an hour or two of sunlight daily. After danger of severe spring frost is past, potted hydrangeas may be set outdoors in a partially shaded place—ideally in morning sunlight. When the blooms have finally faded, cut them off. Prune the shoots back about halfway, or as much as to within two leaf joints from the soil. Repot. Carefully work the old soil away from the roots, and replant in new, using equal parts loam, sand, and peat moss. Keep the plants well watered and fed through the summer. Alternate biweekly feedings of a 4-12-4 fertilizer and ammonium sulfate (1 oz. to 2 gals. of water). The young growing tips may be pinched out until early July. This practice induces branching, and an ultimate yield of more flowers.

Before danger of hard freezes in autumn, put the potted hydrangea indoors, and withhold water until the leaves shrivel and fall. Keep the soil just moist enough so that the stems do not wither, and keep the plant cool (40-50°F.) and in darkness. After Christmas, and before late January, begin forcing the hydrangea into growth by providing a temperature of 50-55°F., a semi-sunny location and humid atmosphere (mist the young leaf buds with tepid water as often as possible). When leaves are making active growth, the temperature may be increased to 60°F. At this time, begin biweekly feedings which continue to the flowering stage. These consist of applying a solution made by dissolving 1 oz. ammonium sulfate and 1 oz. iron sulfate in 2 gals. water. To produce blue flowers, make, at two-week intervals after growth becomes active, from three to six applications of 1 tsp. aluminum sulfate per 6-in. pot, watering the aluminum sulfate in.

Florists' hydrangeas can be cultivated outdoors where wintertime temperatures do not fall below 20°F. In colder climates, gardeners are sometimes successful with them by surrounding the plants with a deep wire cage which is packed full of leaves in autumn after the first frost. CULTURE: See above.

Saxifraga

DESCRIPTION: *S. stolonifera,* from China and Japan, has rounded, bristly leaves arranged in loose rosette form. The leaves are deep olive-green, patterned with light-gray areas along the veins, spotted purple beneath. The small white flowers are borne in airy clusters on tall, thin stalks. Unaccountably, this plant is accorded popular names which are very misleading—"strawberry-geranium,"

Saxifraga stolonifera

and sometimes "strawberry-begonia." *S. sarmentosa tricolor* or 'Magic Carpet' is a smaller-growing plant with leaves beautifully variegated with cream and pink.
CULTURE: Light, semi-sunny to semi-shady. Temperature, cool, not over 72°F. in winter. Humidity, 30% or more, with ample fresh air. Soil, equal parts loam, sand, and peat moss; keep evenly moist, occasionally allowing to approach dryness. Propagate by removing the young plantlets which form at the ends of threadlike, bright red runners.

Tolmiea

DESCRIPTION: *T. menziesii,* from the California coast to Alaska, is a lightly hairy, soft-leaved perennial which grows in an open rosette. It is notable for the development of baby plants at the base of mature leaves, and a well-grown plant is a mound of foliage with the lower circles of leaves all bearing small plants upon them, hence "piggyback plant," sometimes "pickaback."
CULTURE: Light, semi-sunny to semi-shady. Temperature, cool, not over 72°F. in winter. Humidity, 30% or more, with ample fresh air. Soil,

equal parts loam, sand, peat moss, and leaf mold; keep evenly and abundantly moist. Propagate by pin-ning baby plants to damp soil until they root, then cut from the parent plant.

FIGWORT FAMILY Scrophulariaceae

Herbs, shrubs, trees, and vines from many parts of the world cultivated for colorful flowers.

Allophyton

DESCRIPTION: *A. mexicanum*, the Mexican foxglove, is a beautiful small plant, short-stemmed, with long, broad, leathery, dark-green leaves. The clusters of small, lavender, tubular flowers appear over a long period, borne on slender stems about 4 in. above the foliage. Each flower resembles a miniature foxglove with a large lobed white lip and purple-violet throat. The flowers are fragrant during the early morning hours, practically odorless at other times.
CULTURE: Light, semi-sunny to semi-shady. Temperature, cool, not over

Allophyton mexicanum

75 °F. in winter. Humidity, 30% or more. Soil, equal parts loam, sand, and peat moss; keep evenly moist. Propagate by sowing seeds in late winter or spring.

Asarina

DESCRIPTION: *A. antirrhiniflora*, from California, Texas, and Mexico, is a thin-stemmed perennial vine distinguished by white-throated, purple, trumpetlike blossoms over a long period. *A. barclaiana*, from Mexico, is a strong climber with downy leaves and trumpet flowers of white through rose to purple, downy outside, and with a greenish tube. *A. erubescens*, from Mexico, has larger flowers than *A. barclaiana*, and their rose-red coloring and shade misled someone into calling this a "creeping gloxinia," an erroneous name which has become popular. All asarinas may sometimes be listed as "maurandia," or "maurandya."
CULTURE: Light, sunny to semi-sunny. Temperature, average house. Humidity, 30% or more. Soil, equal parts loam, sand, peat moss, and leaf

Asarina antirrhiniflora

mold; keep evenly moist. Propagate by sowing seeds, or by rooting cuttings in a glass of plain water.

Calceolaria herbeohybrida

Calceolaria

DESCRIPTION: *C. herbeohybrida,* and its many hybrid strains, known as "pocketbook plant" because of the flower's shape, originated from species native to the cool Andes of Chile. These are annual plants, often sold in full bloom by florists. To prolong the striking floral display, keep the plant cool (not over 70°F.), moist (but never really wet), in 30% or more humidity, in shade; and provide some fresh air. When flowering ceases, discard the plant.

CULTURE: See paragraph above.

Propagate by sowing seeds in April or August. The seeds require coolness even during the heat of summer, when this may be impossible in most climates. Seedlings started in the spring or late summer will mature the following late winter or early spring.

Cymbalaria

DESCRIPTION: *C. muralis,* from Europe, is a small creeping perennial with rounded, scalloped leaves and tiny, yellow-throated, lilac flowers which resemble miniature snapdragons. It is known the world over as "Kenilworth ivy."

CULTURE: Light, semi-sunny to semi-shady. Temperature, cool, not over 72°F. in winter. Humidity, 30% or more; mist the foliage frequently with tepid water. Soil, equal parts loam, sand, peat moss, and leaf mold; keep evenly moist. Propagate by sowing seeds, or by rooting stem cuttings in a glass of plain water, or in a regular rooting medium such as moist vermiculite.

Cymbalaria muralis

SELAGINELLA FAMILY

Selaginellaceae

The annual and perennial herbs in this family belong to one genus, and all are mossy or fernlike.

Selaginella

DESCRIPTION: *S. emmeliana,* from South America, is called the "sweat plant." This popular name, appearing at first to be a misnomer, refers to this plant's fondness for a close, steamy atmosphere as inside a closed terrarium or "sweat jar." It forms a rosette of bright, lacy, fernlike fronds. *S. kraussiana,* from South Africa, is known as "spreading clubmoss," and spread it does, by sending down roots at every node along the stems. The tiny leaves are bright green; in the variety *aurea* they are splashed with creamy white; and in the dwarf, tuft-forming variety *brownii* they are emerald green. *S. lepidophylla,* from Peru, Mexico, and Texas, is called "resurrection plant" because it can be fully dried into a tight brownish ball, yet brought back to life by placing the roots in shallow water. *S. uncinata,* from Southern China, makes an iridescent blue-green ground cover for terrariums or bottle gardens. CULTURE: Light, semi-shady to shady. Temperature, average house. Humidity, 50% or more. Soil, equal parts loam, sand, peat moss, and leaf mold; keep evenly moist. Propagate at any time by rooting cuttings in warmth and high humidity.

NIGHTSHADE FAMILY

Solanaceae

Nearly all kinds of plants from tropical as well as temperate parts of the world make up this important family. They have alternate leaves and the flowers of most are regular.

Browallia

DESCRIPTION: *B. speciosa major,* from Colombia, forms a bushy plant of bright- to dark-green leaves, set with innumerable white-throated violet-blue flowers. The "orange browallia" is *Streptosolen jamesonii,* also of the Nightshade family, but not discussed separately as its culture is like that set forth here for browallia. CULTURE: Light, semi-sunny to semi-shady. Temperature, cool, not over 75°F. in winter. Humidity, 30% or more, with ample fresh air. Soil,

Browallia speciosa major

equal parts loam, sand, peat moss, and leaf mold; keep evenly moist. Propagate by sowing seeds from midwinter to late spring, or by rooting cuttings in autumn or spring.

Brunfelsia

DESCRIPTION: *B. calycina floribunda,* from Brazil, is a small evergreen shrub which bears showy tubular flowers from fall until spring. These open a deep lavender color, and fade to near-white, hence the popular name "yesterday, today, and tomorrow plant."

CULTURE: Light, semi-sunny. Temperature, average house, preferably not over 75°F. in winter. Humidity, 30% or more, with ample fresh air.

Brunfelsia calycina floribunda

Soil, equal parts loam, sand, and peat moss; keep evenly moist. Prune back as necessary in spring or early summer to keep a convenient size for the window garden. Propagate by stem cuttings in spring.

Capsicum

DESCRIPTION: *C. annuum,* and its many varieties, originally from South America, make valuable pot plants. They form small bushes of bright-green leaves, first laden with white, starry flowers, followed by chartreuse, to purple, to flaming scarlet peppers of

Capsicum annuum conoides 'Acorn'

various sizes and shapes. They are edible, but hot; and do not confuse them with the related *Solanum pseudocapsicum,* which see.

CULTURE: Light, sunny to semi-sunny. Temperature, average house. Humidity, average house. Soil, equal parts loam, sand, and peat moss; keep evenly moist. Propagate by sowing seeds in spring or early summer. Seedlings kept outdoors during warm weather will set on more fruit than those kept inside. These peppers are generally treated as annuals, but sometimes they live over from year to year.

Cestrum

DESCRIPTION: *C. nocturnum,* from the West Indies, is a gangly evergreen shrub of bright-green leaves, with tubular white flowers borne in the leaf axils. One of these small blossoms will send a heavy fragrance through the house on a summer evening. This plant is known popularly as "night jessamine."

CULTURE: Light, sunny to semi-sunny. Temperature, average house. Humidity, average house. Soil, equal parts loam, sand, peat moss, and leaf mold; keep evenly moist. Keep pinched back to induce bushy growth. Propagate by rooting cuttings in the spring.

Solanum

DESCRIPTION: *S. pseudo-capsicum,* from Madeira, is the well-known Christmas pot-plant called "Jerusalem cherry." It has pointed-oval leaves and is noted primarily for the abundance of brightly colored globular fruit, usually bright scarlet-orange, and often measuring an inch or more in diameter. These "cherries" are not edible; do not confuse them with the related *Capsicum annuum,* which see.

CULTURE: Light, sunny to semi-sunny. Temperature, cool, not over 75°F. Keep out of drafts. Humidity, 30% or more. Soil, equal parts loam, sand, and peat moss; keep evenly moist.

Propagate by sowing seeds in late winter or spring. Old plants may be held over by cutting back in the spring, and keeping the soil nearly dry for several weeks.

Solanum pseudo-capsicum

TEA FAMILY   Theaceae

Tropical shrubs and trees, mostly evergreen, cultivated for showy flowers. *Thea sinensis* furnishes the tea leaves of commerce.

Camellia

DESCRIPTION: Asiatic, evergreen shrubs cherished for waxy, long-lasting flowers. Their alternate, toothed leaves are of leathery texture, attractive around the year. Careful choice of six or seven different varieties will provide a season of bloom from mid-September through March. Though they are usually thought of as shrubs for southern gardens, a number of outstanding camellias will grow into compact, bushy specimens which can be kept to a practical size for an indoor garden—ideally a cool, sunny plant room.

There are hundreds of different camellias, each of which has certain desirable, or sometimes undesirable,

Camellia japonica

characteristics. For growing in the window garden, consider length of blooming season, growth habit (choose kinds naturally compact, because they are easily kept pruned to a symmetrical bush which doesn't grow out of bounds), and whether or not it is a profuse bloomer, even while young.

The most enjoyable method of assembling a camellia collection is to visit commercial and public displays of camellias when they are in full flower. A visit made from mid-September to November would acquaint you with early-blooming varieties; December to February, the midseason ones; March and April, those which are late-blooming. Study catalogue listings of camellias before you make final choices. They may be shipped either as potted or bareroot plants.

CULTURE: Light, sunny to semi-sunny in fall, winter, and spring in the window garden; filtered morning or afternoon sun outdoors in summer. Temperature, 40-50°F. for camellias in flower, 55-65°F. afterwards. Humidity, 50% or more, with ample fresh air. Soil, acid (pH 4.0 to 5.5), using equal parts loam, peat moss, leaf mold, and sand. Keep evenly moist. Mature plants usually require repotting every three years. Do this just before growth starts in spring. After camellias have flowered, it is important to push them into new growth. Use a solution of ammonium sulfate (1 tsp. to 1 gal. of water); apply as you water the plants. Fertilizing is done only during the summer growing months. This may be started as early as March, but not continued past August. A cottonseed-meal fertilizer, mixed especially for camellias, is desirable. Apply three times during the season, the first of April, June, and August.

SUMMERTIME CARE: If possible, move tubbed camellias outdoors in warm weather to a place protected from hot, drying winds. They need early morning or late afternoon sun. Sprinkle frequently with water from the hose to increase humidity in the air around them. Watch carefully all summer for insects; when spraying, do not use a pesticide which contains DDT as camellias are harmed by it. Individual camellia flowers will be larger and more perfect if disbudding is practiced. Allow the one tip bud of each cluster to mature. Disbudding is done as soon as the buds are large enough to tell one from another.

PROPAGATION: Root cuttings of the current season's mature wood, from August 15 through early February. The cuttings may be from 3 to 6 in. long and have from one to six leaf nodes. A cutting with only one node needs a live bud at the top and 1½ in. of stem below the leaf. Root in a mixture of equal parts of peat moss and sand that is kept warm (around 72°F.). Cover the cuttings with glass or polyethylene so that they will be in high humidity. Rooting takes two or three months. Cuttings may then be transplanted into regular camellia soil in 2½-in. pots, then to 4-in. ones.

LINDEN FAMILY   Tiliaceae

Herbs, shrubs, and trees from many parts of the world, cultivated for fiber, ornament, or timber. Only one genus is of interest to the indoor gardener.

Sparmannia

DESCRIPTION: *S. africana,* from South Africa, is a fast-growing, lustrous-stemmed plant which resembles a linden in foliage. The leaves are large, soft, hairy, light green, and lightly lobed. Unless roots are restricted, the plant may become tree-like, developing many trunks or main stems. Flowers are white, the petals reflexed to expose yellow filaments, and are in terminal clusters which rival hydrangeas in size and beauty. Popular names include "African hemp" and "parlor linden."

Sparmannia africana

CULTURE: Light, semi-sunny to semi-shady. Temperature, average house. Humidity, average house, with ample fresh air. Soil, equal parts loam, sand, and peat moss; keep evenly moist. Propagate by rooting tip cuttings. Prune heavily after flowering.

NETTLE FAMILY   Urticaceae

Tropical as well as temperate herbs, shrubs, and trees, differing remarkably in growth habit and appearance. Some of the genera have stinging hairs, but those cultivated indoors are harmless.

Helxine

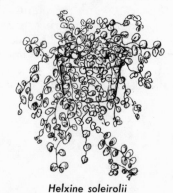

DESCRIPTION: *H. soleirolii,* from Corsica and Sardinia, is a tiny creeping plant with a multitude of common names, among them "Irish moss," "Corsican curse," and "mind-your-own-business," but "baby's-tears" is the universally accepted one. The watery stems of helxine are thread-thin, much branched and intertwining, and the plants form dense mats of fresh green foliage. Individual leaves

Helxine soleirolii

are slightly larger than a pinhead. Baby's-tears is useful as a ground cover in terrariums and bottle gardens. It can be grown as a specimen plant if given sufficient moisture. One way to do this is to set the pot on moist sand, then, as the plant creeps down over the pot sides, place an inverted pot beneath it to provide more moist area for the stems to crawl on.

CULTURE: Light, semi-shady to shady. Temperature, average house, preferably not over 75° F. for long periods. Humidity, 50% or more, with some fresh air. Mist foliage often with tepid water. Soil, equal parts loam, sand, peat moss, and leaf mold; keep evenly moist. Propagate by division of the clumps, or by rooting cuttings.

Pellionia

DESCRIPTION: *P. daveauana,* from Burma, Malaya, and southern Vietnam, has close-set pairs of silvered

Pellionia daveauana

leaves edged brownish purple, with pink creeping stems. *P. pulchra,* from Vietnam, has oval leaves of light greenish gray netted with black or brown veins. These are useful as basket plants, or as ground covers in large planters.

CULTURE: Light, semi-shady to shady. Temperature, average house. Humidity, 30% or more. Soil, equal parts loam, sand, and peat moss; keep evenly moist. Propagate by rooting cuttings at any time.

Pilea

DESCRIPTION: *P. cadierei,* from Vietnam, and its variety *minima,* are succulent, well-branched upright plants of bright green, quilted leaves, silver-marked (hence, "aluminum plant") on the raised portions. *P.*

Pilea cadierei

involucrata, from Peru, is commonly called "panimiga," or "South American friendship plant." It has oval, deeply quilted leaves, coppery red-brown and hairy, with tiny green flowers in clusters at the axils of terminal leaves. *P. microphylla,* from the West Indies, has much-branched, fleshy, semi-upright stems covered by bright-green leaves not more than ¼ in. in diameter. Its common name, "artillery plant," refers to the way ripe pollen is forcibly ejected from the plant. This pilea is best renewed each year from cuttings. *P. nummularifolia,* from the West Indies to Peru, is a creeping plant with small, round, slightly hairy leaves, and a tendency for the stems to root at each node. It is often called "creeping Charlie," but this is not the garden weed, *Nepeta hederacea,* of the same popular name. CULTURE: Light, semi-sunny to semi-shady. Temperature, average house. Humidity, average house, preferably over 30%, with some fresh air. Soil, equal parts loam, sand, peat moss, and leaf mold; keep evenly moist. Propagate by rooting cuttings.

VERBENA FAMILY   Verbenaceae

Mostly tropical herbs, shrubs, trees, and woody vines cultivated for showy flowers.

Clerodendrum

DESCRIPTION: *C. fragrans pleniflorum,* from China and Japan, is a large shrub when cultivated outdoors in the South, but as a pot or tub plant it can be kept under 2 ft. The pale pink, double blossoms within reddish purple calyxes yield such a fragrance that this clerodendrum is often known simply as "Cashmere Bouquet." *C. thomsonae,* from tropical West Africa, is called "glory-bower," or "bleeding-heart vine." It is an evergreen, twining, shrubby vine which can be kept to convenient indoor size by pruning during its semi-dormant period in winter. The flowers have inflated white calyxes, out of which the deep crimson, pendent flowers are borne. CULTURE: Light, sunny to semi-sunny.

Clerodendrum thomsonae

Temperature, average house, although coolness (about 60°F.) is preferable in winter. Humidity, 30% or more. Soil, equal parts loam, sand, peat moss, and leaf mold; keep evenly moist, except on the dry side during semi-dormancy in winter. Feed biweekly from spring to fall. Propagate by rooting cuttings of half-ripened wood in summer, or by removing suckers which form around the base of mature plants.

Lantana

DESCRIPTION: *L. camara,* from the West Indies, and its varieties, are shrubby, spreading perennials which will bloom the year round if they receive sufficient sunlight and moisture. The flowers are borne in dense heads, about 2 in. across, usually creamy yellow, or deep yellow aging to orange and red. *L. montevidensis,* from Uruguay, is less shrubby and, when planted in a hanging basket, makes a beautiful cascade of green foliage and countless heads of lavender blossoms. CULTURE: Light, sunny. Temperature, average house, preferably not over 75°F. in winter. Humidity, 30% or more; mist leaves frequently with

Lantana camara

water to prevent drying and to discourage insect infestation. Soil, equal parts loam, sand, and peat moss; keep evenly moist, except slightly drier during the dead of winter when the top growth should be cut back to 8 in. or less. Feed biweekly except during the shortest days of winter. Propagate by rooting cuttings in spring, summer, or fall.

GRAPE FAMILY   Vitaceae

Mostly woody vines, from temperate as well as tropical parts of the world. They climb by means of tendrils, and the genera grown indoors are cultivated for their handsome foliage.

Cissus

DESCRIPTION: *C. antarctica,* from New South Wales, the "kangaroo vine," has leathery, brown-veined, dark-green, toothed leaves. *C. discolor,* from Java, is probably the most colorful of all vines grown indoors. Its moss-green leaves are variegated with red-purple, overlaid with a silver sheen. The leaf reverses are purple, with red stems. This cissus is altogether a choice plant which needs more moisture, warmth, and humidity, and less sunlight, than the other species; it is often called "rex-begonia vine." *C. quadrangularis,* from Arabia, tropical Africa, India, and Moluccas, is an unusual succulent with square, segmented stems, an occasional three-lobed leaf, and stout tendrils by which it climbs. This cissus can stand full sun, cool temperatures (60-72°F.), and needs only enough water to maintain its leaves. *C. rhombifolia,* from northern South America and the West Indies, has three-parted leaves of metallic green,

Cissus discolor

brown-veined and hairy beneath. It is the popular "grape-ivy." *C. striata,* from Chile, the "miniature grape-ivy," has five-parted, bronze-green leaves with pale veins and deep-red reverses. It makes a good plant for terrarium landscapes.

CULTURE: Except as noted above, the following conditions apply: Light, semi-sunny to semi-shady. Temperature, average house, preferably not over 75°F. in winter. Humidity, average house. Soil, equal parts loam, sand, and peat moss; keep evenly moist, occasionally allowing to approach dryness. Propagate by rooting cuttings.

Leea

DESCRIPTION: *L. amabilis,* from Borneo, has bronzy velvet, slightly toothed oval leaflets which are reddish when young. The leaflets have red midribs and white veins. The palmate leaves of *L. coccinea,* from Burma, are glossy, toothed, and wavy-edged, with new growth tending to be copper-tinged. Flowers are in flat-topped clusters, red in bud, opening pink. Leeas are beautiful small shrubs or trees, often flowering when quite small, and always attractive because of interesting foliage.

Cissus striata

CULTURE: Light, semi-sunny to semi-shady. Temperature, average house. Humidity, 30% or more. Soil, equal parts loam, sand, and peat moss; keep evenly moist. Propagate by rooting cuttings at any time.

GINGER FAMILY   Zingiberaceae

Aromatic tropical herbs cultivated for ornament and flavoring.

Amomum

DESCRIPTION: *A. cardamon,* to about 2 ft. in cultivation, from Java, sends up lance-shaped leaves of dark green from a creeping rootstock. The foliage yields a spicy aroma when bruised and, when good care is given, the plant has conelike spikes of yellow flowers among the leaves. CULTURE: Light, semi-sunny to semi-shady. Temperature, average house. Humidity, average house, preferably 30% or more. Soil, equal parts loam, sand, and peat moss; keep evenly moist. Propagate by dividing the clumps.

Costus

DESCRIPTION: Costus species, called "spiral gingers," because the leaves

grow up the stems like a spiral staircase, are ornamental foliage plants which have also exceptionally attractive flowers. *C. igneus,* to 3 ft., from Brazil, has bright, shiny green leaves

Costus sanguineus

stained red beneath, and red stems. Its 3-in. flowers are of brilliant orange, and open flat to display the ragged petal edges.
CULTURE: Light, semi-sunny to semi-shady. Temperature, average house. Humidity, 30% or more. Soil, equal parts loam, sand, peat moss, and leaf mold; keep evenly moist. Propagate by dividing the clumps in spring.

Curcuma

DESCRIPTION: *C. roscoeana,* from Burma, is a robust perennial which grows from a tuberous rootstock. It is noted for having large spikes of concave or hooded orange bracts from which the yellow flowers scarcely emerge.
CULTURE: Light, semi-sunny to semi-shady. Temperature, average house. Humidity, 50% or more. Soil, equal parts loam, sand, peat moss, and leaf mold; keep evenly moist in spring and summer, nearly dry in fall and winter. Propagate by dividing the tubers at repotting time in spring.

Hedychium

DESCRIPTION: Hedychium species, known as "ginger-lilies," are tropical plants which are very ornamental in both foliage and flower. Although many are too large for indoors, some have canes less than 6 ft. tall, and thus can be grown in tubs or large pots where space permits. *H. flavum,* to 5 ft., from the Indian Himalayas, has highly fragrant light-yellow blossoms and long, slender, smooth leaves. *H. greenei,* to 6 ft., from Bhutan, has red-stained, long, heavy leaves and brilliant red flowers.
CULTURE: Light, semi-sunny. Temperature, average house. Humidity, 30% or more, with ample fresh air.

Soil, equal parts loam, sand, and peat moss; keep evenly moist to wet, except nearly dry for a few weeks immediately after the flowering season. Propagate by dividing the tubers following a rest period.

Kaempferia

DESCRIPTION: *K. decora,* to 1½ ft., from Portuguese East Africa, has canna-like foliage and primrose-yellow flowers 2 in. across. It is one of the showiest of all summer-blooming pot plants. *K. roscoeana,* to 1 ft., from Burma, is called the "peacock plant" because of the iridescent bronze overlay on the foliage. It bears 1½-in. violet-shaped, lavender flowers all summer. There are several other kaempferias which are outstanding for the indoor garden. They include *K. galanga,* from India, *K. gilbertii,* from southern Burma, *K. grandiflora,* from Kenya, *K. involucrata,* from Sikkim, Assam, and Upper Burma, and *K. rotunda,* from Himalaya, India, and Ceylon.
CULTURE: Light, semi-sunny to semi-shady. Temperature, average house. Humidity, 50% or more. Soil, equal parts loam, sand, peat moss, and leaf mold; keep evenly moist, except nearly dry through late fall and win-

Kaempferia roscoeana

ter. Propagate by division of clumps, or by sowing seeds.

Zingiber

DESCRIPTION: Zingibers are grown for scented or variegated foliage, or for the commercial value of their roots. The true ginger, *Z. officinalis,* to 4 ft., from India to the Pacific Islands, has slender, reedlike stems and narrow, glossy leaves almost like a bamboo. *Z. zerumbet,* from India, larger and with broader leaves, is noted for its spikes or cones of bracts which resemble a pine cone and turn red in the fall. Its variety *darceyi* is a rare form with white and green leaves margined in pink.

CULTURE: Light, semi-sunny to semi-shady. Temperature, average house. Humidity, 50% or more. Soil, equal parts loam, sand, peat moss, and leaf mold; keep evenly moist. Propagate by division of the clumps in spring.

part III

A USEFUL
MISCELLANY

GLOSSARY

ALTERNATE LEAVES Those appearing alternately along a stem.

ANNUAL A plant which grows to maturity in one season, sets seeds, and dies.

ANTHER Part of stamen which bears pollen.

AXIL The upper angle formed by a leaf or branch and the stem from which it grows.

BIENNIAL Plant which requires two years in which to reach maturity, set seeds, and die.

BRACT Modified leaf, often near or with a plant's flowers, and sometimes so colorful and showy as to be called a "flower." The bracts of poinsettia, beloperone (shrimp plant), and cornus (dogwood) serve as good examples.

BULB Term used to describe a swollen stem (usually underground) which is covered by much modified, food-storing leaves. Roots come from the bottom of the stem, and the scalelike leaves serve to protect the bud. A parchmentlike covering is usually present; tulips and onions are good examples.

CALYX A term used when referring to all of the sepals of a flower, whether they are separate or united.

CLONE (Sometimes spelled CLON.) The name used to designate a number of plants, all of which have been derived from one original individual through vegetative propagation. They are genetically identical. Seed-grown plants may appear to be the same, but they are not genetically identical.

COMPOST Decomposed vegetable matter, of vital importance to the outdoor garden, and useful in potting mixes as "garden loam" if it is first put through a ¼- or ½-inch screen and then pasteurized (see Chapter 2).

COMPOUND LEAF One composed of more than one leaflet per leaf stalk, as in the rose.

COROLLA The unit formed by the petals of a flower. These may be separate, as in those of the garden geranium, or united, as in the morning-glory.

CULTIVAR Term used to describe a plant which is maintained only in cultivation; for discussion, see page 51.

CUTTING Term used to describe some vegetative plant part removed for the purpose of growing another plant, identical to the parent.

DECIDUOUS Leaf-losing, a term which applies ultimately to all plants, but used commonly with reference to trees and shrubs which drop their leaves each autumn.

DORMANT Term applied to a plant which is not growing, either because of unfavorable conditions, or because it is resting at the end of a growth cycle.

ELLIPTICAL LEAVES Those which are oval and narrowed at each end.

EPIPHYTE A plant which in nature finds lodging on another, usually larger, but only for the purpose of being better situated to receive light, air, and moisture, and not for parasitic reasons. "Tree perching" is frequently used to describe this kind of plant. Many orchids and bromeliads are "tree perchers" in nature.

FAMILY Term used in connection with botany to indicate a

grouping of plants according to their resemblance and similarity. This may be apparent only on careful study of all
plant parts.

FLAT   Shallow box with drainage holes in the bottom, used for
starting plants. The standard size is 16x22 inches, with a
depth of 2 to 4 inches, but any convenient dimensions may
be used.

FORCE   To induce a plant to reach maturity out of season;
spring-flowering daffodils blooming on a window sill in
February, for example.

FROND   Always the leaf of a fern, but sometimes used with
reference to those of a palm.

GENUS (GENERA, plural)   The main subdivision of a plant family.
For example, the genus *Saintpaulia* is part of the Gesneriad
family or *Gesneriaceae*. Each genus may be further divided
into species, the species into varieties, cultivars, and minor
groups.

GERMINATION   The point at which a seed sprouts and becomes
a plant.

HERB   Commonly, a plant used for flavoring, fragrance, or
medicinal purposes. Botanically, a plant of fleshy, not woody,
stems.

HOSE-IN-HOSE   A term used when one flower appears to grow
from within another. This occurs usually in natural doubling
of the flower, or when the calyx and corolla are of the same
color. Some azaleas have hose-in-hose flowers; also campanulas (the cup-and-saucer Canterbury bells).

HYBRID   The result of crossing two different plants.

INFERIOR OVARY   One which appears beneath the point at
which the calyx is inserted; typical of amaryllis and rose
families.

IRREGULAR FLOWER   One made unsymmetrical by parts of
different sizes.

LEAF BLADE   The expanded or flat part of a leaf, as distinguished
from its petiole (or leaf stalk).

LEAFLET   One segment of a compound leaf.

LEAF MOLD Partially decayed or decomposed leaves, used in potting mixtures after first being put through a ¼- or ½-inch screen and pasteurized (see Chapter 2).

LEAF STALK A petiole.

LOAM A mellow soil, composed of about equal parts silt and sand and less than 20% clay. A handful of it moistened will form a sturdy ball, and even when nearly dry it holds together well.

MIDRIB The main or central vein of a leaf.

NODE The joints or swellings which occur at regular intervals along a plant stem. It is at these points that leaf and bud growth begins.

OBOVATE LEAVES Those of ovate shape, except attached to the stem at their narrow end.

OPPOSITE LEAVES Those set directly across from each other along a stem.

OVATE LEAVES Those which are egg-shaped, attached to the stem at their broad end.

PALMATE LEAF One whose sections radiate from a common point; handlike.

PANICLE A loose, open flower cluster which blooms from the bottom or center toward the top or edges.

PEAT MOSS Partially or wholly decayed plant parts, derived chiefly from bog mosses; a valuable ingredient for potting mixtures. There are many peat mosses sold; German peat is preferred for indoor gardening, then Canadian, and Michigan peat as a last resort.

PEDUNCLE The stalk of a solitary flower, or that of the main stalk which supports a flower cluster. Each flower in a cluster is held on a pedicel which is connected to the peduncle.

PELTATE Term used to describe a leaf whose stalk is attached away from its margin, often in the center.

PERENNIAL A plant which lives on and on, theoretically without end so long as its environment is favorable.

PERFECT FLOWER One which bears both male and female

organs of reproduction; one which includes stamens and a pistil.

PERLITE   An almost weightless, gritty, white substance used in gardening as a substitute for sand.

PETAL   The segment of a flower, sometimes separate from others, sometimes joined together.

PETIOLE   The stalk of a leaf, by which it is attached to the plant's main stem, or branch.

PINCH   To remove with scissors, or nip out with the fingers, the young growing tip of a stem, thus inducing it to branch.

PINNATE   Term used to describe a compound leaf whose leaflets appear opposite each other along a common axis; featherlike.

PISTIL   The ovary, style, and stigma of a flower's female reproductive parts.

PLUNGE   To set a plant container in water for the purpose of moistening the soil.

POT-BOUND   Term used when the roots of a pot plant circle endlessly around and through the soil, filling it to the point of being unable to progress further.

RACEME   Term used to describe an elongated flower cluster, which blooms from the bottom upward.

RAY   The flat, marginal flower in the head of a member of the *Compositae*.

REGULAR FLOWER   One whose parts are of equal size, regularly and symmetrically arranged.

RHIZOME   A thickened, fleshy, rootlike stem, occurring underground, or creeping along the soil's surface.

ROSETTE   A cluster of leaves radiating symmetrically from a central stem. These occur usually at or near the soil's surface, but are sometimes at the top of a tall stem.

RUNNER   Name given to a prostrate shoot from a plant which runs along the ground, rooting at each joint as in strawberries.

SEPAL   An individual part of the calyx.

SIMPLE LEAF   One which has only one blade attached to the main leaf stalk.

SPECIES   Term used to designate a major subdivision in a plant family. First the genus, as *Saintpaulia* in the family *Gesneriaceae*, second the species, as *Saintpaulia ionantha*. Species occur in nature and consist of plants which share distinctive characteristics.

SPHAGNUM MOSS   Gray or tan bog mosses dried and used as a planting medium for many kinds of plants. A handful, moistened and wrapped around the base of a cutting, will encourage rooting. Milled sphagnum is sterile and fine-textured, of value especially for starting dust-size seeds.

SPIKE   Term used to describe a racemelike cluster of flowers, except each is stalkless or nearly so.

STAMEN   The male reproductive parts of a flower, including the stalk, or filament, and the anther containing the pollen.

STIGMA   Termination of the style and ovary, the point at which pollen is received.

STOLON   Term used to describe a creeping, trailing, or horizontal stem, the tip of which terminates in a new plant; often called a "runner."

SUCCULENT   Term which refers to plants made drought-resistant by special water-storing powers. Some kinds actually store moisture in leaves, stems, and roots; others, through their physiological make-up, are able to exist through long seasons of dryness.

SUPERIOR OVARY   One which appears above that point at which the calyx is inserted.

TENDER   Unable to survive cold; usually applied to plants which are harmed by temperatures at or below 32°F.

TENDRIL   A threadlike prolongation of stem or leaf by which climbing plants cling to their means of support.

TUBER   A fleshy stem, mostly underground, with small leaf structures from which buds are borne; the tuber of a potato makes a good example.

TUBEROUS-ROOTED   This term refers to a swollen root, as in the dahlia and sweet potato, distinguished from a tuber which is a swollen underground stem.

UMBEL   A flower cluster, either flat or round, in which the individual flower stalks arise from one point; Queen Anne's lace (of the Carrot Family), and hoya or wax plant (of the Milkweed Family) serve as good examples.

VARIETY   A subdivision in a plant family, used to designate a natural variation in a species; this contrasts with the term "cultivar" which designates a new plant brought about in cultivation.

VERMICULITE   A sterile planting medium, like mica, used for rooting cuttings; frequently combined with loam and peat moss as a substitute for sand.

WHORL   Three or more leaves, flowers, twigs, or other plant parts arranged in a circle and radiating from one point.

PERIODICALS ABOUT
INDOOR PLANTS

The Begonian, monthly of the American Begonia Society, Inc., 139 North Ledoux Road, Beverly Hills, California 90211.

Bonsai Magazine, ten times a year publication of Bonsai Clubs International, 445 Blake Street, Menlo Park, California 94025.

The Bromeliad Journal, bimonthly publication of the Bromeliad Society, Inc., P.O. Box 3279, Santa Monica, California 90403.

Cactus and Succulent Journal, bimonthly publication of the Cactus and Succulent Society of America, Inc., Box 167, Reseda, California 91335.

Cymbidium Society News, monthly publication of the Cymbidium Society of America, Inc., 6787 Worsham Drive, Whittier, California 90602.

Epiphyllum Bulletin, publication of the Epiphyllum Society of America, 218 East Greystone Avenue, Monrovia, California 91016.

Geraniums Around the World, quarterly publication of the International Geranium Society, 11960 Pascal Avenue, Colton, California 92324.

Monthly Fern Lessons, with newsletter and annual magazine, publications of the Los Angeles International Fern Society, 2423 Burritt Avenue, Redondo Beach, California 90278.

The National Fuchsia Fan, monthly publication of the National Fuchsia Society, 10934 East Flory Street, Whittier, California 90606.

Gesneriad Saintpaulia News, bimonthly publication of the American Gesneria Society, 11983 Darlington Avenue, Los Angeles, California 90049.

Plantlife-Amaryllis Yearbook, bulletin of the American Plant Life Society, Box 150, La Jolla, California 92037.

American Fern Journal, quarterly publication of the American Fern Society, Biological Sciences Group, University of Connecticut, Storrs, Connecticut 06268.

The Gloxinian, bimonthly publication of the American Gloxinia/ Gesneriad Society, Inc., P.O. Box 174, New Milford, Connecticut 06776.

Seed Pod, quarterly publication of the American Hibiscus Society, Box 98, Eagle Lake, Florida 33139.

Princepes, quarterly publication of the Palm Society, 1320 South Venetian Way, Miami, Florida 33139.

The Camellia Journal, quarterly publication of the American Camellia Society, Box 212, Fort Valley, Georgia 31030.

American Orchid Society Bulletin, monthly publication of the American Orchid Society, Inc., Botanical Museum of Harvard University, Cambridge, Massachusetts 02138.

Bonsai (quarterly) and *ABStracts* (monthly newsletter), publications of the American Bonsai Society, 953 South Shore Drive, Lake Waukomis, Parksville, Missouri 64151.

American Ivy Society Bulletin, periodical of the American Ivy Society, 128 West 58th Street, New York, New York 10019.

Light Garden, bimonthly publication of the Indoor Light Gardening Society of America, Inc., 128 West 58th Street, New York, New York 10019.

African Violet Magazine, bimonthly publication of the African Violet Society of America, Inc., Box 1326, Knoxville, Tennessee 37901.

Gesneriad Saintpaulia News, bimonthly publication of Saintpaulia International, P.O. Box 10604, Knoxville, Tennessee 37919.

Plants Alive, monthly magazine about indoor gardening, 2100 North 45th, Seattle, Washington 98103.

Under Glass, bimonthly devoted to home greenhouse growing; c/o Lord & Burnham, Irvington, New York 10533.

WHERE TO BUY
INDOOR PLANTS AND
SUPPLIES FOR GROWING THEM

Sources for Plants

Abbey Garden, P.O. Box 30331, Santa Barbara, California 93105—
Complete range of cacti and other succulents. Catalog $1.00.

Abbot's Nursery, Route 4, Box 482, Mobile, Alabama 36609— Camellias.

Alberts & Merkel Brothers, P. O. Box 537, Boynton Beach, Florida 33435—
Orchids and other tropicals. Catalog 50¢.

Antonelli Brothers, 2545 Capitola Road, Santa Cruz, California 95010—
Tuberous begonias, gloxinias, and achimenes.

Ashcroft Orchids, 19062 Ballinger Way N.E., Seattle, Washington—
Botanical orchids.

Bart's Nursery, 522 Fifth Street, Fullerton, Pennsylvania—Bonsai
materials.

Buell, Albert H., Eastford, Connecticut 06242—African violets, gloxinias, and other gesneriads. Catalog $1.00.

Burgess Seed and Plant Company, Galesburg, Michigan 49053—Dwarf
fruit and other house plants.

Burnett Brothers, Inc., 92 Chambers Street, New York, New York 10007
—Freesias and other bulbous plants.

Burpee, W. Atlee, Company, Philadelphia, Pennsylvania 19132; Clinton,
Iowa 52733; and Riverside, California 92502—Seeds and bulbs.

Cook's Geranium Nursery, 712 North Grand, Lyons, Kansas 67544—
Geraniums. Catalog 50¢.

Conard-Pyle Star Roses, West Grove, Pennsylvania 19390—Miniature
roses.

DeGiorgi Company, Inc., Council Bluffs, Iowa 51504—Seeds and bulbs.

DeJager, P., and Sons, Inc., 188 Asbury Street, South Hamilton, Massachusetts 01982—Bulbs for forcing.

Farmer Seed and Nursery Company, Faribault, Minnesota 55021—Dwarf citrus and other house plants.

Fennell Orchid Company, 26715 S.W. 157 Avenue, Homestead, Florida 33030—Orchids. Catalog $1.00.

Field, Henry, Seed and Nursery Company, Shenandoah, Iowa 51601—House plants and supplies.

Fischer Greenhouses, Linwood, New Jersey—African violets, other gesneriads, and supplies.

French, J. Howard, Baltimore Pike, Lima, Pennsylvania 19060—Bulbs for forcing.

Green Acres Nursery, 14451 N.E. Second Street, North Miami, Florida 33161—Palms.

Hausermann's Orchids, Box 363, Elmhurst, Illinois 60128—Unusual species orchids.

Hilltop Farm, Route 3, Box 216, Cleveland, Texas—Geraniums and herbs.

Howard, S. M., Orchids, Seattle Heights, Washington 98063—Miltonias, odontoglossums, and allied cool-growing genera.

Ilgenfritz, Margaret, Orchids, Monroe, Michigan 48161—Orchids.

Jones and Scully, Inc., 2200 N.E. 33rd Avenue, Miami, Florida 33142—Orchids and other tropicals.

Kartuz, Michael J., 92 Chestnut Street, Wilmington, Massachusetts 01887—House plants. Catalog 50¢.

Logee's Greenhouses, 55 North Street, Danielson, Connecticut 06239—All kinds of house plants, including rare and unusual kinds. Catalog $1.00.

Lyons, Lyndon, 14 Mutchler Street, Dolgeville, New York 13329—African violets and other gesneriads.

McLellan, Rod, Company, 1450 El Camino Real, South San Francisco California 94080—Orchids and supplies.

Merry Gardens, Camden, Maine 04843—Complete selection of house plants and herbs. Catalog $1.00.

Mini-Roses, Box 4255, Station A., Dallas, Texas 75208—Miniature roses.

Nies Nursery, 5710 S.W. 37th Street, West Hollywood, Florida 33023—Palms.

Nuccio's Nurseries, 3555 Chaney Trail, Altadena, California 91002—Camellias.

Park, George W., Seed Co., Inc., Greenwood, South Carolina 29647—All kinds of house plants, seeds, bulbs, and supplies.

Reasoner's Tropical Nurseries, Inc., P.O. Box 1881, Bradenton, Florida —Tropicals.

Rivermont Orchids, P.O. Box 67, Signal Mountain, Tennessee—Orchids.
Spidell's Fine Plants, Junction City, Oregon 97448—African violets and other gesneriads.
Stewart, Fred A., Inc., 1212 East Las Tunas Drive, San Gabriel, California 91778—Orchids and supplies.
Tinari Greenhouses, 2325 Valley Road, Huntington Valley, Pennsylvania 19006—African violets, other gesneriads, supplies, and equipment.
Wilson Brothers, Roachdale, Indiana 46172—Geraniums and other house plants.
Yoshimura Bonsai Company, Inc., 200 Benedict Avenue, Tarrytown, New York 10591—Bonsai and supplies.
Ziesenhenne, Rudolph, 1130 N. Milpas Street, Santa Barbara, California—Begonias.

Sources for Greenhouses

Aluminum Greenhouses, Inc., 14615 Lorain Avenue, Cleveland, Ohio 44111.
American Leisure Industries, Inc., P.O. Box 63, Deep River, Connecticut 06417.
Casa-Planta, 9489 Dayton Way, Suite 211, Beverly Hills, California 90210.
Geodesic Domes, R.R. 1, Bloomington, Illinois 61701.
J. A. Nearing Company, Inc., 10788 Tucker Street, Beltsville, Maryland 20705.
Lord & Burnham, Irvington-on-Hudson, New York 10533.
Redfern's Prefab Greenhouses, 55 Mt. Hermon Road, Scotts Valley, California 95060.
Redwood Domes, 2664 Highway 1, Aptos, California 95003.
Peter Reimuller, Box 2666, Santa Cruz, California 95060.
Sturdi-Built Manufacturing Company, 11304 S.W. Boones Ferry Road, Portland, Oregon 97219.
Texas Greenhouse Company, Inc., 2717 St. Louis Avenue, Fort Worth, Texas 76110.
Turner Greenhouses, P.O. Box 1260 Goldsboro, N.C. 27530.

Sources for Fluorescent Lighting Equipment

Craft-House Manufacturing Company, Wilson, New York 10706—Lighted plant stands.
Floralite Company, 4124 East Oakwood Road, Oak Creek, Wisconsin 53221—Fluorescent fixtures, mist sprayers, tubes, timers, trays, labels, and other equipment; supplies also.
General Electric Company, Lamp Division, Nela Park, Cleveland, Ohio—Manufacturers of fluorescent and incandescent lamps.

House Plant Corner, P.O. Box 810, Oxford, Maryland 21654—Lighted plant stands, other equipment, and all kinds of supplies.

Neas Growers Supply, P.O. Box 8773, Greenville, South Carolina 29604 —Tabletop units, other equipment.

Park, George W., Seed Co., Inc., Greenwood, South Carolina 29647— Fluorescent equipment of all kinds and supplies.

Shoplite Company, 566 Franklin Avenue, Nutley, New Jersey 07110— Fluorescents, incandescents, in regular and special sizes.

Sylvania Electric Products, Inc., 60 Boston Street, Salem, Massachusetts 01971—Manufacturers of all types of fluorescent lights.

Tube Craft, Inc., 1311 West 80th Street, Cleveland, Ohio 44102—Carts and other lighting equipment for growing plants.

Westinghouse Electric Corporation, Westinghouse Lamp Division, Bloomfield, New Jersey—Manufacturers of fluorescent lamps.

INDEX

The **bold** figures indicate pages on which illustrations appear.